Multinationalism, Japanese Style

Terutomo Ozawa

MULTINATIONALISM,
Japanese Style

◇◇◇◇◇◇◇◇◇◇◇◇◇◇◇◇◇◇◇◇◇◇◇◇◇◇◇◇◇◇◇◇◇◇◇◇◇

The Political Economy of
Outward Dependency

PRINCETON UNIVERSITY PRESS

PRINCETON, NEW JERSEY

Copyright © 1979 by Princeton University Press
Published by Princeton University Press, Princeton, New Jersey
In the United Kingdom: Princeton University Press, Guildford, Surrey

All Rights Reserved
Library of Congress Cataloging in Publication Data will be
found on the last printed page of this book

This book has been composed in Linotype Times Roman.

Clothbound editions of Princeton University Press books
are printed on acid-free paper, and binding materials are
chosen for strength and durability.

Printed in the United States of America by Princeton
University Press, Princeton, New Jersey

To Hiroko, Edwin, and Clare

Contents

List of Figures and Tables

Figures

Tables

Abbreviations

ADMA	Abu Dhabi Mine Areas
BTN	Brussels Tariff Nomenclature
CIECD	Council on International Economic Cooperation and Development
CIPEC	Intergovernmental Council of Copper Exporting Countries
D & I	Develop and Import
DAC	Development Assistance Committee of the Organization for Economic Cooperation and Development
DC	Developing Country
DFI	Direct Foreign Investment
DW	Deadweight
EEC	European Economic Community
FAO	U.N. Food and Agricultural Organization
GATT	General Agreement on Tariffs and Trade
GNP	Gross National Product
GSP	Generalized System of Preferences
IBA	International Bauxite Association
IMF	International Monetary Fund
JETRO	Japan External Trade Organization
JICA	Japanese International Cooperation Agency
JOEA	Japan Overseas Enterprise Association
JPDC	Japan Petroleum Development Corporation
KEPZ	Kaohsiung Export-Processing Zone
LDC	Less Developing Country
LDP	Liberal Democratic Party
LNG	Liquefied Natural Gas
LPG	Liquefied Petroleum Gas
MAFEZ	Masan Free Export-Processing Zone
MITI	Ministry of International Trade and Industry
MNC	Multinational Corporation
MNE	Multinational Enterprise
OECD	Organization for Economic Cooperation and Development
OECF	Overseas Economic Cooperation Fund

Abbreviations

OFCF	Overseas Fishery Cooperation Foundation
OPEC	Organization of Petroleum Exporting Countries
R & D	Research and Development
SUMOC	Superintendency of Money and Credit
UNCTAD	U.N. Conference on Trade and Development
USIMINAS	Usinas Siderurgicas de Minas Gerais

Foreword

SOME years ago, I was taken to task by a businessman for speaking about American multinationals. Our company, he said, is no longer American; that is why we say that it is multinational. Unhappily, large numbers of students of multinational business have acquiesced in this interpretation. Some have gone so far as to suggest that the spread of the multinational firm promises to undermine national sovereignty and to bring us at last to the millennium of abstract economic theory. Governments with narrow, parochial concerns will no longer be able to interfere with market forces, and it will be meaningful for the first time to explain and assess international trade and investment in cosmopolitan terms—to ask how they affect worldwide efficiency and global economic welfare.

It would be silly to deny that multinational firms have unusual attributes and attitudes. It is doubly dangerous, however, to disregard the birthplace of the firm or present residence of the head office—or the fact that the two are the same in almost every instance. It is dangerous to do so because one must not forget that economic actors function in real time. They are creatures of history, policy, and circumstance. Furthermore, the decisions of important economic actors can have political consequences, even when the actors confine their own activities to the economic stage and do not seek to influence policies directly.

These dangers are acute in the study of multinational business. Forgetting that most of the multinationals are American in origin and present residence, economists allow themselves to believe that their explanations of the spread of multinational business apply without qualification to time or place. It is said,

for example, that multinational firms are concentrated in oligopolistic industries, invest heavily in research and development, and produce highly differentiated goods. It is not always
noticed that research-intensive, differentiated goods are typical
American exports. Thus the characteristics ascribed to multinational businesses may be in reality those of American competitive success in international markets. Forgetting that American business began to become multinational more than half a
century ago, before the American government had started to
think about foreign economic policy in comprehensive terms,
economists and political scientists allow themselves to believe
that American policies reflect a considered, consistent judgment
about the costs and benefits of foreign direct investment rather
than being an accretion of arrangements and decisions whose
origins had very little to do with their present roles. It is said,
for example, that, by allowing the deferral of tax payments on
income that is reinvested abroad rather than being paid out to
the parent company, American tax policies favor foreign investment. It is rarely noticed that tax deferral, whether it be good
or bad policy, began as a natural application of the principle
that income is not taxable until the taxpayer receives it—a
principle well established in domestic tax law and extended
almost absent mindedly to the treatment of dividends from
foreign subsidiaries.

It would be wrong to say that American business began to go
abroad early in this century without the knowledge, approval,
or support of the American government. It would be equally
wrong to say that it went abroad as the agent of American
diplomacy or foreign economic policy. As a matter of fact, most
of the cases in which the American government intervened in
support of an American company were instances in which the
company was already doing business and was threatened with
the loss of established rights or privileges.

Even individuals who do not fall into any of these traps

find it hard to deal objectively with the causes, costs, and benefits of multinational business, viewed from the standpoint of the home country, because they have had to make their assessments in the context of an American experience that is full of contradictions. Businessmen hold prominent positions in every American administration. Companies seek openly and often successfully to influence legislation and executive rule making. When the Clean Air Act was passed, the story goes, Japanese automakers hired engineers, and Americans hired attorneys. Yet business and government continue to regard each other as implacable antagonists.

Matters are no simpler when American relations with other countries are studied. Radical critics of American foreign policy find it easy to believe that there is an identity of view, if not a master plan, that governs comprehensively the dealings of American ambassadors and business executives with foreign governments. Was it not the case, they say, that an American firm sought to undermine the government of Salvatore Allende even as the American government was trying to do the same thing? Was it not the case that the United States sought to extend to the foreign subsidiaries of American firms its embargoes on trade with China and Cuba? Yet American businessmen complain that they cannot obtain adequate support from the State Department in their dealings with foreign governments, and congressional critics charge that the major oil companies helped the Arab countries to enforce their so-called embargo against the United States.

This book may help correct some of the biases and fill some of the gaps in the thinking about multinational business. It views old problems and hypotheses from a fresh and important perspective. Its virtues reside in its subject and its execution.

The subject is important because Japan is different in so many ways from the United States. It is different in the structure and problems of its economy, domestic and foreign; in the character of relations between business and government, real and rhetorical; in the aims and conduct of its foreign policy. Furthermore, Japanese firms are distinct from American ones. They are financed and managed differently, and they compete differently with one another in goods and factor markets. Most important, Japanese firms have begun only recently to go abroad in large numbers, and Japanese policy toward Japanese multi-nationals did not evolve after the fact.

Accordingly, recent Japanese experience can be studied to test well-known hypotheses about multinational business, to see if they are truly general or are merely rationalizations, ad hoc and ex post, of the American experience; to examine in a different framework the roles of government and market forces in shaping decisions to invest abroad; and finally to observe how heavily the attitudes of *host* countries are affected by political, cultural, and other national attributes of multinational businesses.

These are some of the issues examined in this book, and they are studied skillfully. Terutomo Ozawa surveys and contrasts competing hypotheses about the causes for the spread of multi-national business and tests them against Japanese experience. He demonstrates, for example, that the advent of Japanese multinationals cannot be explained by some of those hypotheses, because many of the firms are small and belong to highly competitive industries producing standardized products. He weighs carefully the roles of public policy and market forces, tracing with particular clarity the effects of changes in Japan's factor endowment on incentives to invest abroad, the bearing of resource dependency, and the influence of new competition from less-developed countries in Japan's traditional export markets. He looks at the role of the Japanese trading companies in fostering and financing foreign investment and finds in addition important connections between Japanese government programs designed to assist Japanese firms and those designed to assist economic development in neighboring countries.

This book cannot be the last word on the subject. It should not be so, for the subject is young. But those who undertake to study it more closely will not find it easy to achieve the rigor and insight of Ozawa's contribution.

PETER B. KENEN

Princeton University
January 11, 1978

Preface

THE phenomenal growth of Japan's economy and trade in recent decades has been both marvelled at and very often feared by trade partners throughout the world. Yet Japan is in the midst of accomplishing still another feat: She is steadily cementing a base for her multinational corporations, which now offer not only a new form of competition in the markets of advanced Western countries but also greater direct participation in the industrialization programs of Third World economies and thus perhaps a wider range of sources of external economic assistance for host countries. Japan presently ranks fourth in total value of outstanding foreign direct investment, next to the United States, Great Britain, and West Germany. Japan's rate of increase in this new economic activity has, in the recent past, been much higher than any other country's. In many developing countries Japan already has attained the first or the second place as a foreign investor. Clearly, international competition is taking on the new form of direct overseas production in addition to continuing the old form of competition in trade.

An important element of Japan's economy is illustrated by the frequent reference to Japanese economic efforts as "Japan, Inc."[1] Close collaboration and coordination between government and industry has been practically a national necessity for Japan's resource-poor economy and huge (110 million) population—first, to reconstruct her war-devastated industry and second, to catch up with the advanced West. Although this symbiotic relationship has, on the whole, been weakened considerably in recent years precisely because of its success in bringing about the accomplishment of national goals of high economic growth and trade expansion, it is now being reinforced to promote the overseas advance of Japanese industry by way of direct foreign investment, an activity which has only recently grown in significance.

The emergence of government-business relationship in Japan's multinationalism is perhaps what should be expected. For whereas trade is a form of international economic activity essentially left to the forces of the market mechanism (namely, "arm's-length" transactions), direct overseas production is an activity closely coordinated and directly performed by and within a single economic organization, an activity that "transcends the market mechanism." For a variety of reasons, which are explained in this book, Japan has been driven to take up direct overseas production as a national desideratum. Besides, the governments of the host countries exercise more and more control over access to their local markets and resources by foreign corporations. In this new era of multinationalism encumbered by rising neo-mercantilism in both the host and the home country, a close collaboration between government and industry seems to be justified more than ever before. In order to study Japan's multinationalism it is necessary to move into the realm of political economy and to go beyond the conventional limits of economics. Hence, this book carries a subtitle, "the political economy of outward dependency."

Recognizing the broad politico-economic implications of overseas investment, this book explores, in both "positive" analytical and factual terms, the following major premise:

> Japan has been driven to resort to overseas production as a matter of national economic survival, although the majority of individual firms (aside from large trading companies and a handful of giant corporations) are incapable of doing so on their own and are "immature" in size, technological sophistication, and financial strength by Western standards. Ironically, however, from a macroeconomic viewpoint, those types of industrial activities in which these "immature" Japanese firms are engaged are judged both appropriate and ready to be trans-

planted overseas. Consequently, a multitude of supportive functions, both financial and managerial, are being mobilized or newly arranged by both government and industry to defray part of the private costs and to realize the social benefits of overseas production. Overseas production is now emerging as an integral part of both Japan's economic growth strategy and her foreign economic diplomacy.

There is an abundance of recent studies of Japan's multinationalism.[2] However, these studies are mostly descriptive; they do not, except for a few attempts cited in this book, relate their analyses to existing theories of direct foreign investment. Moreover, although the peculiarities of Japan's overseas investment activities are cited in these studies, they are regarded essentially as signs of industrial immaturity, that is, something aberrant—hence, soon to disappear as Japanese industry becomes more sophisticated technologically. There is a lack of theoretical conceptualization of those underlying institutional forces and arrangements that may make the currently observed peculiarities persist for a much longer period of time than one may expect. This book places greater emphasis on "positive" analytical considerations on these institutional parameters (presented particularly in chapter 2) and examines the phenomenon of Japan's overseas production under the broad hypothesis stated above. It is hoped that this book, by presenting a new perspective, will stimulate further theoretical and empirical work on this fascinating topic.

This book draws upon and expands substantially the findings of my previous research, some of which has been published in journals and elsewhere. I am grateful to those publishers who permitted me to incorporate, either partly or wholly, the following articles:

Labor-Resource-Oriented Migration of Japanese Industries to Taiwan, South Korea, and Singapore. Economic Staff Working Paper No. 134. Washington, D.C.: International Bank for Reconstruction and Development, 1972.

"The Emergence of Japan's Multinationalism: Patterns and Competitiveness." *Asian Survey* 15 (1975): 1036-1053.

"International Investment and Industrial Structure: New Theoretical Implications from the Japanese Experience." *Oxford Economic Papers* 31 (1979): 72-92.

"Japan's Mideast Economic Diplomacy." *Columbia Journal of World Business* 9 (1974): 38-46.

"Japan's Multinational Enterprise: The Political Economy of Outward Dependency." *World Politics* 30 (1978): 517-537.

"Japan's Resource Dependency and Overseas Investment." *Journal of World Trade Law* 11 (1977): 52-73.

"Multinationalism, Japanese Style." *Columbia Journal of World Business* 7 (1972): 33-42.

"Peculiarities of Japan's Multinationalism: Facts and Theories." *Banca Nazionale del Lavoro Quarterly Review*, no. 115, December 1975, pp. 404-426.

"Japan's Direct Investment in Brazil." *Columbia Journal of World Business* 11 (1976): 107-116. (Co-authored by Moyses Pluciennik and K. Nagaraja Rao.)

I owe another debt of gratitude to the many Japanese corporations which generously provided me with opportunities to interview their executives or officers. Without their kind assistance I would have been unable to gain sufficient insight into the myriad problems involved. Special thanks are extended to Mitsui, Mitsubishi, Marubeni-Iida, Kanematsu Gosho, Nissho-Iwai, Ataka, Hitachi, Toshiba Electric, Sanyo Electric, Toray Industries, Teijin, Toyota Motor, Isuzu Motors, Nippon Gakki, Asahi Chemical, Sekisui Chemical, Dai Nippon Printing, Snow Brand Milk, and Takasago Perfumery.

My opportunities to dwell upon and organize the topic were considerably enhanced during my sabbatical at the Center for Policy Alternatives, M.I.T., for the academic year of 1975-76. I am indebted to J. Herbert Hollomon, Director of the Center, for his kind hospitality.

Considerable improvements in the content and organization of this book have resulted from the penetrating comments of Peter B. Kenen of Princeton who took the trouble of reading an earlier draft of this book in its entirety during his busy European trip in the early summer of 1977. I am grateful for his valuable suggestions. Mieko Nishimizu of Princeton also reviewed the earlier draft and gave me constructive criticisms. Any remaining errors and deficiencies are mine—perhaps a reflection of my stubbornness.

Multinationalism, Japanese Style

Chapter 1

Emergence of Japan's Multinationalism

JAPANESE corporations have emerged as multinationals, both suddenly and recently. Japan's rate of growth in direct investment capital outflows has been much higher than that of any other industrial country; according to estimates made by Japan's Ministry of International Trade and Industry (MITI), the average annual growth rate between 1967 and 1974 was 31.4 percent for Japan, 26.1 percent for West Germany, 10.7 percent for Canada, 10.4 percent for the United States, 9.9 percent for France, and 9.3 percent for the United Kingdom.[1] Although Japan's postwar overseas investment began in 1951 (when she invested in an iron-ore development project in Goa, India), it is only since the mid-1960s, particularly since 1968, that her direct foreign investment has been large enough to be identified as a new trend toward multinationalism.

Before World War II Japan did set up production facilities abroad. But they were located in Japan's former colonies, namely Manchukuo, Korea, and Formosa, and were confined mostly to such industries as mining, transportation, communication, and some sectors of the heavy and chemical industries. Because Japan regarded these territories as her own, overseas investment in them was essentially the same as domestic investment except that development in the territories was more closely planned and controlled, as part of Japan's colonial policy, by the government then in power.

Until very recently Japan has had a long-standing policy of building industries at home by providing all sorts of protective and promotional measures. Japan strove to develop herself as an industrial workshop, importing raw materials and exporting finished products, and was extremely wary of any action that might have encouraged industrialization in other Asian countries, particularly in resource-exporting countries, lest she lose vital supplies of industrial materials. Suddenly, however, Japan has begun to make all-out efforts to establish manufacturing operations overseas as well as ventures in extractive industries in which Japan, as a resource-poor country, is naturally interested.[2] Through overseas investment activites Japan is perhaps the most active of the industrialized countries in disseminating industrial knowledge to assist economic development in less-developed countries, and her overseas manufacturing ventures are concentrated in developing countries.

What has abruptly motivated the Japanese government and industry to become an eager disseminator of industrialization, to switch from a traditional, ethnocentric policy of building industries at home to a new, more geocentric orientation of economic growth?[3] How have Japanese firms attained the necessary competitive advantages to manufacture directly in foreign markets, because operation in an alien market environment inevitably puts the foreign manufacturer at some disadvantage compared to local firms, particularly in advanced countries? This chapter will focus on these questions and related ones by analyzing the sudden growth and the general characteristics of Japan's direct overseas operations.

Structural Transformation and Outward Expansion

Because overseas investment activities emanate from economic activities at home, it is necessary to first familiarize ourselves with the major features of Japan's economic growth in the period after World War II. What is perhaps unique about Japan's postwar economic growth is that it was accompanied by a number of rapid structural changes. Not only was there a substantial reallocation of resources, particularly labor, from the primary sector (notably agriculture) to the secondary sector (especially manufacturing) and to the tertiary industries, a typical phenomenon commonly observable in a successful process of economic development, but also the Japanese experience was strongly characterized by a swift structural transformation within the manufacturing sector itself, a transformation from low-productivity, light-manufacturing industries to high-productivity, growth industries. The latter consisted initially of capital-intensive heavy and chemical industries and added gradually research and development (R & D)-intensive, high-value added, and less resource-consuming industries such as electronics. For instance, the proportion of textiles in Japan's domestic industrial output declined from 15.7 percent in 1955 to 6.0 percent in 1968, whereas that of electric and nonelectric machinery increased from 8.0 percent to 18.1 percent and that of transport equipment rose from 5.3 percent to 11.0 percent over the same period.[4]

Many new industries have been fostered under a variety of active government promotional programs "known as the 'industrial structure policy' in supplementing the market mechanisms."[5] Hugh Patrick and Henry Rosovsky observe:

> The policy was a mixture of key-sector and infant industry approaches. Designation as a key industry brought favorable tax and depreciation treatment, loans on favorable terms, duty-free equipment imports, and protection from import competition. As the economy grew and evolved, the key industries of the occupation period—steel, shipbuilding, electric power, coal, and fertilizer—needed and received relatively less help, and were superseded by new key industries such as petrochemicals, automobiles, and computers.
>
> As the economy grew and its capabilities and structure evolved, the government bureaucracy envisaged a shift of emphasis from labor-intensive, technologically unsophisticated industries, such as cotton textiles, into more technologically advanced industries for which demand would be large and labor productivity high, such as cars, television, and computers.

> These were infant industries in which costs were initially high;
> protection of the home market from imports enabled them to
> cut costs through learning by doing, economies of ever-larger
> scales of production, and further technological innovations.[6]

This does not mean, however, that the Japanese government,
specifically the MITI, which is in charge of the industrial structure policy, has selected all the promising industries for the
private sector to develop. In fact, some of the most impressive
growth industries, such as optical goods and motorcycles, were
not singled out by the MITI.[7]

Although it is debatable to what extent a plethora of governmental measures has really contributed to an astonishingly rapid
industrial expansion of the Japanese economy, the pro-business
attitude of the Japanese government has no doubt sustained and
promoted a favorable industrial climate. The government placed
economic growth among its highest priority goals, as epitomized
by the era of the ten-year income doubling plan initiated in
1961. An impressive array of new products were introduced
one after another, a process facilitated by relatively easy access,
through licensing agreements, to modern technologies developed
in the West during and after World War II. Consequently, new
products, those that were included in the official production index only after 1950,[8] accounted for roughly 40 percent of Japanese industrial output in 1970. This wave of new products (many
of which developed into entirely new industries) sustained capital investments and made the Japanese economy grow by leaps
and bounds. Most growth industries introduced into Japan also
quickly developed into strong export industries, earning valuable foreign exchange with which Japan was able to purchase
industrial raw materials, fuels, and foodstuffs—the vital supplies
that natural-resource-indigent Japan badly needed. During the
1950s and most of the 1960s, the structural transformation of
the Japanese economy was thus designed to re-establish Japan
more strongly than ever before as an industrial workshop proc-

essing imported raw materials and exporting manufactured goods (that is, by means of the conventional *trade route*).

Yet it was not without strain that Japan's industrial transformation proceeded, the basic source of which was the "successful" process of structural transformation itself; it has sharply demarcated the Japanese economy into two industrial sectors the destinies of which are diametrically opposite; one is a relatively expanding "growth" sector and the other a relatively contracting "senile" sector.[9] The situation is perhaps aggravated because industrial policy has been "inconsistent" in the sense that the government is hesitant to let the senile industries take their natural course and quickly die out.

There is good reason. Although outsiders tend to entertain the erroneous impression that Japanese industry is comprised mostly of *zaibatsu*-related super-giant firms, small- and medium-sized enterprises (defined as those with either 300 or fewer employees, or a paid-in capital of 100 million yen or less) account for as much as 99.5 percent of the total number of manufacturing factories, employ nearly 70 percent of the total manufacturing labor force, and are credited with about half the total value of shipments in manufacturing in Japan, according to Japan's Small and Medium Enterprise Agency.[10] (These shares of the small- and medium-sized firms are somewhat exaggerated due to the "factory base" statistical procedure employed by the agency. The factories with 300 or fewer employees include some of those belonging to larger firms. Even when this bias is taken into account, this group of manufacturers still comprises a significant part of Japanese industry.) And the electoral power of the Liberal Democratic Party (LDP), which has been in power throughout Japan's impressive growth, is, interestingly enough, "not Japan's great urban industrial-commercial centers but small towns and farms."[11] Heavily concentrated in the latter electoral district are traditional light manufacturing industries such as textiles, tablewares, toys, and other sundries—labor-intensive industries mostly composed of small firms. According to Philip H. Trezise and Yukio Suzuki:

> The impact of small business on Japanese politics tends to be diffused among the numerous Diet members who receive support from small local enterprises and political leaders whose home constituencies include a concentration of small firms in such industries as textiles and stainless steel tableware. But this influence can be important on specific issues. During the textile trade dispute between the United States and Japan in 1969 the small textile firms helped to rally Diet support of the chemical fiber makers and the large textile fabric companies whose interests were principally engaged. According to a senior Ministry of Finance participant in the policy debate on yen revaluation in 1971, the opposition of Kakuei Tanaka, then MITI minister, was a result of pressures from his Niigata prefecture electoral district, in which the tableware industry is centered.[12]

Thus Japan's labor-intensive (hence, cheap-labor-dependent) senile industries, in which small- and medium-sized firms are predominant actors, are receiving what Trezise and Suzuki call "a patchwork of assistance measures" that include special measures of assistance for overseas migration. In other words, a dual industrial structure in which large-scale firms engaged in capital-intensive operations and small-scale firms engaged principally in labor-intensive operations coexist has been permitted to exist under the political aegis.

Yet market forces have relentlessly continued to weaken these senile industries. Perhaps the most severe blow came from the labor market in the form of a declining supply of factory workers combined with rising wages—a phenomenon that began to appear in the early 1960s in theretofore labor-abundant Japan. This change clearly indicated the emerging incompatibility of Japan's factor endowments conditions with her labor-intensive industries. In a study on changing factor endowments in Japan from 1956 through 1969, Peter S. Heller states:

Within the last two decades [Japan] has evolved from a bat-
tle-torn, moderately-developed economy to the third largest
economy in the world and its economic growth rate has far out-
paced that of other [countries]. This structural transformation
in its production structure has been accompanied by a striking
shift in its factor endowment position. Rapid rates of capital
formation and demographic restraint led to the disappearance
of "easy labor market conditions" in the factor markets by the
early 1960s, and Japan's factor endowment position has rapidly
converged toward a capital-abundant position characteristic of
the [developed] countries.[13]

As a result of this quick shift in Japan's factor endowments
toward a relatively more capital-abundant position, real wages,
for example, tripled in the twenty-year period between 1952 and
1972.[14] Not only did a rapid industrial expansion itself increase
the over-all demand for workers and hence wages, but also, and
more important, as workers were attracted and absorbed into
more productive and higher-paying jobs in the expanding sector,
wages in the contracting sector rose concomitantly. Because the
competitiveness of Japan's light manufacturing industries, particularly in world markets, was based on relatively low labor
costs (that is, on a relatively labor-abundant position), her export shares of the world market in light manufactured products
began noticeably to decline, yielding to competitors in lower-
wage, developing countries. The adverse effect of labor shortages on the contracting sector and the reaction of that sector
will be detailed in chapter 3. Here it is only necessary to point
out that rising labor shortages at home compelled those firms
operating in labor-intensive industrial segments, particularly
small- and medium-sized enterprises, to seek abundant labor in
developing countries by way of direct foreign investment. In
other words, overseas investment began to serve as a means
to preserve Japan's trade competitiveness based on the dual industrial structure, which previously had existed only at home

but which was now encouraged to spread across national borders.

Another source of strain in Japan's industrial structure resulted from the very success of Japan's industrial strategy of making herself the workshop of the world. As this small island nation soon depleted her available industrial space, the costs of pollution and ecological destruction became intolerable. These external diseconomies were aggravated by the shift of industrial structure toward the heavy and chemical industries whose mode of production is prone to pollution. Additional difficulties arose because these industries are also highly intensive in the use of raw materials and fuels that Japan must import. In order to pay for these vital imports, Japan had to push for more manufactured exports at the risk of creating economic and political tensions in foreign markets. Thus the more successful the development of these industries, the more frequent Japan's confrontation with thorny issues both at home and abroad; the environmental costs of a workshop economy were ominously large at home, and the political and economic costs of conflict with other trading countries threatened abroad. Besides, as Japanese industry became more and more dependent on overseas markets for a growing part of its sales of output as well as of its purchases of vital resources, it also made itself increasingly vulnerable to possible restrictions on both exports and imports by Japan's trading partners. This trade dependency inevitably led to a strong motivation to resort to direct overseas production on the part of Japan's export-oriented growth industries (for example, electrical and electronics machinery) as well as her import-dependent resource-processing industries (for example, aluminum and petro-chemicals). These developments constitute important macroeconomic forces underlying Japan's outward expansion by means of direct foreign investment.

In sum, in order to understand the nature of Japan's overseas investment activities it is essential to remember the effects of the structural transformation of the Japanese economy, a transformation that has necessitated the preservation of the dual industrial structure, even across national boundaries, and the escape outward of Japanese industry from newly emerged environmental constraints at home. Although Japan's structural transformation initially centered in the trade route, it has gradually come to be developed by the overseas investment route.

Postwar Trend

With the preceding brief description of macroeconomic forces at work in the Japanese economy as a background, it is possible to examine more specifically how the trend toward multinationalism has developed. As shown in table 1.1 (for the definitions of statistics on Japan's overseas investment, see the appendix), only since 1968 has Japan's overseas investment (measured in terms of the annual value of overseas investment projects approved by the government) grown truly large.[15] Note the phenomenal acceleration in the early 1970s; the amount of overseas investment approved in the two years 1972 and 1973 alone exceeded the cumulative total of the preceding twenty years. From 1966 to 1971 it increased at the average annual rate of 29.4 percent; it then grew prodigiously, by 52.7 percent in 1972 and by 51.6 percent in 1973. Although the trend seems to have been decelerating ever since, the annual growth rate is still impressively high, 20 percent, and this growth rate is much higher than that of any other industrial country.

The postwar development of Japan's overseas investment activities may be divided into three broadly demarcated subperiods.

1. *1951-1967*.

During the first half of the 1950s, Japan's overseas investment averaged annually less than $10 million, due largely to the limitations imposed by the precarious position of her foreign exchange reserves. The initial projects approved by the govern-

Table 1.1

Value of Japan's Direct Foreign Investment (DFI)
Approved by the Japanese Government
(in millions of U.S. dollars)

Fiscal year[a]	Direct foreign investment (DFI)	Cumulative value	Growth rate %
1951-1961	$ 447	$ 447	
1962	98	545	21.8
1963	126	671	23.1
1964	119	790	17.7
1965	159	949	20.1
1966	227	1,176	23.9
1967	275	1,451	23.4
1968	557	2,008	38.4
1969	665	2,673	33.1
1970	904	3,577	33.8
1971	858	4,435	24.0
1972	2,338	6,773	52.7
1973	3,494	10,267	51.6
1974	2,396	12,663	23.3
1975	3,280	15,943	25.9
1976	3,462	19,405	21.7
1977	2,806	22,211	14.5

Source: Figures up to 1976 are compiled from **MITI**, *Wagakuni Kigyo*, 1977, p. 54. Statistics for 1977 are from a news release of the Ministry of Finance reported in *Japan Economic Journal*, July 25, 1978, p. 2.
[a] Japanese fiscal year starts on April 1. Hence, the data cover the period up to the end of March 1978.

ment were the re-establishment of the sales offices of major trading companies and some export-oriented manufacturing firms, mostly in the United States, and the setting up in 1953 of Alaska Lumber and Pulp, a wholly-owned Japanese subsidiary to develop pulp in Alaska. Thus Japan's overseas investments in the early 1950s were designed to help restore the Japanese economy as an exporter of manufactured goods, and to secure overseas resources, aims similar to those of the prewar years.

Overseas investment was initially regulated for balance-of-payments reasons under the Foreign Exchange Control Law of 1949. Every investment project, including any additional capital investment from Japan in existing overseas ventures, was subject to case-by-case screening and approval by the Ministry of Finance, which made decisions in close consultation with other government agencies, especially the MITI. Although no requirements for approval were officially announced, it was generally understood that (1) direct foreign investment must either promote exports from Japan or lead to the overseas development of natural resources vital to Japanese industry; (2) foreign investment must not jeopardize the competitive position of other Japanese firms at home; (3) foreign investment must not interfere with the effectiveness of domestic monetary policy.[16] The official attitude toward overseas investment was clearly ethnocentric, even mercantilistic, in orientation. As will be seen below, however, these implicit requirements frequently have been violated, and, in recent years, replaced by a more global orientation of industrial activities.

Starting around 1955, Latin American countries, notably Brazil, Mexico, and Argentina, began to attract the attention of Japanese industry. By the end of the 1950s, major trading companies, vying with each other to secure footholds on the local markets, had established branches throughout the region. The most popular among the Latin American countries was Brazil, where Japanese firms in a variety of industries, including iron and steel, shipbuilding, machinery, and textiles, began to produce on a relatively large scale. These manufacturing ventures were made in response to the import substitution policy then pursued by Brazil. Other Latin American countries, such as Bolivia, Chile, and Peru, also attracted Japanese investments in mining, especially the development of copper mines.

During the early 1960s, however, inflation, political instability, and rising nationalism in Latin America somewhat slowed the pace of Japan's overseas investment in the region, while

Japan's neighboring Asian countries, Taiwan, Thailand, Hong Kong, and Singapore, began to emerge as the host countries for Japan's offshore ventures in both commercial and manufacturing operations. Yet Japan's investment in Asia during the early 1960s remained relatively insignificant, particularly in manufacturing, because it was aimed mostly at small local markets. Among the exceptions was a sudden rush of Japanese firms to Singapore in 1963 when several joint ventures were set up to capitalize on the formation of the Malaysian Common Market. One exceptionally large project was an oil exploration investment, worth approximately $52 million, made in North Sumatra in 1960.

In the latter half of the 1960s, for the first time, the amount of direct foreign investment approved by the government rose notably. It started to exceed the $200 million level in 1966. This surge was due partly and importantly to an increased flow of overseas investment in neighboring Asian countries. Taiwan, Hong Kong, Thailand, and Singapore, in particular, attracted Japanese manufacturers of labor-intensive products who produced not only for local markets but also for export to third-country markets as well as back to Japan. Many factors contributed to this new development. Perhaps the foremost reason was the labor shortage of young workers (nineteen years old and under) in Japan that began to appear in the early 1960s and grew into a serious problem thereafter. This segment of the labor market was particularly important to Japan's small- and medium-sized enterprises producing labor-intensive manufactures for export. Just as the labor market began to tighten in Japan, other Asian countries began to pursue an "outward-looking" strategy of economic development by encouraging the inflow of foreign capital and technology to build export industries. In 1965, for example, Taiwan opened the Kaohsiung Export Processing Zone (KEPZ) that provided profitable production bases for many export-oriented Japanese manufacturers.

2. *1968-1973.*

In 1968, Japan's overseas investment reached a decisive level—$557 million, doubling the previous year's figure of $275 million. This period started out with considerable strength in Japan's balance-of-payments position and hence with an unexpectedly large accumulation of foreign reserves. During the first four years of this period, Japan registered a surplus, successively each year, not only in the trade balance but also in the over-all balance of Japan's international payments. All the preceding years had been, although headed definitely in the direction of improvement, dominated by payments deficits—a source of persistent constraint on the outflow of investment capital from Japan. The trade surplus during this period, however, jumped from $2.5 billion in 1968 to a record high of $7.8 billion in 1971. Because of this favorable trade balance, Japan's foreign exchange reserves soared, despite a substantial outflow of investment capital, from $2 billion at the beginning of 1968 to $8 billion on the eve of ex-President Nixon's announcement of new economic policies in August 1971.

The sudden rise in Japan's overseas investment at the start of this period was due partly to an increase in Japan's investments in the United States, which were heavily concentrated in commercial and service sectors, such as branches, sales and service offices, and warehouses. Japanese companies already operating in or about to enter the United States found it difficult to secure the necessary financing locally because of tightened monetary conditions in the United States; however, it was easy to take out capital from home because of eased regulations on capital outflows from Japan. Other developments also affected overseas development. Further expansion took place in Japan's labor-oriented manufacturing investments in neighboring countries, including South Korea, which, having restored normal diplomatic relations with Japan in 1965, began to invite foreign investment with attractive measures such as the opening of the

Masan Free Export Processing Zone (MAFEZ) similar to Taiwan's KEPZ. Japan also continued her search for raw materials and energy sources by making so-called "develop-and-import" (D & I) investments in resource-rich countries, and, starting in 1971, Brazil again became a popular site for Japan's manufacturing investments.

Also controls on capital outflow were quickly lifted. In October 1969, when a new system of automatic approval by the Bank of Japan (for those projects worth less than $200,000) replaced case-by-case screening by the Ministry of Finance, restrictions on overseas investments began to be liberalized. The $200,000 limit for automatic approval was raised to $1 million in September 1970, and was completely eliminated in July 1971. Behind this move was the appreciation of the yen which occurred then for the first time since the end of World War II. The devaluation of the dollar at the end of 1971 and again in February 1973, coupled with the floating of the yen, had made the yen appreciate about 35 percent against the dollar by the summer of 1973. The first round of the yen's appreciation did not deter Japan from accumulating international reserves. Her trade account kept registering surpluses, and "hot money" continued to flow into Japan in anticipation of a further appreciation of the yen—an expectation that proved largely self-fulfilling as a result of such massive speculation. Japan's international reserves hit a record high of $19.07 billion at the end of February 1973.

This continuous accumulation of reserves took place despite drastic action taken by the Japanese government. Japan went through three stages of the so-called yen defense program to reduce an embarrassingly large stock of reserves and to "defend" the yen from further appreciation. The first such program was introduced in June 1971, the second in May 1972, and the third in October 1972. Various measures were taken to encourage imports and capital outflows, each time more progressively than before, and to discourage exports and capital inflows on a temporary basis. In principle, all overseas investments were completely liberalized in June 1972. Japan's direct foreign investment, encouraged by the program, recorded a phenomenal rise. The yen's appreciation itself brought about a subsidy effect on investing Japanese companies, because they were able to acquire foreign productive assets at much lower costs than before. The government's blessings to industry were after all the decisive factor behind the gushing outflow of investment capital. In addition to liberalizing capital outflows, the government newly instituted a special loan program for overseas investment which included a lower rate of interest and expanded availability of long-term funds in foreign exchange. It also introduced a tax-exempt loss reserve program for overseas ventures; under this system the investing firm would be allowed to put aside in a so-called loss reserves taxable income up to a certain percentage of the value of its investment abroad.

In the wake of the massive outflow of long-term investment capital, Japan's balance-of-payments surplus soon disappeared. In April 1973, Japan experienced an over-all payments deficit of $1.16 billion even though her trade account recorded a small surplus. Yet already accumulated reserves continued to provide ample exchange for investing Japanese companies. Japan's overseas investment during this period began to expand actively into new fields such as real estate, tourism (for example, hotels and golf courses), and financial institutions, such as banks, security firms, and insurance companies. Reflecting a growth-led appetite for industrial resources, particularly energy resources, a vast amount of investment capital was poured into resource-rich countries, including Indonesia, Brazil, and Mideast oil-producing countries.

Then came the Mideast war of October 1973. The Arab oil embargo and, more important, the quadrupled oil prices drastically changed the picture of Japan's international payments. Because Japan is almost totally dependent on imports for her oil supply (99.7 percent in 1972), glum predictions were made about Japan's economy and her trade balance. As a result, the government first imposed restrictions on overseas investments in real estate and later announced its decision to ask industry, through "administrative guidance," to postpone some of the less urgent overseas investments already approved. Yet the momentum for overseas investment, built under the favorable trade surpluses in the earlier period, showed only a temporary slowdown. It now seemed to have gathered more force, because the energy crisis would require more and more participation in the development of energy resources abroad to secure supplies, and because Japan became more willing than ever to transfer energy-consuming industries to countries where energy supplies are abundant. As might be expected, however, Japan's strategy for financing her overseas investment shifted from one of dependence on her trade surpluses to one of taking advantage of capital available overseas. In this respect petro-dollars became a new source of capital that Japanese firms were eager to tap for their overseas ventures. In fact, the establishment of overseas branches by Japanese banks in the Middle East quickly demonstrated this new attitude.

Another characteristic of the early 1970s was the growing disillusionment on the part of the Japanese public with the results of economic growth, a government policy impetuously pursued throughout the postwar period. Pollution, congestion, and environmental decay—social costs of economic development aggravated by industrialization centered in the heavy and chemical industries—had reached intolerable levels. For the first time in Japan's industrial history genuine concern for the quality of life became a public issue. Moreover, an unexpectedly strong antagonism against Japanese exports in the world market forced Japan to reflect on her "export-or-perish" attitude and to realize the need to reorient her economic drive.

With these developments as a backdrop, the Japanese government adopted an epoch-making policy to restructure Japan's industry, a proposal made by the Industrial Structure Council, the MITI's consultative organ. The policy emphasized a shift from "pollution-prone" and "resource-consuming" heavy and chemical industries toward "clean" and "knowledge-intensive" industries, and assigned overseas investment a new role—that of a catalyst to "houseclean" the economy.[17] Overseas production was also intended as a substitute for export, alleviating, it was hoped, the rising outcry against imports in foreign markets.

After the 1973 Arab oil embargo Japanese industry also began to look seriously at the Middle East as another host region for overseas production. Government and industry began a concerted effort to capture the Middle Eastern market through "economic development assistance."

3. *1974-1977.*

The momentum for overseas investment declined sharply in 1974—down by as much as $1,098 million from the previous year's. The stringent anti-inflationary measures taken by the government drove the economy into a deep recession. A record number of companies went bankrupt, and unemployment rose (for example, in March 1975 unemployment exceeded 1 million for the first time in the past eight years, registering a rate of 2.2 percent). An economic slump at home naturally forced Japanese companies to curtail their overseas investment plans. Lack of funds necessitated cancellation or postponement of large-scale projects in areas such as petro-chemicals and steel-making in the early part of this period—much to the disappointment of developing host countries. Worsened political relations with some Asian countries, such as South Korea (where a Korean national residing in Japan made an abortive assassination attempt on the life of President Park) and Thailand (where there was a flare-up of anti-Japanese demonstrations), also adversely affected the outflow of Japan's overseas investments.

Nevertheless it is still noteworthy that the total value of investment projects approved by the government stood above the $2 billion level in 1974 and that it quickly returned to the $3 billion level in the following year. This seems to attest to a strong current underlying the persistent trend of Japan's overseas industrial expansion. Domestic conditions provided a partial reason for continual expansion. For example, a record-breaking wage hike of 31.4 percent in the spring of 1974 further aggravated the domestic conditions of industrial production already seriously affected by the soaring prices of fuels and raw materials. Because of this huge wage increase it was predicted that production costs of consumer durables such as radios and televisions in Japan would soon exceed those in the United States. These expectations of continued inflation and wage spirals at home, which would surely be greater than corresponding increases in productivity, gave an additional incentive to Japanese companies to transfer part of their corporate production overseas.

Moreover, Japan's balance-of-payments position, which had temporarily become precarious as a result of increased bills for imported oil, soon showed an impressive strength mainly because of a surprisingly strong growth in her exports. Hence, once an economic upturn was in sight, the interest of Japanese firms in overseas production was rekindled. At this time, the Japanese government also began to fulfill previous commitments to provide economic assistance to developing countries. After a considerable delay to work out a final agreement in each case, official loans finally were extended to such "show-case" projects as a power-and-aluminum project in Indonesia (the Asahan project), another power-and-aluminum project in Brazil (the Amazon project), a petro-chemical complex in Singapore, and another petro-chemical project in Saudi Arabia. In addition, another sharp increase in the value of the yen relative to the dollar began in 1977 and gave Japan's export industries further impetus to manufacture their products overseas (for example, the consumer electronics industry). Industries were motivated mainly to circumvent protectionism, to minimize the exchange risk for export earnings in foreign currencies (the U.S. dollar and those other currencies tied to the dollar) and, at the same time, to take advantage of a newly gained currency premium on the yen in acquiring foreign assets.

Regional Patterns of Direct Foreign Investment

The Japanese government recently has begun to realize that direct foreign investment is an important catalyst in implementing its ambitious plan to reorganize and upgrade Japan's economic structure while integrating her industrial activities with those of the rest of the world, supplementing the traditional route of trade. Japan now desires to transfer by means of overseas investment some of her traditional industries (particularly those that are less skill-intensive, resource-consuming, or pollution-prone) to developing or resource-rich countries and to encourage simultaneously the development of modern, technology-intensive, and "clean" industries at home. Heretofore Japan's direct foreign investment activities have evolved largely in response to changing economic conditions in the world market. Among the important developments are a rising clamor against Japanese exports, the eagerness of developing countries to attract foreign capital and technology, the so-called chasing-up competition from these countries against Japan's traditional industries, the soaring labor costs and rising social costs of industrial growth at home, and the recent changes in the value of the yen. A successful cartel organized by the Organization of Petroleum Exporting Countries (OPEC) countries is still another significant development.

The combination of these events has rendered obsolete and even deleterious to Japan the conventional approach of home-centered economic expansion (namely, importing raw materials, turning them into manufactures at home, and then exporting the latter back to the world). In short, overseas production has become not only a useful supplement to but also a desirable substitute for Japan's trade. This new mode of commercial relations is reflected in the industrial and regional distributions of Japan's overseas investments, as shown in tables 1.2 and 1.3.

One feature seems unique—a heavy concentration of investments in commerce and services, accounting for as much as 39.5 percent of the total amount of Japan's overseas investment (table 1.2). The fact that 42.3 percent of this category of investment is made in North America (table 1.3) indicates the importance of that region for Japan's postwar economic development through trade. The United States by adopting a free trade policy, phenomenally increased its imports from Japan, initially, price-elastic, labor-intensive products (such as textiles, toys, and sundries) and later, mostly income-elastic, high-value manufactures (such as automobiles and televisions) that Japanese industry had succeeded in producing competitively, using technologies purchased mostly from the United States itself.[18] These Japanese exports, notably consumer durables, required the establishment of marketing networks, especially in advanced Western markets, to take care of inventories, advertising, sales promotion, and after-sale services. On the regional level, therefore, overseas investment in commerce and services accounts for 67.9 percent of Japan's total investment in the United States and as much as 81.1 percent of that in Europe (table 1.2).[19]

In the early postwar period, the foreign exchange earned through exports was sparingly allocated to buy foodstuffs, industrial raw materials, fuels, and capital equipment. As Japan's capacity to earn more foreign exchange developed later on, her overseas investment to develop the supply sources of vital resources expanded boldly, for some projects involved huge sums of capital outlays even by international standards. This pattern of behavior could be expected of a country that lacked natural resources yet emphasized the development of resource-consuming heavy and chemical industries. Here the economics is not a cost-pinching, short-term calculation but a security-primacy, long-term calculation. Japan's demand for and dependence on

Table 1.2

Sectoral Distribution of Japan's Direct Foreign Investment
within Different Regions at the End of March 1976

Region	Extractive sector %	Manufacturing sector %	Commerce and services %	Total %
North America	10.9	21.2	67.9	100.0
Europe	4.2	14.7	81.1	100.0
Latin America	22.7	53.3	24.0	100.0
Asia	32.8	48.3	18.9	100.0
Oceania	49.0	34.1	16.9	100.0
Middle East	66.9[a]	7.1	26.0	100.0
Africa	61.8	12.0	26.2	100.0
Total	28.1	32.4	39.5	100.0

Source: Compiled from MITI, *Wagakuni Kigyo*, 1976, p. 103.
[a] Japan's purchase from Britain of the equity ownership ($780 million)
of Abu Dhabi Marine Areas (ADMA) is included here, although the
Japanese official statistics treat this as part of investments in Britain.

Table 1.3

Regional Distribution of Japan's Direct Foreign Investment
by Industrial Sector at the End of March 1976

Region	Extractive sector[a] %	Manufacturing sector[a] %	Commerce and services[a] %
North America	9.5	16.1	42.3
Europe	1.6	4.9	22.3
Latin America	14.6	29.7	11.0
Asia	30.9	39.5	12.7
Oceania	10.2	6.1	2.5
Middle East	26.3	2.4	7.2
Africa	6.9	1.2	2.1
Total	100.0	100.0	100.0

Source: Compiled by MITI *Wagakuni Kigyo*, 1976, p. 103.
[a] Subject to rounding errors.

overseas resources have increased enormously—so much so that the conventional trade mechanism, because it inevitably involves uncertainties, has become obviously inappropriate. Thus a develop-and-import strategy through direct foreign investment has become a sine qua non, since it helps to secure, even if partially, the supply sources by involving them in ownership and management. Therefore, Japan's overseas investment shows a relatively high proportion of investments in extractive ventures (table 1.2).[20]

What is uinque about Japan's direct foreign investment, however, is the migration of Japan's manufacturing industry to neighboring Asian countries and Latin America. There are two basic motives for this geographical transplant of Japan's manufacturing activities; one is to circumvent the import substitution policy of the host country; the other is to set up a production base to utilize low manufacturing costs overseas. The first motive was predominant throughout the 1950s and the early 1960s and was generally observable in Japan's investment in Latin America; the second gained in importance beginning in the mid-1960s, particularly following each of the currency realignments in 1971 and 1973, and explains, on the whole, Japan's manufacturing ventures in Asia.

As shown in table 1.3, Asian countries account for about 40 percent of Japan's overseas investment in manufacturing. Japanese ventures in this region are not only supplying local markets but also increasingly exporting to third markets, particularly to advanced Western countries, as well as back to Japan. The manufacturing activities transferred to this region are mostly those labor-intensive, low-technology sectors in which Japan used to enjoy decisive trade advantages but in which she can no longer compete internationally if production is to be continued at home.

This newly evolving triangular trade system enjoys not only the low-cost production available in developing countries but, and more important, the marketing networks so extensively developed by Japanese firms, notably the trading companies, in the world market. The global marketing channels that Japan established initially for her own exports are thus evolving into outlets for exports produced in developing countries with Japanese capital and technology.

With the foregoing analysis in mind, it is interesting to observe the differences that have emerged between Japan's overseas investment patterns in the advanced West and those in the developing regions (table 1.2); the ratio of overseas investment in commerce and services is comparatively high in North America and Europe; in contrast, it is the ratio of overseas investment in manufacturing that is relatively high in Asia and Latin America. Although Japan's manufacturing investment in Latin America is aimed mostly at relatively large local markets, it may become export-oriented once host countries adopt a more outward-looking development strategy, one emphasizing exports rather than import substitution, as Brazil has done so successfully in the recent past.

"Immaturity" of Investing Japanese Firms

As the analysis of how Japanese multinationalism has evolved in the postwar period has emphasized, both internal and external macroeconomic constraints on Japan's industrial production at home and her overseas trade conditions have impelled her industry to expand overseas; this development, therefore, was primarily not an aggregation of microeconomic behaviors that naturally evolved from individual firms attaining the internal capacity to produce overseas on their own. In this respect the behavior of the majority of Japanese investing firms, manufacturers in particular, is unlike the typical behavior of Western, notably U.S.-based, multinational corporations. Much Japanese participation in overseas manufacturing ventures, especially in Asia, is in the individual instance "immature" by Western standards in terms of scale of operation, technological sophistication, and financial strength. By examining closely these "immature" characteristics of Japanese multinationals, it is possible to see how this apparent weakness is overcome.

In the case of U.S. multinationals it is said that large size is a necessary, if not a sufficient, condition. Raymond Vernon states:

> Even if the tie between the problems of corporate multinationality and the phenomenon of corporate size had not been so commonly taken for granted, other indications would have focused the search on the largest U.S. corporations. A relatively few large U.S. corporations account for most of the foreign direct investment of the U.S. economy, a higher proportion in fact than their share of U.S. industry itself. With the emphasis on size, therefore, the search turned to the usual group that epitomizes U.S. industrial giants: *Fortune's* list of 500 U.S. industrial firms.
>
> Large size is a necessary but not sufficient condition for including an enterprise in the ambit of this study. A few industrial giants are not engaged in manufacturing, for example, airlines and public utilities; these were passed over. Moreover, some giants fail to venture abroad in spite of their size; about one quarter of *Fortune's* 500 in 1964, for instance, had no overseas manufacturing subsidiaries at all. In addition to size, therefore, a second criterion of selection was needed, reflecting the propensity of the large corporation to venture widely abroad.[21]

Size is the most dominant feature of U.S. multinationals. Thomas Horst observes: "The conclusion I have come to, after an exhaustive examination of the data is that *once interindustry differences are washed out, the only influence of any separate significance is firm size.*"[22]

In contrast, nearly one-half of the total number of Japan's overseas investments are made by small- and medium-sized enterprises (those with either a total number of employees of 300 or fewer, or paid-in capital of 100 million yen or less, as defined earlier). As table 1.4 indicates, the ratio of manufacturing in-

Table 1.4

Number of Japan's Overseas Manufacturing Investments Made by Small- and
Medium-Sized Firms Compared to Total Number of Firms at the End of 1975

	North America	Latin America	Asia Total	Taiwan	South Korea	Others	Europe	Middle East	Oceania	Africa	Total
A. Investments by small- and medium-sized firms[a]	107 (7.8)[b]	86 (6.3)	1,128 (82.3)	302 (22.0)	473 (34.5)	353 (25.8)	17 (1.2)	2 (0.2)	13 (1.0)	17 (1.2)	1,370 (100.0)
B. Total number of investments	307 (9.3)[b]	383 (11.7)	2,283 (69.6)	515 (15.7)	676 (20.6)	1,092 (33.3)	140 (4.3)	29 (0.9)	67 (2.0)	71 (2.2)	3,280 (100.0)
A/B (%)	34.9	22.5	49.4	58.6	70.0	32.3	12.1	6.9	19.4	23.9	41.8

Source: Adapted from Japanese Government, Small and Medium Enterprise Agency, *Chusho Kigyo Hakusho*, 1976, p. 41.

[a] The number of approved manufacturing ventures by small- and medium-sized enterprises (those either with the total number of employees of 300 or less, or with the paid-in capital of 100 million yen or less—but 50 million yen or less prior to 1972). The number of ventures listed here covers only securities investments and does not include additional investments to existing ventures.

[b] Figures in parentheses indicate the regional distribution in percent.

vestments made by these small firms to the total number of manufacturing investments is as high as 41.8 percent on the whole. The ratio becomes even higher in some of the Asian countries; it is 58.6 percent in Taiwan and as high as 70.0 percent in South Korea. This clearly reflects both Japan's peculiar industrial structure, still "dominated" by relatively small- and medium-sized enterprises, and the unique process by which the labor-intensive, low-productivity end of the dual industrial structure is being gradually pushed out of Japan and sent to more labor-abundant neighboring countries through direct foreign investment. Taiwan and South Korea alone host 56.5 percent of Japan's manufacturing ventures made by small- and medium-sized enterprises. In fact, 82.3 percent of them are concentrated in Asia. (Even when investments made by large-scale firms are included in the total, Asia is still decisively important as a host region for Japanese firms. Nearly 70 percent of the total *number* of Japan's manufacturing ventures is located in Asian countries. This fact also indicates that Japanese manufacturing investments in Asia are, on the whole, on a much smaller scale than those in other regions, because Asia accounts for about 40 percent of the total *value* of Japan's manufacturing investments.)

Moreover, there are other important differences between Japanese and U.S. multinationals. Those manufacturing industries in which U.S. multinationals are most active are identified as the ones that are R & D-based, differentiated in product, and highly concentrated in structure (namely, oligopolistic), and not as "those relatively labor-intensive and declining industries."[23] "They portray a group of enterprises of extraordinary size and high profitability, committed to activities that involve the relatively heavy use of skilled manpower and of advertising outlays—in short, a group of enterprises bearing the characteristics usually associated with oligopoly."[24]

In comparison, however, the pattern of Japan's multinationalism is almost the opposite; it is clustered in relatively competitive industries that produce standardized or traditional goods such as textiles, sundries, metal products, and the relatively un-sophisticated product lines of electrical appliances (for example, batteries, fans, irons, and radios) and chemicals (for example, paints and plastics). This characteristic is exhibited in table 1.5. Interestingly enough, the more competitive the industry is

Table 1.5

Worldwide and Asian Distribution of the Value of Japan's
Overseas Manufacturing Investments by Industry

Industry	World-wide %	Asia %	Asia's share in each industry %
Food	5.5	4.3	29.4
Textiles	22.2	38.3	65.5
Timber and pulp	10.2	5.9	22.0
Chemicals	15.3	7.0	17.4
Ferrous and non-ferrous metals	15.3	8.7	21.6
Nonelectrical machinery	7.4	4.2	21.8
Electrical appliances and machinery	10.3	13.6	50.2
Transport equipment	6.4	6.1	36.5
Sundries	7.3	11.6	60.7
Total[a]	100.0	100.0	

Source: Computed from data in MITI, *Wagakuni Kigyo*, 1975, p. 233.
[a] Subject to rounding errors.

(that is, the more standardized the product is), the greater the incidence of Japan's manufacturing investment in developing Asian countries. Note that textiles, electrical appliances, and sundries taken together account for 63.5 percent of the value of Japan's manufacturing investments in Asia, and that 65.5 percent of the total value of Japan's investments in textiles, 50.2 percent of that in electrical appliances, and 60.7 percent of that in sundries are located in Asia.

Thus, by the usual standards of U.S. multinationals many Japanese firms investing in overseas manufacturing may be judged "immature" or even "misfits" in both firm size and the technological sophistication of their products. Small firm size usually is associated with a weak financial position. Many of those small firms concentrated in Japan's declining industrial sector are not only financially weak but also managerially incapable of taking up direct overseas production on their own. How, then, do these individual Japanese firms overcome their internal weaknesses in directly operating overseas? Are there any unique features in the Japanese or the host economy which have helped or are helping them establish corporate production overseas?

"Arranged" Competitiveness

Support from General Trading Companies

Before attempting to answer the above questions, it should be noted that investment in commerce is an exception to the rule outlined above. Here Japanese industry has unmatched strength, because it has the powerful trading companies known as *sogo shosha*. The trading companies are industrial organizations unique to Japan, organizations whose existence is almost unparalleled elsewhere.[25] There are literally thousands of trading companies in Japan (anywhere from 3,000 to 7,000, depending on the criteria used for classification), but the most significant are the so-called Big Ten trading companies, whose total sales at present amount to almost 30 percent of Japan's Gross National Product (GNP).[26] They have traditionally been commission brokers, operating at a thin margin of profit but engaged in large volumes of trade. For example, the combined share of the Big Ten trading companies in Japan's foreign trade in 1973 was 51 percent in exports and 63 percent in imports,[27] and they were the first group of Japanese firms to make overseas investments to set up global marketing networks.

Indeed, the big trading companies now play a vital role in assisting small Japanese enterprises to establish manufacturing ventures overseas, and they provide the organizational skill needed for large-scale, resource-development ventures. In 1976, for example, the first five of Japan's top overseas investors were trading companies: Mitsui, Mitsubishi, Marubeni, C. Itoh, and Sumitomo. They alone accounted for 43 percent of the total value of outstanding overseas investments made by Japan's top fifty overseas investors among whom five other big trading companies (Nissho-Iwai, Nichimen, Ataka, Toyo Menka, and Kanematsu-Gohsho) are included.[28]

In overseas manufacturing activities trading companies are usually engaged in light-manufacturing ventures in collaboration with small Japanese firms whose products they used to export from Japan. Trading companies then traditionally have been a specialized export division of Japan's light manufacturers who, because of their small size, cannot afford (or are managerially unable) to have an export division of their own and who remain essentially production units. Trading companies have also been financiers for small manufacturers. Thus an intercompany division of corporate functions between small light manufacturers and trading companies has long been a unique feature of Japan's export-oriented light industries.

When a labor shortage at home and rising competition from developing countries threatened Japan's light manufacturers, starting in the mid-1960s, trading companies were naturally interested in trying to save their established business. One solution was to encourage their affiliated small firms to move to labor-abundant neighboring countries by providing all necessary assistance. In locating their production units in developing Asian countries, trading companies often chose local partners who were either their own former distributors or independent local producers (that is, potential competitors). As a result, many Japanese manufacturing ventures in light industries exhibit the following pattern of capital ownership: The trading company involved owns from 25 to 30 percent; the affiliated Japanese manufacturer, about the same; and local interests, the balance.

Because trading companies were originally specialized in marketing a given product line, overseas production tends to be centered in their specialty. For example, C. Itoh, Marubeni, Nichimen, Tomen, and Kanematsu were initially textile wholesalers; hence they are relatively more active in overseas textile ventures: Iwai and Ataka were originally iron and steel product wholesalers; hence they are active in metal product ventures. On the other hand, Mitsui, Mitsubishi, and Sumitomo, being *zaibatsu* trading companies, are relatively less centered in light industries and more widely dispersed industrially in overseas ventures.[29]

Host Country Environment

Political instability aside, Japanese ventures in developing countries enjoy a variety of economic advantages. First, there are few local competitors. The less industrially developed the host country, the less the local competition. Although there may be some competition from Western manufacturers also operating in the developing host country, they mostly tend to operate in less labor-intensive industries, so they rarely offer serious competition. In fact, Japanese investors regard their *own* compatriots as tougher competitors in developing countries than local or third-country firms.[30] Moreover, the host country may even discourage local competition among investing foreign interests lest their scale economies be jeopardized.

Second, especially in Asia, the Japanese are most eagerly taking advantage of abundant low-cost labor and of other financial advantages offered by host countries, such as tax holidays and freedom from duties on imported capital goods and materials. Because of their geographical proximity Japanese firms enjoy an absolute advantage in utilizing tax-free export processing zones both in Taiwan and South Korea. Japanese manufacturers abroad may even enjoy the preferential tariffs recently conferred by their own country and others on the importation of manufactures from the developing countries.

Government Support and Debt Financing

Perhaps the most important supportive feature in Japan's overseas industrial expansion is the role of the Japanese government in encouraging, assisting, and occasionally even participating, albeit indirectly, in private overseas ventures. First, the Japanese government officially treats private overseas investments as an integral part of Japan's overseas economic assistance. Because of the sharp increase in private overseas investments, Japan was able to claim that in 1973 more than 1 percent (1.42 percent) of her GNP was transferred to less developed countries in the form of development assistance; she thereby exceeded the "one percent target" of economic foreign aid internationally agreed upon in the United Nations.[31] It is debatable, however, whether private overseas investments should be construed as foreign aid; strictly speaking, foreign aid is "a transfer of real resources or immediate claim on resources (for example, foreign exchange) from one country to another, which would not have taken place as a consequence of the operation of market forces or in the absence of specific official action designed to promote the transfer by the donor country."[32] Private overseas investments are certainly determined by "the operations of market forces" and do not involve the idea of "economic sacrifice" implied in the term "foreign aid."

It is understandable that for reasons of international diplomacy the Japanese government is tempted to magnify the flow of resources for economic assistance by including private overseas investment. Whether it is appropriate to include private overseas investment in a definition of foreign aid is debatable. However, the treatment of market-encouraged private-resource flows as an inseparable part of Japan's official development assistance presents quite a realistic picture of the manner in which "foreign aid" is provided by Japan. For there is a growing trend toward coordination and collaboration between the Japanese government (official foreign aid) and industry (private overseas investment) in Japan's productive activities overseas.

In 1972, the Japanese Economic Planning Agency noted a close association between the two flows:

> In the case of all DAC [the Development Assistance Committee of the (OECD) Organization for Economic Cooperation and Development] members. . . . Government aid is extended to countries in a lower stage of industrialization while direct investment is made in countries in a higher stage of industrialization. As for Japan, Government aid and private investment are almost equally distributed. This is partly because Japanese aid is concentrated in Southeast Asia where the rate of industrialization in mining and manufacturing is 10-20 percent in most countries. Such a pattern of aid often presents the problem of private direct investment being concentrated in the same region that Government aid is concentrated. It is necessary, therefore, to create basic conditions for development by expanding Government aid and to diversify private direct investment to include as many regions as possible.[33]

Although the statement does not explain why Japan's official aid and private investment coincide, the reason is obvious: in the 1950s, Japan's reparation program helped to pave the way for the advance of Japan's trade and private overseas investments into the Asian region; in the 1960s, aid loans further opened up many markets in Asia and Latin America; and in the 1970s, massive aid loans are being extended to the Middle East, accompanied by the advance of Japanese industry to the region. In fact, a greater dispersion of Japan's economic assistance has occurred since 1972—with the share of Asia declining and the share of Latin America and the Middle East rising.[34] Yet this has happened precisely because other regions have emerged as equally important areas for Japan's overseas investment. The flows of official aid and private investment have become more concurrent than before. Such a trend is definitely expected to be intensified, because the Japanese government is officially determined to make economic assistance more "effective" by calling upon Japan's private enterprises to assist in the actual implementation of investment projects. Instead of merely leaving the use of aid to the discretion of the aid-receiving country, the Japanese government wants to require feasibility studies, planning of the necessary infrastructure and plants, and acquisition of managerial and technical training.[35] This approach constitutes a new form of "tied aid," designed to foster both Japan's exports *and* her direct foreign investment.

Furthermore, Japan's official bilateral aid exhibits an unusually high ratio of loans to grants. From 1972 to 1974, for example, this ratio was as high as 72.2 percent, as compared to the average of 35.6 percent for all the DAC member-countries of the OECD.[36] The "tied aid" characteristic is no doubt stronger in loans than in grants, because loans are offered for specific projects that the lender must approve in terms of their economic feasibility and rationality—usually from his own vantage point. Official loans often are extended in return for purchases of industrial plants and equipment from the lending country. Japan is making relatively more active use of this particular form of bilateral aid than any other country.

In addition to foreign aid, the Japanese government also provides private Japanese firms with "internal aid," with which they then finance their overseas investment. For example, the Export-Import Bank of Japan extends large loans to Japanese investors who are allowed to use them for three purposes: (1) to finance their equity ownership in overseas ventures; (2) to provide debt capital to their overseas ventures; and (3) to finance the purchase of plants and equipment from Japan to be installed in overseas ventures. Another governmental agency, the Overseas Economic Cooperation Fund (OECF), invests public funds in those large-scale resource-development or processing projects that are set up as joint ventures with the government of a developing host country—projects that, because of the large-scale operation involved, the private Japanese sector alone cannot finance. The investment takes the form of equity capital participation (the agency usually becomes the largest shareholder) in an investment syndicate organized by a group of Japanese firms, representing the Japanese interest in overseas ventures. The Japanese International Cooperation Agency (JICA) also extends loans and performs other functions (for example, technical assistance for the development of infrastructural facilities required by an "economic development" project in which Japanese industry is participating).

In order to assist Japan's small firms in light industries and the developing countries interested in hosting joint ventures with these Japanese firms, another governmental agency, the Japan Overseas Development Corporation,[37] conducts preliminary surveys on the practicality of proposed ventures in the host countries and extends to those small Japanese firms participating in its approved ventures interest-free loans with the maximum term of twenty years covering the maximum of four-fifths (normally two-thirds) of the required capital. In addition, the government-affiliated financial institutions established specifically to assist small firms (such as the Small Business Finance Corporation, the People's Finance Corporation, and the Central Bank for Commercial and Industrial Cooperatives)[38] are all active in providing advice and commercial loans for overseas investment.

Japanese firms are also given a tax incentive for overseas investment. Under a program called "Loss Reserves for Overseas Investment and Related Expenditures," the investing firm is allowed to put aside its taxable incomes in reserves up to an amount equivalent to a specified percentage of the value of its overseas investment (inclusive of loans). This tax deferment is for five years, after which the reserves must be redistributed back to taxable income within the subsequent five years. The ventures involving the extraction of mineral and energy resources abroad are allowed to accumulate loss reserves up to 100 percent of expenditures for prospecting and up to 40 percent of the value of overseas investment. For all other overseas ventures, the investing firm can set aside up to 30 percent, regardless of industries, provided that they are located in developing countries. (The same tax incentive originally was given to Japanese ventures in advanced countries, but was eliminated in April 1975. However, it is possible that the government may restore it.)

The result of all these governmental efforts to supplement the financial strength of Japanese multinationals is clear. By the end of March 1975, 34.2 percent of their overseas investment capital was borrowed from government-affiliated financial institutions; 32.8 percent from private financial institutions (mostly city banks whose liquidity is in turn controlled by the Bank of Japan); the balance, 33.0 percent, was financed internally by the individual firms.[39]

Not only are investing Japanese firms dependent on loans to finance their own equity interest, but their overseas ventures are in turn dependent on the use of debt capital (that is, on direct overseas loans). Direct overseas loans are made in foreign currency, capital goods, and services by Japanese firms to their affiliated overseas ventures. Reflecting this widespread practice, the official statistics of Japan's direct foreign investment are comprised of five categories: (1) securities investments (involving the acquisition of equity interest in return for investments in the form of capital, physical equipment, and industrial property); (2) direct overseas loans; (3) the acquisition of real estate; (4) the establishment of branch offices; and (5) direct overseas investment (by firms as Japanese corporate persons without their being incorporated locally). The first two forms of investment alone account for more than 90 percent of the total value of Japan's investment—55.3 percent for securities investment and 36.7 percent for direct overseas loans (see table A.1). The inclusion of loans in Japan's direct foreign investment is an unusual arrangement; the normal practice of the International Monetary Fund (IMF) and the United States is to exclude loans from such a classification on the grounds that loans do not accompany ownership and managerial controls.[40]

The internal nature of these loans enhances the managerial control of Japanese interests in overseas production, so perhaps their treatment as direct foreign investment is justified. In addition to taking the form of capital goods and services supplied by Japanese parent companies or partners, these loans are also extended to local joint-venture partners who are short of capital to finance their portion of equity ownership—not an uncommon situation in the developing host countries. Under this sort of financial arrangement, the Japanese partners are likely to end up exercising a much stronger managerial control than their equity share implies.

In sum, the financial strength of Japan's overseas advance is built upon *three layers* of debt financing: (1) official aid loans extended by the government to induce the host countries to acquire Japanese capital goods and services for infrastructural projects (which create a favorable climate for direct foreign investment by Japanese industry); (2) bank loans acquired by investing Japanese firms from both the government-affiliated institutions and the private banks to finance their share of equity interest in overseas ventures; and (3) direct overseas loans provided by Japanese firms to their overseas affiliates (and often also to the local joint-venture partners who use the funds to finance their equity ownership).

This pattern of heavy dependence on debt perhaps reflects the general financial structure of Japanese corporations. In 1975, for instance, the average ratio of equity to debt capital was 16.2 percent for Japanese enterprises, compared to 52.1 percent for U.S. enterprises, 49.8 percent for British firms, and 35.7 percent for West German firms.[41]

This financial practice, which has enabled Japanese firms to grow rapidly throughout the postwar period,[42] is now extended equally to Japan's overseas investment and has become recognized as an important source of Japanese advantage in overseas ventures. Indeed, the constant need for growth (a larger share of the market) created under these financial arrangements may itself be an important driving force behind the overseas expansion of Japanese firms. Throughout the postwar period of the "economic miracle," heavy debt-financing for growth was encouraged by the Japanese government. In part, this was a way of supplying funds to the capital-short economy in order to avoid dependence on foreign capital. Now the individual firm with insufficient financial strength to invest overseas is similarly provided with funds by the Japanese government and its closely controlled financial sector.

Conclusions

One major characteristic of Japanese multinationals that emerges from the preceding analysis is that they are strongly influenced by the macroeconomic factors of their own economy and by those of the host countries. Among the significant factors, both internal and external, are: the great dependency of their economy on foreign markets, both for export and import (particularly of natural resources); the rising environmental costs of industrialization at home; the phenomenal increase in the prices of domestic industrial inputs (notably, land and labor); the aspirations of developing countries to industrialize and their eagerness to attract Japanese capital and technology (particularly in labor-intensive light industries); and the rising protectionism against Japanese exports in the world market. In short, Japanese multinationals are responding to, and taking advantage of, both the needs of their own economy and the new requirements of foreign markets.

The overseas investment activities of many Japanese manufacturers may look "immature" in firm size and technological sophistication by Western standards. Even by Japanese standards many small light manufacturers for whom the need to defend both their export and domestic markets by means of overseas production is the greatest are managerially, technologically, and financially not ready to go overseas on their own (that is, without external assistance). But ironically, from a macroeconomic viewpoint, they are judged both appropriate and ready to be transplanted overseas. In Japan, labor-intensive, pollution-prone, or heavily-resource-consuming industries need to be phased out because of a rapidly changing factor endowment position, the rising social costs of industrialization, and the increased vulnerability of import dependence on overseas resources. Hence external assistance is given to defray part of the private costs and to realize the social benefits of overseas investment.

Chapter 2

Peculiarities of the Japanese Experience:
Theoretical Considerations

A variety of theories have been advanced to explain the present trend of business firms toward multinational operations, a trend of massive outward expansion which was first noticed in the United States but is now spreading to other industrial countries. Recently, several survey articles interpreting and categorizing these various theories have been published. Two papers (J. H. Dunning, 1973; G. C. Hufbauer, 1975), for example, survey and evaluate major theories and empirical studies; another (T. G. Parry, 1973) discusses policy issues; and a series of U.N. reports from 1973 to 1974 on multinational corporations focuses on the political questions involved, particularly those that the host countries of the Third World raise.[1] The theoretical works so far written obviously revolve around the behavior of Western multinationals, notably U.S. multinational corporations, with their Japanese counterparts being treated either as a special case or as mere newcomers who will inevitably follow the same path of their Western predecessors. Some writers are more cautious, cautious enough to point out some differences in the industrial pattern of Japanese multinationals and to urge a further and more systematic analysis.[2] This chapter evaluates the applicability of existing theories to the Japanese case and postulates a new analytical framework within which to interpret the uniqueness of Japan's multinationalism.

Relevance of Western Theories

In this section, the major theories advanced by Western economists to explain the behavior of Western multinationals are reviewed, and their relevance as applied to the behavior of Japanese multinationals is reviewed with the necessary theoretical modifications.

Industrial Organization Approach

One well-accepted theory emphasizes industrial organization. To explain the pattern of "horizontal" foreign investment (namely, investment designed to produce the same line of products across national boundaries), Stephen H. Hymer, Charles P. Kindleberger, and Richard E. Caves, among others, emphasized that direct foreign investment occurs in industries characterized by oligopolistic market structures in both home and host countries.[3] The products involved in overseas production are therefore either distinct in their technical makeup or highly differentiated in their market acceptability, and are produced by a group of a few relatively large firms. By definition, this oligopolistic market is composed of individual firms each of whom enjoys monopolistic profits through possessing and controlling some type of firm-specific, rent-yielding attributes (for example, either a superior technology or greater knowledge about production, marketing, and management). The basic assumption here is that the firm that invests for direct production in a foreign market is, all other things being equal, at a disadvantage compared to local firms because of its unfamiliarity with local market conditions (that is, it must incur higher information costs than do its local counterparts). Therefore, some special advantage possessed by the investing foreign firm must be great enough to offset the higher information costs of its alien status if it is to operate competitively in a foreign market.

This theoretical approach also explains why an investing firm prefers to own its foreign subsidiary outright or as nearly so as possible. The firm is understandably reluctant to share with local interests the quasi-rents resulting from its advantages.[4] If its advantages are built on some technical knowledge internal to the firm, the need for quality controls and other engineering supervision may also make the firm wary of losing control of management.[5] The desire for managerial control may be even stronger if a firm's advantage is based only on a differentiated "product image" it has carefully cultivated over a long period of time, as is the case with soft drinks and convenient foodstuffs.

According to this view, there would be no direct foreign investment in a perfectly competitive market, since, as Kindleberger has pointed out, there ought to be some type of "market imperfections" in the market for direct foreign investment to take place:

> For direct investment to thrive there must be some imperfection in markets for goods or factors, including among the latter technology, or some interference in competition by government or by firms, which separates markets. . . .
>
> That product differentiation breeds direct investment is indicated by its prevalence in branded products such as pharmaceuticals, cosmetics, soft drinks, and specialty foodstuffs, and in concentrated industries such as automobiles, tires, chemicals, electrical appliances, electronic components, farm machinery, office equipment. It does not occur in standardized goods produced by competitive industries such as textiles, clothing, flour milling, and distribution (except for Sears Roebuck in Latin America).[6]

Raymond Vernon similarly observes:

> Multinational enterprises are not identified with the manufacture of such standardized products as steel bars and rods, gray cloth, or plywood; but they are identified with products whose specifications are in flux. The dichotomy is not all that clear, of course. A few seemingly standardized products, such as automobiles, appear to enlarge their scale economies of production or distribution with such regularity and persistence that the advantages of the multinational enterprises are maintained.[7]

Yet a vast majority of Japan's overseas ventures in manufacturing are located in neighboring Asian countries and in Latin America. Especially in the former, these ventures, set up primarily by small- and medium-sized companies, produce mostly standardized, low-technology products. These are therefore relatively small-scale operations, so there is not much possibility of scale economies in production or of product differentiation.

There is, however, an emerging pattern of overseas investment by large Japanese companies that fits the Hymer-Kindleberger-Caves model. These ventures are located mostly in advanced countries, especially in the United States, and in high-technology sectors that require firm-specific advantages. This type of direct investment accounts for still only a small segment of Japan's overseas investment in manufacturing.

The competitiveness of a vast majority of Japan's manufacturing ventures originates in the backward industrial environment of the host countries of the Third World, a condition that gives quasi-advantages to those Japanese firms that have gained business experience in a more advanced market environment at home or elsewhere. In this respect, this type of investment can still be interpreted as meeting a part of the theoretical requirement mentioned above that stresses the existence of some market imperfection for overseas investment to transcend the normal channel of trade. Yet the Hymer-Kindleberger-Caves model is postulated on the oligopolistic market structure of a particular industry in *both* the home and host countries. On the other hand, the market imperfections that give advantages to Japanese ventures in Asia and Latin America are caused largely by the underdeveloped market structures of the host countries rather than by the oligopolistic characteristics of business internal to the investing Japanese firms. Besides, the "markets" of the host countries, being still underdeveloped, hardly exhibit any meaningful characteristics that can be conveniently classified as oligopolistic. (Indeed, by definition, oligopoly is a state of market conditions that develops in industrialized market economies.)

When these trends are placed in perspective, an important question arises: If most Japanese manufacturing ventures in developing countries derive their quasi-advantages rather from the economic weaknesses (backwardness) of the host country than from their own firm-specific advantages, are their so-called advantages not really transient—much less enduring than the oligopolistic advantages inherent in the individual firms, especially given that their overseas investment itself contributes to the economic development of the host countries? The answer seems to be yes. There is, however, one type of advantage accruing to Japanese firms which may be relatively lasting: the world-wide marketing networks of Japanese companies, set up initially to foster Japan's exports but now increasingly used to market products manufactured in her offshore production bases. Even though small Japanese firms themselves may lack marketing capacities, trading companies as partners assist them either indirectly or participate with them directly in overseas ventures. Thus access to the export market is assured whenever it is needed. In contrast, lack of marketing skills and lack of networks in world markets are among the crucial weaknesses of developing countries in undertaking by themselves the production and export of standardized goods, even when they have a strong basis for developing a comparative advantage.

This type of Japanese enterprise is likely to conflict with local interests, because these ventures are largely in those industries that the developing countries, once having acquired basic skills and capital, desire to manage and are capable of doing so on their own. Under these circumstances, the outcry against Japanese economic domination is bound to be heard. As a consequence, the Japanese are often forced—if not in the early stages of their advance into a developing country then in the later stages when they have demonstrated successful operations—to form joint ventures and to transfer a great share of ownership to the local interests. Local protest of this nature has occurred most vociferously in Thailand. Japanese industries, constantly in search of countries which still offer favorable manufacturing conditions, may migrate from one Asian country to another. A pattern of transmigration has already appeared: Taiwan, Hong Kong, Singapore, and South Korea, once most eager to attract labor-intensive, low-technology industries, are now more selective in hosting Japanese ventures; hence, Japanese companies have begun to move to other countries, such as Malaysia, Indonesia, and the Philippines, which have recently emerged as attractive offshore-production bases.

Another interesting development in the industrial organization approach was recently emphasized by John K. Galbraith in discussing the organizational and motivational characteristics of oligopolistic modern corporations.[8] His approach supplements the Hymer-Kindleberger-Caves model, which interprets direct investment as a market behavior, predetermined by the oligopolistic structure of industry rather than molded by any internal psychological drive of the individual firms. This type of analysis is largely in line with the neoclassical economic approach that identifies a firm's behavior with the particular type of market structure in which it operates.[9]

Galbraith interprets overseas investment essentially as the rational behavior of big oligopolistic corporations nurtured in an advanced capitalist economy like that of the United States. In a mature stage of capitalism what he calls "a technostructure" comes into existence. The technostructure is "a complex of scientists, engineers, and technicians" in the fields of management, marketing, and production, hired by a big corporation. It is a planning system built on "collective intelligence" and on "the authority of organization." According to Galbraith, this modern efficiency-oriented business organization strives to eliminate uncertainties in the market, first at home and then overseas, as its span of operation expands: The function of the multinational corporation "is, simply, the accommodation of the technostructure to the peculiar uncertainties of international trade. It transcends the market internationally as it does nationally. . . . By re-creating itself in other countries the technostructure, in effect, follows its product to other countries."[10] Galbraith thus brings in the unique organizational form of the modern corporation as an additional factor to explain overseas investments. The existence of an oligopolistic market is simply a necessary but not a sufficient condition for direct investment to occur; the firms in such a market must reach a mature stage of organization to form a technostructure, and the United States arrived first at such a stage.

> Here, it follows, is the explanation of the eminence of American corporations in transnational operations. It is not because they are American. Where foreign firms have developed large and powerful technostructures, as in the case of Philips, Shell, Unilever, Nestlé, Volkswagen, they have exploited transnational operations as vigorously as any American firm. But the United States, befitting its higher level of industrial development, has the most advanced planning system. Accordingly it has far more corporations that are prepared for transnational operations than any other country. What has been called the American challenge is not American; it is the challenge of the modern planning system. This, because of size of country, absence of adverse feudal tradition, legal system, geography, resources and much else, has reached its highest development in the United States.[11]

Several Japanese corporations perhaps have already grown large enough to form a technostructure. One can easily list Japan's big companies—Nippon Steel, Toyota, Nissan, Mitsubishi Heavy Industries, and many others including trading companies—as technostructures in the Galbraithian sense. Indeed, the trading companies, which are actually nothing but planning complexes of "collective intelligence," are the spearheads of Japan's multinationals. Many Japanese manufacturing ventures in Asia and Latin America were, as pointed out earlier, established by small- and medium-sized companies or what may be described as "pretechnostructural" organizations, but they can secure assistance from the trading companies. Moreover, the Japanese government itself (notably the MITI), which is also an efficient technostructure for economic planning, is now actively engaged in planning, assisting, and guiding Japan's overseas investments. The much-publicized concept of "Japan, Inc." itself reflects the existence of macroeconomic technostructure in the Japanese economy. Thus the Galbraithian theory has interesting implications for the analysis of Japan's multinationalism not only as a theory of the organization of modern corporations but also as a theory of the structure of an economy. The sudden emergence of Japan's multinationalism is not so much a result of the development of technostructures in her individual corporations as a product of her entire economy, which strives to adapt itself to rapidly changing world economic environments, a dynamic adaptive process planned and implemented through a close collaboration between industry and government.

The Product Cycle Approach

The postwar industrial world has been characterized by the appearance of a rapid succession of new products, some of which develop into new industries on their own. Synthetic materials and electronics products are prime examples. Many of these innovations originated in the United States. In fact, a 1970 OECD study shows that U.S. firms are credited with about 60 percent of the 110 significant innovations introduced into the world economy since 1945.[12] Once successfully introduced in the United States, these innovations quickly spread to the rest of the world, first to European countries and Japan and then gradually to developing countries in Latin America and Asia. As a result, world trade in new products has flourished, but with shifting patterns of comparative advantage as innovations spread from one industrial center to another. This dynamic trade pattern is captured in the so-called product cycle theory of trade.[13]

This theory postulates that new products or processes (notably high-income products and labor-saving processes) are likely to be first introduced in a developed country like the United States that enjoys the advantages of a large affluent market with the world's highest standard of living, and a relatively abundant supply of technological and entrepreneurial resources, including scientists, engineers, and daring businessmen. Thus the U.S. firm that innovates a new product can exploit its monopolistic position first at home and then in the markets of other industrialized countries with similar demand structures. But when the market for the product develops overseas as a result of the very success of the firm's exporting, and as the technology to produce the new product is perfected and standardized, firms in other industrialized countries are motivated first to produce for their own markets and later even for export. They enjoy a variety of local advantages, including their familiarity with the local markets and lower labor costs, which are a predominant cost factor in the mature stage of the product cycle. These foreign producers may eventually succeed in exporting the product back to the United States.

Since new products or processes are bound to be imitated by and produced in other countries, innovating firms may decide to move into foreign markets themselves in order to retain control of new products by establishing their own production facilities, either wholly- or jointly-owned. "An enterprise innovates in response to the conditions in its home market. For a time, it exports on the basis of its innovational lead. Eventually, overseas demand expands, competitors appear, and costs grow important. The enterprise asks whether it can prolong its innovational lead or salvage what it has been exporting. At that point, its decision turns on a number of considerations involved in setting up a branch plant in the home market."[14]

According to this view, overseas production of a new product is essentially defensive in nature; it is an alternative to the export of a new product that helps the firm preserve the otherwise fleeting advantage embodied in the innovation. The firm is compelled to set up production abroad to ward off foreign competition; the firm then acts passively in contrast to the aggressive behavior implied in the Galbraithian model of the technostructure, which posits an aggressive effort by the efficient planning system to triumph over both domestic and overseas markets. Many American, as well as some European, overseas investments may be explained by the product cycle approach.

Yet the product cycle model does not directly apply to the case of Japan's manufacturing ventures overseas. Japanese industry, having been, for the most part, an interceptor of Western technologies throughout the postwar period, has not introduced any significant innovations that would invite massive imitations overseas as envisaged in the model.[15] This theory, then, needs to be analyzed from the viewpoint of the followers rather than that of the innovators; thus far the latter approach has been the main theoretical construct used.

The question which must be asked is: Under what circumstances would the followers, who develop advantages in the mature stage of product cycle because of their lower production costs in their own market, also be induced to opt for overseas production? There are two sets of possible circumstances and thus two broadly different investment patterns.

First, the followers themselves may be interested in transferring production to other countries where production costs have either become much lower than at home or are expected to drop soon. After all, it is the standard production costs such as labor costs, not the innovative costs of R & D that are of primary importance to the followers. In the course of establishing trade competitiveness the followers themselves are most likely to accumulate valuable experiences in producing a new product in a relatively more labor-abundant environment than that in which the original innovator operated. They may therefore become both more adept and more willing to move to a more labor-abundant third country when their cost advantage declines. After all, the original innovator's advantage is in the effective use of production factors most intensively employed in the initial stages of the product cycle (that is, technology resources), whereas the advantage of the followers is in the use of factors most intensively employed in the later stages (mainly labor). Hence the followers develop a competitive advantage in transplanting their operations in a relatively more labor-abundant third country. Stephen P. Magee's observation is relevant:

> Factor price structures differ between the developed countries (DCs) and the LDCs [less developed countries]. This affects which portions of the production function will be developed in each stage of the cycle. Early in Vernon's cycle, products are produced in the United States and other DCs. Given the relatively high cost of unskilled labor, these production processes are less unskilled-labor intensive than would be desired later in the production process. Production isoquants are "created" in segments covering only the empirically relevant price ranges; the classic production isoquant which spans the entire region in capital-labor space with costless substitution of factors (as taught in all elementary economics courses) is a fiction. When a capital-intensive production function is taken from the DCs to the LDCs, the firm substitutes relatively cheap unskilled labor for other factors. However, the degree of substitution is limited by the past investments which the firm has made in developing unskilled-labor intensive production techniques. Such investments are frequently small. There are several reasons why such production technologies have not been developed. The abundance of cheap unskilled labor in LDCs is not empirically relevant when production functions are being created: production occurs in LDCs so late in the cycle that discounting gives their relative factor price structures a small weight.[16]

However, the followers necessarily end up making "investments"—in the form of experiences, if not in the form of R & D —in developing those unskilled-labor intensive segments of the production isoquants more suitable for operation in LDCs. In short, the original innovator operates in an economic environment that gives him a comparative advantage in introducing a new but incomplete production function with its unskilled-labor intensive segments unexplored, whereas the followers residing in a relatively more labor-abundant environment (such as Japan, particularly during the 1950s and the early 1960s) enjoy a comparative advantage in filling in those segments and transplanting the production technique to more labor-abundant third countries when their own labor cost advantage disappears. The follower's move to a labor-abundant country is also encouraged by offers of favorable production incentives by the host country to attract foreign manufacturers who seek low-cost labor. This type of investment behavior fits nicely into the factor endowments framework to be discussed below.

A second set of circumstances under which the followers invest overseas arises when they themselves have made substantial improvements in the new products and have succeeded in differentiating their products through the development of their own brand names. In this case, their motives and investment behavior can be explained by the industrial organization approach (that is, by a market behavior typical of oligopolistic firms). Another and more important alternate set of circumstances arises where the technological capacity of such firms advances by means of learning-by-doing until they attain technological independence, in which case they quickly pass through the follower stage and become innovators themselves. But so long as this technological maturity is attained mainly as a result of exporting to some foreign markets, which are economically more advanced than their home market, rather than "in response to the conditions in [their] home market," they may naturally be interested in setting up plants in such advanced markets when their exports are threatened by protectionism.

Once having established direct production, they are also likely to capitalize on market conditions that they cannot enjoy at home such as the innovation-conducive atmosphere and the technological resources of advanced markets. For example, the source of competitiveness of U.S. firms in R & D-based industries was a combination of abundant technological resources and affluent mass-markets. This competitiveness, once practically monopolized by U.S. firms because of their closeness to the market, is now available, through direct foreign investment, to foreign firms as well. All this explains, at least in part, why followers-turned-innovators tend to invest in the original innovator's market. Indeed, there seems to be a strong tendency on the part of Japanese followers-turned-innovators to invest in the advanced markets at a much earlier stage of innovation than the stage at which U.S. innovators invest overseas. The Japanese are eager to capitalize on technological resources in the advanced Western countries and to capture the most promising markets for their innovations without creating trade friction.

As we have seen earlier, Japan's manufacturing ventures in Asia are on the whole a product of the first set of circumstances. They have been attracted primarily by lower production costs, especially lower labor costs. In contrast, Japan's manufacturing ventures in the United States, still limited in number, are mostly a result of the second set of circumstances (that is, of oligopolistic maneuvering and innovation-seeking investments). The latter behavior is particularly of interest, because it signals a new level of the Japanese industrial offensive in the United States. Some technologically mature Japanese firms (notably some of those in electronic consumer goods) are in the U.S. market. Even some Japanese textile firms are building their own textile mills in the United States for the purpose of quickly monitoring the rapidly changing fashion market for high-value, fashion-oriented lines of products. Clearly, these manufacturers have graduated from the status of outside interceptors of innovations originating in the United States and have moved right into the center of the world's most innovation-conducive market in order to continue to improve their technological capacities. These Japanese firms are in a post-product-cycle stage of industrial adaptation.

It should be noted that a framework for our analysis of Japan's recent experience with overseas manufacturing in labor-abundant neighboring countries may be called more appropriately an industry-cycle approach in contrast to the product-cycle approach. A well-established "mature" industry may become less competitive as a result of a quick change in the relative factor endowments of the economy. The less R & D-based, the less differentiated in product, and the more competitive in structure the industry is, the more readily it succumbs to international competition. Other economies that happen to find themselves better suited for that particular industry in terms of their factor endowments may become "followers." Hence the "losing" economy may itself be induced to take the initiative in transplanting that industry to potential "follower" economies. In contrast to the product-cycle approach, the industry-cycle approach rests not on product-specific, R & D-originated technological transmission but on an economy-wide change in a country's factor endowments.

The Factor-Endowments Framework

The Heckscher-Ohlin factor-endowments theory of international trade describes the pattern of trade between countries in terms of relative differences in their factor endowments (for example, a relatively capital-abundant country tends to exhibit a comparative advantage in producing and exporting capital-intensive goods, while a relatively labor-abundant country finds itself comparatively more competitive in labor-intensive goods).[17] T. M. Rybczynski first extended this analytical framework to an analysis of a change in factor endowments and the effect of that change on the composition of industrial outputs of different factor intensities under a particular set of conditions.[18] Then

Robert A. Mundell applied it to a study of a tariff-induced capital movement between two countries.[19] Capital movement occurs from a capital-abundant country to a capital-scarce country when the latter impedes the importation of capital-intensive goods from the former. In the capital-receiving country, the capital inflow causes its equilibrium production point to shift in such a direction that a capital-intensive industry (namely, that country's comparatively disadvantaged industry) expands, while a less capital-intensive industry (namely, that country's comparatively advantaged industry) contracts. This pattern of output change is posited in the well-known Rybczynski theorem.[20] In the capital-investing country exactly the opposite phenomenon is observed. As a consequence, the basis for trade (that is, the existing pattern of comparative advantage between the two countries) is in the end eliminated by the capital movement.

Mundell was the first to show this substitution relationship between trade and factor movement, and his analysis preceded (hence, remarkably predicted) the massive pouring of U.S. direct investment capital into Europe that took place in response to the establishment of the European Economic Community in 1958, a common market that set up discriminatory tariffs against the nonmember countries. Mundell's "substitutes-relationship" case has been elaborated on and "perfected" by others.[21] Some also tried to make a case for "complements-relationship" (that is, that direct investment enhances trade).

One complements-relationship case was presented by Andrew Schmitz and Peter Helmberger in their analysis of direct investment in extractive industries.[22] Their model is, however, a partial-equilibrium analysis involving one particular industry. They assume that one country with a large domestic demand for a particular natural resource is also a capital-surplus country. The other country is assumed to be more favorably endowed with that resource but unable to extract it because of a lack of capital and adequate technology. Under this set of assumptions, it is easy to see how direct investment made by the capital-surplus country in the resource-rich country leads to the creation of new trade in the extracted resource with an export of that resource from the latter to the former. The Schmitz and Helmberger model does fit very nicely into Japan's "develop-and-import" investment in overseas natural resources. Yet it is still necessary to search for an appropriate theory to explain Japan's manufacturing investment within the general equilibrium framework.

Kiyoshi Kojima presented another complements-relationship case. His model, constructed within the general equilibrium framework of the Heckscher-Ohlin theory, is quite ingenious and applies equally to both Japan's extractive and labor-resource-oriented manufacturing investments. Kojima first offered what he called "a macroeconomic approach to foreign direct investment" by contrasting an essential difference in trade orientation between the overseas investments of Japan and the United States.[23] Other than her commerce-oriented investments, Japan's overseas investments are aimed mostly at exploiting natural resources in resource-rich countries or manufacturing labor-intensive products in labor-abundant developing countries. Most outputs from the first type of investment are shipped back to Japan, while the manufactures from the second type are increasingly exported back to Japan or to third-country markets, a phenomenon observed in chapter 1. In contrast, American overseas manufacturing investments are designed mostly to produce highly sophisticated, technology-based products for local markets, as envisaged in the direct foreign investment theories of the industrial organization and the product-cycle approach. Kojima characterized the Japanese type as "trade-oriented," the American type as "anti-trade-oriented."

Later Kojima proceeded to give his observation a theoretical underpinning by presenting a complements paradigm opposite to the Mundell substitutes paradigm—that is, with the inflow of capital the host country's production frontier expands in such a direction that the less capital-intensive industry, that country's comparatively advantaged industry, expands, while the capital-intensive industry, that country's comparatively disadvantaged industry, contracts; the result is an enhancement of the basis for trade.[24] (In technical terms, this complements-relationship case is shown by Kojima for the host country in terms of the Rybczynski line which slopes in quite an opposite direction to the one used in the Mundell model. It slopes in such a direction that with the inflow of capital the labor-intensive industry expands and the capital-intensive industry declines—in a direction quite opposite to that predicted by the Rybczynski theorem.)[25]

Because such a complements-relationship case cannot be produced under the assumption of homogeneous "money" capital allocable to any industries, Kojima redefines the concept of direct investment capital. He begins with Harry Johnson's definition: "the essence of direct foreign investment is the transmission to the 'host' country of a 'package' of capital, managerial skill, and technical knowledge."[26]

The main role of foreign direct investment is to transplant superior production technology through training of labor, management and marketing, from the advanced industrial country to lesser developed countries, or, in brief, it is the transfer of superior production functions which replace inferior ones in the host country. The foreign direct investment is to be a starter and a tutor of industrialization in less developed countries. . . .

Direct investment differs from international money capital movement in which money capital as a general, homogeneous factor of production is reallocated in a general equilibrium fashion, instead of a specific way, according to its outflow from the investing country and its inflow into the host country. Thus it necessarily results in the competitive expansion of production that uses the increased general factor (capital) more intensively in the host country than the other production. However, the fact that a subsidiary or joint venture firm is established in the host country is not enough to analyse national (or macro)economic effects, although there is the so-called "enclave" direct investment whose effects are limited. The foreign direct investment gradually has an effect spread over that specific industry in the host country through training of labourers, engineers and managers and makes the establishment of competitive firms by local capital possible, and ultimately improves the production function of that specific industry in general. This is a role of foreign direct investment as a tutor.[27]

Why then is Japan both more willing than any other industrialized country to serve as a "tutor" who transfers industrial knowledge to the comparatively advantaged industries of the developing countries and better able to do so? Here Kojima assumes that "the smaller the technological difference between the investing and host country industry is, the easier it is to transfer and improve the technology in the latter."[28] In developing this assumption, he cites Ozawa's work on Japan's technology transfers to developing countries,[29] which pointed out that Japan has a comparative advantage in transferring to the developing countries the industrial knowledge of labor-intensive, small-scale manufacturing operations because of several unique factors associated with the overall technological level (mostly intermediate), dual industrial structure (small-scale firms coexisting with large-scale firms), and recent development experiences ("modernization" skills acquired) of Japanese industry.

Kojima's argument that the relatively small technological gap between Japan and the developing countries constitutes an advantage for Japan to invest in the latter is an interesting approach, as it is a view quite opposite to the "rent-yielding advantage" characteristic emphasized in the Western oligopoly theory of direct foreign investment: the larger the technological difference between the investing and host country industry, the easier and the more profitable to make overseas investments. The oligopoly theory stresses a technological superiority that is either aggressively taken advantage of (by the "technostructure" firms) or defended (by the "product-cycle" firms), mostly through their wholly- or majority-owned foreign subsidiaries with the inevitable result of an "enclave" type of technology transfers. On the other hand, what Kojima emphasizes is the successful transplant of a particular industry in which Japan is losing competitiveness (the result of a rapid change in her factor endowments) but in which the developing host country, if assisted, is capable of developing a comparative advantage. Viewed from this perspective, the oligopoly pattern may also be characterized as a "domineering" type of knowledge transfer, the Kojima model as a "yielding" type. In fact, the latter agrees with a view presented earlier: the quasi-advantages of Japanese manufacturing investors in the developing countries are transient, because they are derived basically from the economic backwardness of the host country rather than from their own firm-specific advantages.

John E. Roemer has criticized the presumption of "sagacity on the part of the Japanese and shortsightedness of the U.S." implicit in Kojima's thesis, and argued that the pro-trade nature of Japanese manufacturing investment (therefore, its harmony with Japan's national interest) was due merely to "fortuitous circumstances":

> Although the data . . . and the observations about Japanese manufacturing investment drawn from them are consistent with Kojima's hypothesis, these data and observations can be explained by certain fortuitous circumstances which have nothing to do with a more "rational" policy of Japanese investment. Furthermore, it is probable that the pattern will change and that Japan, too, will invest strongly at the "top of the product cycle." The fortuitous circumstances are: (1) Southeast Asia has been Japan's main "sphere of influence," and labor-intensive investment is the natural type of investment to make in that area; (2) the existence of trading companies has facilitated early, small-scale investments in non-competitive industries; (3) a large, unsaturated domestic market made foreign expansion in the advanced sectors less critical during the 1960's.

Thus Japanese foreign investment in the 1960's was atypical; it was marginal investment in the sense that the mainstream economy had no need to expand abroad because of its highly competitive export position and a strong domestic market.[30]

It is clear that Japan did not develop a "rational" policy with regard to her overseas investments in the 1950s and 1960s, and there is no doubt that "Japan . . . will invest strongly at the 'top of the product cycle.'" (Some technologically advanced Japanese firms may invest overseas at a much earlier stage of the innovation phase than their U.S. counterparts in order to take advantage of technology resources and innovation-supportive markets in advanced Western countries and to avoid protectionism.) But it will probably be a few more decades before this type of manufacturing investment becomes the dominant type of Japan's overseas investment. Moreover, to dismiss conditions (1) and (2) as merely "fortuitous circumstances" and the investment pattern of the 1960s as atypical seems to miss the distinct macroeconomic forces influencing Japanese industry.

On the theoretical level, how a macroeconomic mechanism works in motivating direct foreign investment is explained by Kojima:

> Let us now introduce foreign direct investments which are undertaken by a firm in X-industry of country A [Japan] so as to improve technology of the same X-industry in country B [the developing country]. Such direct investment is stimulated by the fact that the production of X-goods . . . under the international commodity price ratio . . . gives lower rewards both to labour and capital in that industry as compared with the other industry Y, and labour and capital must shift from the less profitable X-industry to the more profitable Y-industry . . . This is an internal structural adjustment. But there is another possibility for a firm in X-industry to use its accumulated technology and managerial skills: that is in foreign direct investment.[31]

Thus the economic resources released from the contracting sector can be used by the expanding sector either internally (through intracountry-sectoral transfers) or externally (through intercountry transfers), but it is important to stress two other resource-transfer aspects of this internal structural adjustment although they are not pointed out by Kojima. First, the marginally efficient firms that must exit from the contracting sector are most likely to find it much easier to set up their own lines of business overseas, where factor endowments are more favorable for them than at home (that is, to cross a national border) than to re-establish themselves de novo in the expanding sector at home (that is, to enter a new industry). In fact, many developing host countries encourage this type of industrial transplant by offering various incentives. Thus, within the factor-endowments framework, the marginal firms in the contracting sector greatly prefer to cross the national boundary rather than the product (or industry) boundary, a behavior considered to be one of the typical oligopolistic behaviors emanating from the firm-specific advantages.[32] This particular behavior seems, therefore, compatible equally with the assumption of intraindustry "perfect competition," if not with the intercountry or interindustry "perfect knowledge" assumption. Moreover, the macroeconomic forces of international trade exert pressure for overseas production in a more suitable factor-endowments environment on the marginally efficient firms and not on the most efficient firms. In contrast, in the monopolistic theory, the leading firms (the "technostructures" and the "product-life-cycle" firms) are the first to move to overseas.

This unique Japanese situation explains why financial and other assistance for overseas production is given by the Japanese government and large trading companies to those relatively small firms threatened by competition from developing countries. With the external assistance to fill in their lack of firm-specific advantages an element of market imperfection is purposely introduced into their overseas investment behavior; otherwise they are doomed to perish at home. Thus, this type of investment meets the theoretical requirement of the monopolistic (or oligopolistic) theory of foreign direct investment that stresses the existence of some market imperfection. Yet the prevailing monopolistic theory is postulated on the existence of a monopolistic or oligopolistic market structure in a particular industry in both the home and the host country prior to the firms' decision to invest overseas: "[F]oreign direct investment occurs mainly in industries characterized by certain market structure in both the 'lending' (or home) and 'borrowing' (or host) countries. In the parlance of industrial organization, oligopoly with product differentiation normally prevails where corporations make 'horizontal' investments to produce abroad the same lines of goods as they produce in the host market."[33] In contrast, the extended factor-endowments approach does not require the existence of a monopolistic or oligopolistic market structure in either the home or the host country as a necessary precondition before the firms in a declining industry shift their production overseas. Indeed, the very lack (or the underdeveloped state) of such a market structure at home hastens a decline in their competitiveness to defend their home market, compels them to search for a more favorable factor-endowments milieu abroad, and calls for external assistance in their overseas investment activities.

The competitiveness of Japan's labor-intensive investment in the developing countries is built on a "thin" technological gap. What is transplanted is essentially "general technology" fundamental to the establishment of an industry, a technology hardly considered to be an advantage by Western oligopoly standards. It is a transfer of a conventional industry to a developing country where such industry has not really existed before but where the establishment of such industry is considered desirable from the viewpoint of the developing country's factor endowments. The fact that the Japanese firms in the contracting sector are required to possess only general, industry-specific knowledge in order to invest in the developing countries may explain in part their en masse investment behavior. Thus the so-called bandwagon behavior,[34] another behavior considered to be oligopolistic, can also be observed in the overseas investment activities of Japan's relatively small-scale firms in nonoligopolistic, competitive industries.

Second, when internal structural adjustment is necessitated by the process of exploiting comparative advantage, essentially two types of economic resources are released from the contracting sector: (1) those readily transferable to the expanding sector (namely, homogeneous, nonsector-specific resources); and (2) those specific to the contracting sector and, therefore, nontransferable to the expanding sector (for example, industry-specific technology and experience). Most resources of the first type (such as labor and industrial sites), however, are nontransferable to other countries because of institutional or physical constraints. On the other hand, the second type of resources released actually will be wasted at home unless they are transferred to and employed in other countries where such resources are needed to develop comparatively advantaged industries. In other words, this type of industry-specific resources possesses the characteristics of a public good for the same industry in both the investing and host countries. Thus changing conditions in relative factor endowments assist transfers and utilization of those intraeconomy-nontransferable resources that would otherwise be wasted at home without the opportunities to transplant them overseas—with an obvious positive implication for world welfare.

Japan is perhaps more apt to undergo an internal structural adjustment than the United States, because Japan's industrial policy emphasizes, on the whole, protecting high-technology, high-growth sectors, while the rising protectionism in the United States is forcing itself to protect low-technology, low-growth sectors (such as shoes and textiles);[35] hence, a greater incentive exists for Japan's low-growth sectors (that is, the relatively contracting sector in the context of the preceding discussion) to go overseas than for her high-growth sectors (most of which are, in any event, not yet significantly advanced or competitive enough to generate new product-cycles for the world economy). This is a phenomenon associated with Japan's industrial transformation.

Another possible explanation for the massive outward expansion of Japan's contracting sector (labor-intensive industries) is that Japanese firms in that sector were not able to come up with labor-saving technologies of their own to overcome suddenly emerging labor shortages and rapidly rising wages and, therefore, resorted to an easier alternative, overseas production in low-labor-cost countries. In other words, labor-endowment-seeking overseas investment is a substitute for the development of a labor-saving type of innovation. (This means, particularly for the U.S. economy, that either alternative is deleterious to the interest of labor unions. On the other hand, Japan's company unions may welcome either alternative, so long as their member workers are transferred to other jobs or even higher-skill [hence, higher-paying] jobs within their companies, as is usually the case with large-scale, vertically integrated firms under the traditional system of lifetime employment.) Yet in recent years the so-called U-turn investment (the investment that is made at home, instead of overseas, because of the development of labor-saving innovations or automations) has lately begun to be observed in some industrial sectors of labor-intensive operations.

In addition to the comparative-advantage-induced macroeconomic motive for direct foreign investment envisaged in the Kojima thesis, which explains the outward expansion of Japan's contracting sector (that is, the labor-intensive end of Japan's dual industrial structure), there is another and perhaps more fundamental macroeconomic force, described in the Ricardo-Hicksian model of industrialism, that compels Japanese firms in both the contracting and the expanding sectors to resort to overseas production.

Escape from the
Ricardo-Hicksian Trap of Industrialism

At present, perhaps no other industrial country is so bent on reorganizing its industrial structure as is Japan. Why is Japan so impelled? This question can be best put into a theoretical perspective in terms of John Hicks' analysis of industrialism. In his Nobel memorial lecture and in a subsequent one,[36] Hicks examined how the "impulse of an invention," which he identified as the "mainspring of economic growth" proceeded to work itself out in an industrialized world.

Obviously, in a limited world, the expansion that is due to a single improvement cannot go on forever. If railway-building, for example, went on forever, the world would in the end become cluttered up with railways. The profitability, or productivity, of a railway depends on its location; the time must come when a new railway project which will yield any surplus over cost, must be hard to find. For unlimited expansion of a particular kind, such as that induced by a particular invention, there is not enough space.

Space, however, is not the only issue. Any indefinite expansion must encounter scarcities. Some, such as the bottlenecks previously discussed, are removable; in time they can be overcome. Others—by necessity, or in the world as it is and has been—are irremovable. It is by irremovable scarcities that expansion, such as we have been discussing, is brought to a stop.

The first economist to see this at all clearly was Ricardo. . . . He supposed that the supply of labour was indefinitely extensible; it would increase without limit, so long as subsistence for the increasing labour force could be provided; so his operative scarcity was scarcity of agricultural land. This was responsible for his "declining rate of profit." Because of the scarcity of land, provision of an unchanged subsistence for an increasing labour force would become more expensive from the point of view of the employer, even though there was no rise in the real consumption of the labourer himself. With labour costs rising, the rate of profit would fall. . . .

[I]t would still be true, even in the socialist economy, that irremovable scarcity (of land or of labour) would cause the rate of return on the spreading of the original improvement to diminish. In either case the *impulse* of the original improvement would in time peter out.

When it is so interpreted (or generalized), the Ricardian theory still holds; and I maintain that it is rather fundamental.[37]

The Ricardian model applies to a closed economy without trade (cheap food imports and other imported wage goods would certainly stem rising labor costs), and the irremovable scarcity of key input factors emphasized by Hicks is expected, under normal circumstances, to occur only in the long run when the economy matures.

Nevertheless, the Japanese economy, although open to trade opportunities, soon experienced these growth barriers. As is well known, in postwar Japan the major technological impulse came from outside in the form of technology imports. The government closely controlled the inflow of foreign technologies in order to organize the Japanese economy around the heavy and chemical industries and to strengthen its export capabilities. The Anti-Monopoly Act of 1947, enacted originally at the direction of the occupation authorities to dissolve the *zaibatsu* financial interests, was gradually revised in such a manner as to allow powerful industrial groups to be reshaped in the form of less financially oriented, more functionally integrated conglomerations (namely, *keiretsu* groups).[38] This new industrial organization served to capture economies of scale and to exploit industrial linkages as a group—at the same time, however, it spurred oligopolistic rivalry among the groups. Under the so-called one-set principle the government encouraged each *keiretsu* group to establish a set of modern industries through the introduction of the latest Western technologies. In this process, each group was permitted to enter a new industrial sector only in a staggered sequence so that each was assured of an adequate market but was prevented from securing an excessively monopolistic share of the resulting growth.[39] The end result was an intensification of fierce intergroup competition that came to be popularly called "excessive competition." Stimulated by the large-scale plant requirements of modern technologies, waves of capital investments ensued, supporting a vigorous expansion of the economy and resulting in an impressive rise in labor productivity. But the Japanese economy quickly reached a point at the end of the 1960s where the "trend acceleration" ceased.[40]

In terms of the Ricardo-Hicksian model of industrialism, Japan's industrialization was inescapably headed for a slowdown. In fact, the higher the growth rate of the economy, the sooner the approach of the day of reckoning. Japan, although densely populated and hence a labor-abundant nation, began to experience labor shortages in the mid-1960s, and wage rates, particularly those of young factory workers, started to rise. Moreover, a serious shortage of land soon became apparent. The Japanese economy, confined within a small geographical space, as in Ricardo's microcosm, was clearly pushing against its meager physical limit for industrial expansion. By the end of the 1960s, the Pacific coastal regions of Japan's mainland, known as *Tokaido*, were cluttered with factories, with continuous urban industrial sprawl obliterating the rural areas that had once existed. An extremely high density of industrial activities —indeed, the world's highest density measured in terms of a country's GNP per unit of flat land—resulted in aggravating the malignancies of pollution, congestion, and ecological destruction. Indeed, Net National Welfare (NNW), a measure of national welfare used in Japan, indicated a decline after 1968 despite (or rather because of) a rapid continuous growth of GNP.[41] (It was no coincidence, then, that Japan's overseas investment suddenly grew in 1968 and has been on the rise rapidly ever since.)

In the meantime, the expansionary impact of imported technologies began to lessen as the technology gap was narrowed and as it became increasingly difficult to find suitable foreign technologies. Furthermore, the Arab oil crisis in 1973 and rising economic nationalism in resource-exporting countries suddenly made the vulnerability of Japan's dependency on overseas industrial resources critical. For many years Japan had been fortunate in her ability to import necessary energy and mineral resources at attractively low prices. The conventional trade mechanism was sufficiently reliable to ameliorate the situation resulting from Japan's exiguous natural endowments, a handicap that otherwise would have surely stultified any budding industrialization in that island economy. In fact, the postwar Japanese economy was redesigned to operate, as it had in prewar days, essentially as a "processing economy" importing raw materials, processing them into finished products, and exporting them overseas. But now its processing activities came to be centered, as they had not in prewar days, around heavy machinery, chemicals, and petro-chemical products, instead of light manufactures. Trade was initially the sole link with the outside world, a means by which Japan could obtain the natural resources she lacked. But it soon became evident that access to overseas resources through trade was no longer as secure and as dependable as before, considering the rise in worldwide demands for natural resources and the increased desire on the part of resource-exporting countries to extract as many economic and political benefits as possible from the acquisition of their resources.

Although scarcities of labor and land became quite serious toward the end of the 1960s, Japan fortunately, by then, had succeeded in making another key factor, capital, relatively abundant. This relatively plentiful factor, moreover, came in part in the form of foreign exchange reserves as a result of

Japan's accomplishments in world trade. In order to remove the uncertainties of foreign supplies of industrial resources and to cope with shortages of labor and land, surplus capital began to be exported to other countries in which these productive factors existed in abundance, culminating in a surge of direct Japanese foreign investment that started in the late 1960s. (Japan's balance of payments prior to 1968 had been dominated by deficits, and only after 1968 did her international payments begin continually to turn to a surplus.)

In short, Japan's emergence as a home country for multinationals was motivated by the uncertain supplies of overseas resources and by the irremovable scarcities of labor and industrial space at home. These are problems that Japan could not solve through the conventional trade mechanism. Japan resorted to multinationalism essentially to escape from the threatening Ricardian trap of industrialism into which she was inexorably being led by her own high-powered economic growth. This way of looking at the uniqueness of Japan's overseas investment activities helps explain why such activities suddenly expanded in the late 1960s and continue to grow at a rate faster than that of any other country. Viewed in this light, classical macroeconomic growth theory conveniently provides a relevant framework for interpreting the basic forces that underlie Japan's multinationalism.

By way of contrast, it is interesting to note a micro-oriented historical interpretation of multinationalism held by Western economists. In the words of Harry G. Johnson: "[T]he multinational corporate enterprise represents the contemporary stage of development of the national corporate enterprise, which in its turn developed from the local corporate enterprise, which in its turn evolved from the noncorporate local (though sometimes national or international) enterprise. At each stage of this evolution, there has been protest over and attempts to arrest or control the emergent next stage. . . . The national enterprise has emerged, survived, and prospered because its superior economic efficiency has triumphed over efforts to keep it local and controllable by local political processes."[42]

Johnson's view expressed is very similar to the Galbraithian interpretation (and Hymer's law of increasing firm size)[43] and implies that with or without the Ricardo-Hicksian shortages of key productive factors, the individual firm naturally tends to evolve into a multinational enterprise as it grows in size and organizational sophistication in this age of modern communication and transportation. This pattern of development may be true as a long-term tendency, and it so far duplicates the experiences of Western multinational corporations, notably those of U.S.-based enterprises. But such a view is not quite appropriate to explain the recent Japanese experience; it does not help explain why Japanese national enterprises, small as well as large, suddenly and simultaneously took on multinational characteristics in the late 1960s, even though most of them initially had not yet, by Western criteria, quite reached the stage at which they evolved naturally into multinational corporations because of their "superior economic efficiencies." Japanese firms were driven overseas by such macroeconomic factors as the emerging factor scarcities at home, an increasing uncertainty in the supply of imported key resources, and a decline in the trade competitiveness of Japan's labor-intensive light industries rather than by the growth of their individual internal capacities to operate on a global scale. Indeed, the very weakness of their capacity to go overseas as individual units is leading in part to Japan's unique pattern of government-supported and group-oriented multi-firm investments overseas.

Industrial Immigration

Placed in the above perspective, the behavior of Japanese firms shifting their corporate production overseas can perhaps be likened to that of an immigrant who settles in a foreign country, having left a homeland in which living conditions are de-

teriorating. This analogy seems useful to better understand that
Japanese firms have set up plants even in advanced Western
markets where they rarely possess decisive competitive advantages over local firms, not to speak of the developing countries
where they obviously enjoy quasi-advantages created by the
underdeveloped industrial conditions of the host countries. For
they have invested in advanced economies in part because their
host countries offer (or are expected to offer) better productive
environments than does their home country. Even though they
have no decisive advantages over local firms now, they thus opt
for direct investment in advanced markets in the belief that their
production costs at home will soon catch up with or even exceed those in the host countries. Under these circumstances,
their operations in advanced markets initially are kept small
to minimize the risk of possible miscalculations. (Needless to
say, protectionism in advanced Western countries and the recent
appreciation of the yen, two additional constraints imposed
externally, have further contributed to a deterioration of the
home-based production of Japanese firms.)

In fact, what can be described as an "immigrant psychology
effect" may be observed in their performance; even if an investing Japanese firm possesses no particular advantage over local
firms, it is possible that it outperforms the local firms in productivity and sales simply because the Japanese firm's management is highly motivated to take advantage of local production
conditions that it can appreciate far better than the local firms
can. This type of efficiency fits the concept of "X-efficiency"
advanced by Harvey Leibenstein.[44] He asserts that in microeconomic theory human motivation is often not taken into
account as a contributing factor in productivity but that it is a
major element, if not the only element, of "X-efficiency." The
concept explains, for example, why "there is a great deal of
possible variation in output for similar amounts of capital and
labor and for similar techniques."[45] Indeed, there is evidence,
although limited, that some Japanese ventures in the United

States are outperforming American firms under similar production conditions.[46]

It is also at least true that the Japanese are strongly motivated to make their overseas ventures successful, especially in the United States. Because of the importance of the U.S. market, their home offices usually dispatch their most able managers and trouble shooters to their U.S. ventures. To have an office or, better still, a successful subsidiary in the United States is thought to indicate that a Japanese company has truly attained international standing, a status that can be invaluable to its public relations image at home.[47]

Conclusions

In this chapter the relevancy of existing theories of direct foreign investment for Japan's experience has been examined, and a search for a more appropriate frame of reference has been made.

The prevailing view is that the theories, notably the monopolistic theory, already advanced to explain Western multinationals are considered sufficiently general to cover Japan-based multinationals as well and that any noticeably unique features of Japan's overseas investment can be dismissed as something transitory associated with the early stages of Japan's industrial expansion abroad. As the Japanese economy matures, its industrial market and corporate structure tend to become increasingly similar to, if not identical with, those of advanced Western countries. Hence similar patterns of market and corporate behavior as envisaged in the monopolistic theory of direct foreign investment are expected to be seen in Japan's industrial expansion overseas. Nevertheless, Japan's overseas investments, when they are looked at as a whole, have so far exhibited features quite different from those of any other industrialized country—features, as this chapter has shown, that have some important theoretical implications for the theory of direct foreign investment.

One of the most distinctive features of Japan's overseas manufacturing investment is that such activities occur most frequently in standardized goods produced by competitive industries. Indeed, this starkly contrasts to the behavior of Western multinationals, which largely are centered in technology-based, highly oligopolistic industries. Noting this pattern points up the motivation of Japanese industry to preserve as much as possible its global competitiveness in those industries in which it has until only recently had a comparative advantage in trade but upon which developing countries have encroached. It is contended that the phenomenon of direct foreign investment is equally compatible, under a certain set of circumstances, with a "relatively competitive" market structure (a market devoid of such strongly monopolistic or oligopolistic characteristics as the monopolistic theory postulates).

In short, given the influences of the peculiar macroeconomic forces on the Japanese economy, the *more competitive* the industry (that is, the less technologically sophisticated the product and the smaller the firm-specific advantage), the *greater* the need so far for the Japanese manufacturing sector to resort to overseas production in developing countries—a phenomenon not envisioned in the prevailing monopolistic theory of direct foreign investment. Why Japan's overseas investments are most prevalent in such industrial sectors seems to be best explained in terms of the expanded factor-endowments model that emphasizes the motivation of those sectors to transfer corporate production to developing countries where factor endowments are more favorable. Interestingly enough, within the factor-endowments framework it is also argued that the "bandwagon" syndrome and the "cross-the-national-rather-than-industry-boundary" behavior, both considered typically oligopolistic, are equally compatible under a given set of circumstances with a relatively competitive market structure. Thus this study of the Japanese experience presents a supplementary analytical framework for the prevailing monopolistic theory of international investment.

In addition, the rapidly deteriorating domestic productive conditions—the result of such negative factors as the appreciation of the yen, rising labor and energy costs, environmental decay, and shortages of industrial sites—have been decisive in forcing Japanese firms, small and large alike, to locate their corporate production abroad. Their decision criterion is not so much whether they have a competitive advantage over local firms as whether they are able to acquire better productive conditions overseas than at home. It is in this connection that the framework of "an escape from the Ricardo-Hicksian trap" is most appropriate. It helps us understand a suddenly emerged need to reorganize Japan's industrial structure at home, a rising preference for overseas production over trade, and an outward-push effect felt by Japan's entire economy to extend productive activities overseas. It also helps explain the suddenness and simultaneity of the massive rush of Japanese companies abroad, a trend that has been established ever since the late 1960s.

Yet another important frame of reference is needed for understanding the *relatively effective* operations of Japan's multinationals despite the seeming individual weakness or "immaturity" exhibited by many of them. For both the expanded factor-endowments model and the Ricardo-Hicksian framework explain only the *motivations* of Japan's outward expansion. Here it is necessary to emphasize again a macroeconomic version of the Galbraithian organization theory that stresses the importance of "a planning system" built on "collective intelligence." The organizational and financial assistance given by the Japanese government and Japan's powerful trading companies to the Japanese firms, particularly small ones, which are unable to go overseas on their own, cannot be ignored. There is also a widespread practice of mutual help and collaboration within, and also frequently between, different industrial groups in their overseas ventures. The "administrative guidance" of the Japanese government, the global information (commercial intelligence) networks of general trading companies, and the collective economic power of Japan's industrial groups are the major components of Japan's macro-technostructure. This unique structure, which has so effectively functioned to achieve the national goals of economic growth and trade expansion throughout the postwar period, is now being put to work to supplement Japanese industry with overseas production activities.

Chapter 3

Industrial Transplant in Asia: Spread
of Japan's Dual Industrial Structure

CHAPTER 1 described how Japan's successful industrial transformation, in which she shifted her economic structure more
toward the heavy and chemical industries, has created strain,
because of labor shortages and rising wages, in the labor-intensive segment of her dual industrial structure where small-
and medium-sized firms producing mostly traditional light
manufactures are concentrated.

Rapid economic growth ought to have quickly contracted
the senile sector, but the political reality of Japan's ruling political party, the LDP, compelled the government to prolong the
life span of that industrial sector by means of various measures
designed to rejuvenate it. The transplanting of corporate production to more labor-abundant developing countries has clearly
been one such measure. Interestingly enough, Japan's preferential tariff program for manufactured imports from developing
countries serves as an integral part of Japan's design to assist
her light manufacturing industries to migrate to neighboring
countries. This chapter details this intra-Asian spread of Japan's
dual industrial structure.

Asian Environment

The advance of Japan's industry into neighboring Asian
countries has been phenomenal. Indeed, considering that bitter
memories of Japan's past military occupation and colonialism
bred animosities against the Japanese throughout Asia immedi-

ately after World War II, it is remarkable that during the 1960s Japan's private investments were accepted so willingly by other Asian countries. The investments Japan had made overseas before and during World War II were either destroyed or completely liquidated at the end of the war. Yet by the early 1970s Japan had reemerged as a leading investor throughout Asia.[1]

The events that contributed to the rapid return of Japan's economic influence in Asia took place both inside and outside Japan. Throughout the 1950s Japan was totally preoccupied with the recovery of her own economy and was heavily dependent upon Western countries, especially the United States, for capital, technology, and markets. It was only after her continuous economic expansion in the early 1960s that she began to look seriously to Southeast Asia as an additional market, supplementary to Western markets, for exports and as an alternative source of supply for industrial raw materials.

Moreover, it was not until the late 1950s that Japan began to settle the problem of reparations and to restore normal relations with other Asian countries. From 1954 to 1958, over $1 billion of grant reparations payments and other forms of economic cooperation worth about $700 million were negotiated, and the 1960s saw increasing flows of reparations and economic aid supplementing such payments from Japan.[2] Japan used these flows as an effective conduit for re-establishing commercial relations with her Asian neighbors. Since both reparations and economic aid were tied to the purchase of Japanese industrial products, new markets were opened up for exports. Japanese businessmen, having been cut off from their contact with the Southeast Asian markets for almost ten years after the end of World War II, were given opportunities to get acquainted with local businessmen and markets in the recipient economies.[3] Besides, the reparations agreements often included as an integral part commercial loans and direct investment, an arrangement that encouraged the direct involvement of Japanese industry in key local projects.

Equally important, other Asian countries themselves became more serious about embarking on industrialization. As partly reflected in the United Nations' resolution making the 1960s the "First Development Decade," there was an air of optimism and an emphasis on rationalism (rather than nationalism) in their development programs. In the 1960s several Asian countries, notably Singapore, Taiwan, and South Korea (in addition to Hong Kong, which had long been an open free-market economy) adopted an outward-looking strategy for industrialization by encouraging exports and the inflow of foreign private investment. Singapore set up her Jurong Industrial Park in 1961, Taiwan her KEPZ in 1965, and South Korea her MAFEZ in 1970. No doubt, Japan's quick rise to the status of a major economic power had gained the respect and admiration of her neighboring countries, and they began to take a more pragmatic view of their economic, if not their political, relationship with Japan. Japan's "low posture" diplomacy was also highly instrumental in taking the political sting out of her economic thrust in Asia.

Shortages of Factory Workers

The favorable climate thus created in neighboring Asian countries in the 1960s turned out to be highly attractive to Japanese industry, which was coincidentally confronted by both rising wages and a shortage of young factory workers at home. In the latter half of the 1960s there appeared an acute shortage of young workers, particularly high school graduates, willing to work as blue-collar workers for a variety of labor-intensive operations in modern factories as well as in conventional small shops. As shown in table 3.1, there were shortages of workers in all age groups except the 51-and-over group, but the shortage was most pronounced in the 19-and-under category.

Both the supply and the demand sides of the industrial labor market contributed to this development. First, Japan's over-all

Table 3.1

Ratios of Job Offers to Job Seekers by Age Group in Japan

Year	19 and under %	20-25 %	26-30 %	31-35 %	36-40 %	41-50 %	51-55 %	56 and over %
1965	157	59	63	63	57	47	12	5
1966	200	92	107	106	101	80	20	8
1967	257	110	143	156	158	107	38	12
1968	311	115	153	177	169	119	48	15
1969	452	142	195	219	207	142	58	17
1970	506	131	183	214	194	131	57	15

Source: Economic Planning Agency, *Economic Survey of Japan (1970-1971)*, p. 104.

demographic structure has become older, with a decline in the absolute number of fifteen- to nineteen-year-olds in the labor force—a category previously bolstered by the "baby boom" of the early postwar period. It declined from 12.4 percent of the total labor force in 1955 to 5.7 percent in 1970.[4] Furthermore, rising incomes and Japan's traditional system of corporate promotion based on educational background encouraged an ever-increasing number of young people to seek higher education. For example, the percentage of junior high school graduates who entered employment declined from 38.6 percent in 1960 to 18.7 percent in 1969; the same ratio for senior high school graduates also dropped from 61.3 percent to 58.9 percent.[5]

At the same time as the supply of young workers in the labor market decreased, Japan's economic growth brought about a surge in the demand for young workers who were highly adaptable, both physically and mentally, to modern industrial operations. Thus the labor market for young workers became tighter than that for any other age group.

With an abundance of employment opportunities for young people (for example, in the spring of 1971, when a new crop of junior and senior high school graduates moved into the labor market, there were about seven times more job openings than job seekers in this particular group), young workers became particularly fastidious about working conditions and the social status associated with their occupations. This tendency was manifest in the difficulties Japanese firms had in recruiting young people for physically strenuous work such as metal casting or for "unclean" jobs such as skinning and tanning. They were more interested in "clean" service industries such as department stores, airlines, travel agencies, and other sectors of Japan's booming leisure industry.

Thus, despite their gleaming modern facilities, even big corporations had trouble recruiting young factory workers for assembly-type operations, work considered monotonously tedious by youth, and had to pay unconventionally high wages to attract new workers. By and large, however, the big corporations succeeded in holding down the rise of total corporate wage payments by narrowing the wage differentials between age groups based on the traditional seniority system. In contrast, however, the wage differentials of small- and medium-sized firms were too narrow to manipulate.[6] Moreover, their working facilities were still primitive and therefore the least attractive for youth. Thus the worst squeeze was on the small- and medium-sized manufacturing firms.

As a way to escape from the strained labor market at home Japanese manufacturers, notably small- and medium-sized ones, began to look for labor in such neighboring countries as Taiwan, South Korea, Hong Kong, and Singapore. These countries have a plentiful supply of young labor, because more than half of their population is under 19 years old (see table A.4). Low wages in these Asian countries were an added attraction. Yet because the attractiveness of low labor cost needs to be discounted by the disadvantage of low labor productivity, it was not so much low wages per se as the availability of young factory workers in the neighboring Asian countries that attracted Japanese manufacturers during the latter half of the 1960s. The net result was that Japan's manufacturing ventures in Asia were predominantly those made by relatively small firms.

The fact that a major motive of Japan's manufacturing activities abroad has been the utilization of overseas labor is reflected in an interesting statistical study made by John E. Roemer (see table 3.2). The capital-labor ratios of Japanese manufacturing ventures abroad are much lower—on the average as much as 67 percent—than those at home (with the sole exception of paper and pulp for which Japan's overseas ventures are understandably much more capital-intensive because of the larger scale of operations). It is true that U.S. overseas manufacturing activities are also more labor-intensive than those at home, but the dependency of Japan's overseas manufacturing on overseas labor resources is much greater than that for its U.S. counterpart relative to their respective domestic standards.

Table 3.2

Percentages by which Capital-Labor Ratios of Japanese and U.S. Manufacturing Affiliates Abroad Exceed Their Respective Domestic Capital-Labor Ratios by Sector

Sector	Japan 1972 %	U.S. 1970 %
All manufacturing	−67	−31
Textiles	−60	n.a.[a]
Paper and pulp	+29	n.a.[a]
Chemicals	−80	−8
Metals	−39	−48
Electrical machinery	−79	−63
Nonelectrical machinery	−69	−34
Transport	−62	−6
Precision machinery	−49	n.a.[a]
Sundries	−65	n.a.[a]

Source: Compiled from tables 5.7 and 5.9 in Roemer, *U.S.-Japanese Competition*, pp. 183 and 185.
[a] Not available.

Thus, when it comes to overseas manufacturing activities, the relatively labor-abundant Japan is *more heavily* dependent on overseas labor than the relatively capital-abundant United States. Yet this apparent "contradiction" is exactly what should be expected from the factor-endowments theory of trade; Japan has developed a comparative advantage of trade in labor-intensive products, but her competitiveness has been steadily eroded by a rapid change in her factor-endowments position and by a rising competition from more labor-abundant countries. Hence, those Japanese manufacturers whose operations are heavily dependent on labor are relocating themselves in more labor-abundant developing countries in an effort to retain control over their established markets.

Moreover, the labor-intensive, low-productivity, and low-value-added end of Japan's dual industrial structure has been pushed out of Japan to developing countries, particularly in Asia, and table 3.3 shows the output- (value-added) labor ratios of Japan's overseas manufacturing ventures by region. The ratios are much lower in Africa, the Middle East, and Asia than

Table 3.3

Value-Added Labor Ratios and Relatives for Japanese
Manufacturing Affiliates by Area at the End of March 1972

Area	Ratio	Relative
North America	8.2[a]	342
Europe	3.5	146
Oceania	2.8	117
Latin America	2.5	104
Japan (domestic)	2.4	100
Africa	1.3	54
Middle East	1.1	46
Asia	1.1	46

Source: MITI, *Overseas Activities of Japanese Enterprises*, October 15, 1973, quoted in table 5.8, in Roemer, *U.S.-Japanese Competition*, p. 184. Relatives added.
[a] Unit of denomination not provided.

at home, whereas they are higher in advanced Western regions, especially North America.

In what follows, Japanese investments in Asia's major host countries will be surveyed. For this purpose the beginning of the 1970s will be used as a chronological divider, because in the 1970s the world began to witness a series of epochal events, both economic and political, which drastically affected the investment enviroments of Asian countries.

Taiwan

Throughout the 1960s Taiwan was the most popular country for Japanese manufacturing investment. Its geographical proximity (hence, a low transport cost) and its abundant supply of low-cost labor have no doubt been two major attractions. Perhaps more important, however, are the sociocultural similarities that serve as a psychological inducement for the Japanese. One executive interviewed in Tokyo remarked: "In my mind Taiwan is no different from Kyushu or Shikoku [Japan's major southern islands]." His statement epitomizes the general attitude of most Japanese businessmen toward Taiwan. By and large, they feel psychologically much closer to Taiwan than to Hong Kong, Singapore, or any other country in Asia. Because Taiwan is a former colony of Japan, a large number of people there were educated under the Japanese education system and are accustomed to the Japanese way of life. It is said that Japanese specifications for technically complicated products, such as electronic devices, can usually be handed over to Taiwanese engineers without translation. In most cases technical oral instructions also can be conveyed in Japanese. This ease of communication constitutes a substantial saving of time and energy for the Japanese, who in general are notoriously poor linguists. Consequently, when the Japanese economy began to experience a shortage of factory workers, Taiwan was a logical place to secure needed labor. The country has become popular particularly among small- and medium-sized Japanese enterprises which, although inexperienced in direct overseas investments, have found it quite comfortable to operate there because of the sociocultural affinities. Thus Taiwan has proved to be an ideal overseas base for Japanese industry because of the extremely low cost of "being alien" (a source of economic disadvantage to operate in an alien environment discussed in chapter 2).

A variety of positive measures adopted by the Taiwanese government to encourage foreign capital inflows were also important attractions. These measures included legislation such as the Statute for Encouragement of Investment of 1960 and its subsequent major amendment in 1965 and the gradual simplification of procedural matters relating to investment applications. Anticipating the cessation of U.S. economic aid in 1965, Taiwan in advance of that date began to place greater emphasis on export promotion through absorption of foreign capital and technology as an alternative to earning foreign exchange than on import substitution policies theretofore pursued. This was a total reversal of its traditionally conservative attitude toward foreign capital. In 1963 the Council on U.S. Aid was transformed into the Council on International Economic Cooperation and Development (CIECD), and the Industrial Development and Investment Center was established for the specific purpose of creating a better climate for foreign capital investment. This new policy also led to the opening of an export processing zone (KEPZ), which combined the attractions of a free trade zone and an industrial park, in Kaohsiung in 1965.[7]

Japanese investments were clearly affected by Taiwan's policy changes. Before 1965, when Taiwan decisively moved to the outward-looking strategy, some major Japanese manufacturers of consumer goods, notably electrical household appliances and pharmaceuticals, who had previously been exporting to Taiwan, were compelled to set up joint ventures, a type of investment that can be identified as "tariff-induced." Although some of these manufacturers went on to export part of their output later on, production (initially simple assembly operations of imported inputs) was aimed mainly at local markets. The so-called excessive competition of Japanese industry at home was practically reproduced in Taiwan as several Japanese manufacturers in the same industry simultaneously set up plants lest they be cut off from the Taiwan market by tariffs. No doubt Taiwan also encouraged the entry of several Japanese firms at one time in order to strengthen the bargaining position of local firms that were interested in forming joint ventures. The existence of a strong rivalry among Japan's different industrial groups was another factor for their simultaneous move. Moreover, the products Japanese industry started to produce locally in joint ventures were mainly technologically unsophisticated or standardized (for example, electric fans, irons, rice-cookers, vacuum cleaners, batteries, and the like for the electric appliance industry; and vitamin pills for the pharmaceutical industry). The relative ease of entry into these competitive industrial segments also contributed to the pattern of keen competition.

After 1966 there was a sudden rise in Japan's investment in Taiwan, accompanying a substantial change in the nature of investment, a change which closely reflected the new direction of Taiwan's industrialization policy. Indeed, as much as 86 percent of the total number of Japanese ventures in Taiwan before 1971 were set up during the second half of the 1960s.[8] In contrast to the preceding period, a large number of relatively unknown and small- and medium-sized Japanese enterprises moved in, some of whom had never exported to Taiwan before. Moreover, a majority of investments during the latter part of the 1960s were not so much directed at local markets but were intended mainly to increase their export competitiveness by taking advantage of an abundant supply of factory workers in Taiwan (that is, these investments may be identified as "export-oriented and labor-resource-induced," as opposed to those of the preceding period which were "local-market-oriented and tariff-induced"). At the same time some existing Japanese ventures themselves became export-oriented.[9]

What attracted Japanese industry most was the opening of KEPZ in 1965. With a variety of preferential tax and administrative treatments the zone was designed to attract foreign private capital and technology for export manufacturing.[10] It was intended to create employment locally with the help of foreign capital but without foreign domination of the domestic market. The timing of KEPZ's opening squared perfectly with the newly arisen need of the Japanese economy; had it not been for the "push" effect of Japan's shortage of young factory workers on her overseas investments, KEPZ might not have been so successful. Above all, Taiwan's young demographic structure was a big inducement for Japan's manufacturers of labor-intensive products (about half of the population was under twenty years old, and the age group from fifteen to nineteen years accounted for 18.3 percent of total labor force in 1968).[11]

The importance of Japanese investments in KEPZ is clearly shown in table 3.4. At the end of January 1970 they accounted for no less than 25 percent of both the total number of factories set up and the total value of capital invested there. If local and overseas Chinese capital is excluded, Japan's share was even greater: it was about 74 percent of the total number of factories and 47 percent of the total capital invested by foreign nationals. By either account Japanese industry became the largest foreign investor in KEPZ. It is worth mentioning here in passing that a rise in Japan's export competitiveness during the 1960s also induced, in no small part, many U.S. companies to take advantage of low-cost labor in Taiwan in order to stay competitive. Thus Japan's industrial surge stimulated not only her own investment in Taiwan but also that of American companies.

A shift of Japanese investment toward export markets during the second half of the 1960s is revealed in the findings of a survey conducted by the Japan Chamber of Commerce in Tai-

Table 3.4

Approved Investment in KEPZ by Nationality
at the End of January 1970

Nationality	Number of approved projects	Value of approved investment
Taiwan	40	$ 5,368,150
Overseas Chinese	29	5,852,439
Foreign Nationals	55	19,835,419
a. Japan	41	9,502,600
b. United States	10	7,249,429
c. United Kingdom	2	750,940
d. Holland	1	2,150,000
e. Others	1	170,000
Joint Ventures	42	6,294,211
a. Taiwan-Japan	20	2,100,551
b. Taiwan-Overseas Chinese	6	1,026,250
c. Taiwan-U.S.	6	1,210,841
d. Others	10	1,956,569
Total	166	37,350,129

Source: Chinese Investment and Trade Office (New York) KEPZ Administration of the Republic of China. Mimeograph.

wan in September, 1969.[12] From 1953 to 1965, investments with more than 50 percent of their sales going to local markets were about five times as many as those with more than 50 percent of their sales going to exports. From 1966 to 1969, however, this pattern was reversed: the latter became about twice as numerous as the former.

After 1966 there also appeared another type of investment than the "labor-resource-induced" type discussed above. Big Japanese producers of synthetic fibers (that is, Toray Industries, Mitsubishi Rayon, Kanebo, Teijin, and Daitobo) started to produce intermediate products such as polyester and rayon fibers locally for Taiwan's booming textile industry. Although these investments certainly benefited from an abundant supply of factory workers, they were primarily attracted by Taiwan's expanding local market, which began to show a demand for various intermediate goods large enough to be satisfied by local production instead of by imports. No doubt, local production requirements imposed by the Taiwan government also accelerated this trend. (This type of investment may be called a "backward-linkage-induced" investment.)

Despite the spectacular growth of Japanese investment in Taiwan during the 1960s, investments, taken individually, remained relatively small. At the end of 1970, for example, Japan's investment averaged $339,000 in electronics and electric machinery products and $417,575 in chemicals, compared to the average U.S. investments of $3,975,676 (more than ten times as large) and $2,344,478 (more than five times as large), respectively.[13] Industrial classification also masked differences in the technological level of products manufactured. To some extent Japanese firms' smaller scale of operation even in relatively technology-intensive industries meant investment at the "low" end of technology, although it was due also to the prevalence of joint ventures, which the American firms did not prefer. Moreover, Japanese firms invested more in such labor-intensive industries as textiles, apparel, footwear, wooden and bamboo products, plastic and rubber products, and basic metal products.

South Korea

Although South Korea is geographically the nearest to Japan (less than an hour's flight from the southern tip of Japan), her strained political relations with Japan prevented a quick restoration of economic relationship. Understandably, strong anti-Japanese feelings were openly expressed after World War II, which liberated Korea from thirty-five years of Japanese colonialism. Syngman Rhee's policy deliberately sustained antagonism against Japan "through textbooks, constant reminders of Japanese colonial rule in speeches and declarations."[14] Throughout his presidency during the 1950s, little diplomatic contact was initiated, although trade because of economic necessity was re-opened.

It was only in the early 1960s, after the need for economic development was recognized by later administrations as a major national priority, that serious efforts were made to settle the so-called Japanese issue. By then, Japan had begun to shape up as a world economic power and it was clearly in Korea's interest to restore normal relations. In 1962 Korea adopted a develop-ment policy dependent on an inflow of foreign capital and tech-nology, as Taiwan did, at the prospect of the end of U.S. eco-nomic aid. Such a policy would not be successful without close economic relations with Japan, the newly emerged economic power in Asia. Yet there was strong opposition among political opponents, intellectuals, and students to what they considered a "sell-out" attempt to come to terms with Japan. Hence, a final settlement had to be pushed through by President Park with the use of military power to suppress domestic opposition in August 1965.

However, once normal diplomatic relations had been re-stored, Japanese industry eagerly made investments in Korea, and the latter in turn welcomed such investments. In 1967, for the first time four Japanese companies were granted approval by the Korean government to invest a total of $1.3 million.[15] Thereafter, the number of Japan's direct investments multiplied phenomenally year after year. Indeed, in 1970 and afterward Korea came to rank first, overtaking Taiwan, as the most popu-lar host country for Japanese overseas investment in Asia.

To create job opportunities at home and promote exports and industrial growth, Korea opened an export processing zone in Masan (MAFEZ), in 1970.[16] This industrial zone soon came to be dominated by Japanese industry. As of May 1971, for example, six foreign firms were given approval to operate within the zone, but five were owned either wholly or partly by Japanese companies.[17] The Korean government, naturally concerned about the prospect of turning MAFEZ into a Japanese enclave rather than an international industrial park, had to strive to attract investments from other countries. But the dominance of Japanese industry in MAFEZ has proved to be inevitable because of its geographical proximity to Japan.

Other Major Host Countries

Singapore[18] and Hong Kong[19] constitute another set of important host economies for Japan's overseas investment, although wages in these economies are much higher than in Taiwan and South Korea, so that Japanese industry has not really been able to transplant labor-intensive manufacturing activities on so large a scale as it has done in the latter two economies.

There was, however, a short-lived sudden rush of Japanese investment to Singapore in 1963 when twelve joint ventures were established.[20] These investments were mostly induced by the formation of the Malaysian Common Market, which they intended to penetrate using Singapore as their production base. Although Singapore's Pioneer Ordinance, legislated at that time, did assist such investments, it was not the decisive factor.[21] The subsequent separation of Singapore from the Federation of Malaysia in 1965 played havoc with those Japanese companies which had set up relatively large-scale facilities aimed at the entire Malaysian Market.[22] Then, the pace of Japanese investments in Singapore slowed somewhat for the rest of the 1960s. The interest of those Japanese firms that invested in later years lay in exporting to the world market beyond the Malaysian region proper.[23]

Singapore's comparatively high wages meant that profitability would be assured only for those investments in relatively high value-added industrial sectors and those in which scale economies could be attained. Therefore, as compared to the investments in Taiwan and South Korea, a fairly large unit of investment was required. Consequently, the world's electronics industry, a high value-added one, which saw its rapid growth in the 1960s, found Singapore an ideal place for the offshore production of its components. Indeed, realizing that a great potential existed, the Singapore government itself made efforts to attract the labor-intensive assembly-type subsector of this new growth industry.

U.S. electronics companies such as Texas Instruments, Radio Corporation of America (RCA), Hewlett-Packard, Fairchild, National, and Litton set up semiconductor assembly lines, one after another, in Singapore.[24] Yet Japanese electronics manufacturers did not immediately participate in the "electronics boom" of Singapore. As a result, Japan's share of foreign capital invested in Singapore declined from 15.0 percent in 1963 to 3.9 percent in 1969.[25] Although Singapore is as attractive for U.S. firms as any other Asian country as a manufacturing and distribution center because the United States is far from Asia, Japan is not.[26] In addition, the wage differential between Singapore and Japan was not as great as that between Singapore and the United States. In the late 1960s the ratio of Singapore's wage to Japan's was 1:1.5, while that to the United States was 1:11.1.[27]

More important perhaps, Japan was then still a neophyte in electronics. This industry was initiated in Japan from scratch with technological assistance from the United States and Europe in the late 1950s and gradually developed indigenous technologies through R & D during the 1960s.[28] Because the Japanese government restricted the entry of foreign interests into this "infant technology" industry, Japanese manufacturers were able to enjoy a relatively secure domestic market under governmental guidance and were not, like the U.S. manufacturers, driven by competition (foreign or compatriot) to scramble for overseas production in low-labor-cost countries. It is also possible that Japan's technology-purchase agreements with Western firms included regional restrictions on the export and overseas investment activities of Japanese licensees.

Japanese electronics firms, however, did move gingerly to overseas production later on, but they invested in Japan's close neighbors, Taiwan, South Korea, and Hong Kong instead of Singapore. At the end of February 1971, for example, Taiwan ranked first, with 35 approved investment projects in electronics worth $10,233,000, South Korea second, with 6 projects worth $6,101,000, and Hong Kong third, with 4 projects worth $371,000.[29]

Although Hong Kong attracted Japan's electronics industry because of its proximity to Japan, Japanese investments there initially were centered in commercial activities. Wages in Hong Kong were once extremely low, notably in the early 1950s, as a result of an influx of refugees and returning residents. But with a quick industrialization (industrial production grew at an average annual rate of at least 30 percent between 1950 and 1964, and national income consequently rose faster in Hong Kong than elsewhere in Asia) the wage rates rose rapidly. By 1959 Hong Kong's industrial wages had come to rank third in Asia, after Japan's and Singapore's, and then doubled between 1960 and 1971, surpassing those in Singapore.[30]

It was only after the mid-1960s that Japanese manufacturers began to set up shop in Hong Kong, mostly in synthetic and woolen textiles, apparel, transistor radios, printing and publication, and other relatively skill-requiring, but small-scale industries. Therefore, they did not really have a chance to benefit as substantially from Hong Kong's low-cost labor as did some Western firms that had established production facilities much earlier in textiles, electronics, plastic products, and toys.

Throughout the 1960s, moreover, the wages, the office rents, and the rentals of industrial land in Hong Kong began to climb steeply, making the city economy less attractive for labor-intensive and small-scale manufacturing ventures. In fact, some of these types of foreign ventures, including some Japanese enterprises, started either to contract their operations in Hong Kong or to transmigrate to Taiwan and other Asian countries. Some Hong Kong firms even followed suit themselves.

One Asian economy, although relatively far away from Japan, on which Japan's overseas investment has had perhaps the greatest impact is Thailand. It is in Thailand that Japan became the largest foreign investor for the first time in the postwar period, Thailand quickly restored her economic relations with Japan during that time. In 1949 a bilateral trade agreement was signed. The treaty that had initially been intended to exchange rice for transport equipment paved the way for building an ever-stronger economic bond between the two countries, ultimately making Japan a key supplier of industrial capital and technology and a vital export market for Thailand's primary products. In fact, it became eventually the Thai economic policy to emphasize "much less dependence on the United Kingdom, much more dependence on the United States, but with a steady trend towards substitution of Japan for the United States."[31]

In 1955 Thailand settled the "cash" part of her reparations treaty with Japan, the latter promising to pay 1.5 billion yen. In 1959 Japan also agreed to provide Japanese goods and services worth 9.6 billion yen. The "goods and services" portion of the reparations, in particular, gave Japanese industry ready access to the Thai economy. Thailand was then about to embark on industrialization with a variety of promotional measures.[32] Japan's direct foreign investment was quickly attracted. More significantly, during the Vietnam War, when the Thai economy experienced a boom, many more Japanese ventures were established to cater to the growing Thai markets for consumer goods such as electrical household appliances, textiles, motorcycles, and automobiles.[33]

Throughout the 1960s Japan's direct investment contributed significantly to the capital formation in Thailand's newly promoted industries. By the end of March 1970, for example, Japanese investment accounted for 10.6 percent of the total capital registered under the Thai Investment Incentive Program, which was initiated in 1959, in contrast to the local share of 66.5 percent and the U.S. share of 5.7 percent.[34]

New Waves of Investment in the Early 1970s

During the 1960s Japan's direct investment in Asia, assisted by a favorable investment climate, expanded swiftly and succeeded in capturing a sizable share of the host countries' markets, particularly in those newly established manufacturing industries designed both for import substitution and for export promotion. The presence of Japanese companies in Asian countries became all the more visible to the local people because they were concentrated in the fast-growing local markets for consumer goods. These industries were labor-intensive, and, in a short period of time, tended to be crowded by competing firms of both Japanese and local interests. Increasingly, criticism of Japanese business behavior began to be voiced by the host countries, which were, to begin with, ambivalent about the benefits of economic growth and the loss of economic autonomy brought about by the influx of Japanese capital and technology.

In this respect, perhaps the most drastic change occurred in the investment environment of Thailand. After strong avowals of anti-Japanese sentiment, first openly expressed by student demonstrations in 1972 and later combined with labor strife and social unrest in 1974, the tempo of Japanese investment noticeably slowed down. The turning point was perhaps marked by the withdrawal of the Mitsui and the Mitsubishi groups from a Thai government-sponsored project for constructing a huge petro-chemical complex on the Gulf of Siam.[35]

There also occured a series of adverse international political developments in the early 1970s that affected Japanese investments in Taiwan and South Korea. They were the political pressure of Chou En-Lai's "four principles" imposing a prohibition of investment in Taiwan and South Korea as a necessary condition for trade with the People's Republic of China (May 1970), Taiwan's expulsion from the United Nations (November 1971), and the Nixon-Chou communiqué explicitly stating that Taiwan was part of China (February 1972). At least momentarily, these events did deter the advance of Japanese industry, particularly in Taiwan. Big Japanese corporations eager to do business with the People's Republic of China decided to phase out their Taiwan operations. Several leading Japanese manufacturers who had subsidiaries in Taiwan decided to halt any additional investment, to reconsider the implementation of their new technical-assistance contracts, and postpone any renewal of existing technical-assistance agreements.[36] For example, Hitachi, then operating five ventures (three of them wholly-owned subsidiaries) in Taiwan, declared that it would not make any additional capital investment there. Other major Japanese investors, such as Teijin and Nippon Paint, decided to reduce their corporate visibility in Taiwan by selling ownership interest to their local partners.[37]

Japan's small enterprises in labor-intensive industries, however, showed an unfaltering interest in Taiwan and South Korea. For, unlike big enterprises, they had little stake in the People's Republic of China, and mainland China, which was about to open trade with the West, appeared to be a potential threat to themselves in labor-intensive exports. Some big Japanese corporations also set up "dummy corporations" and continued their business operations incognito.

Similarly, in the face of the detente between the United States and the Communist bloc and the subsequent Japanese move to normalize relations with the latter, South Korea, which had just started to attract direct investment capital from overseas, was especially worried about the possible withdrawal of Japanese investment. Consequently, the Japanese government had to reaffirm its position to strengthen economic cooperation at the ministerial conference with South Korea in August 1971. Japan gave assurance that she would promote private Japanese investments and declared that Japan's economic ties with the Republic of Korea were not expected to have any ill effect on normalization of Sino-Japanese relations.[38]

Despite all these adverse developments that surfaced in the late 1960s and in the early 1970s, Japan's over-all direct investment in Asia rose at an unprecedented pace. From 1971 to 1973 it amounted to as much as $1,640 million, more than doubling the total value of the previous figure ($752 million) from 1951 to 1970.[39]

A sudden and substantial rise in the value of the yen forced by the successive devaluations of the dollar in 1971 and 1973 was the major cause of the renewed interest of Japanese industry in offshore production. The revaluation of the yen decisively eroded the price competitiveness of most of Japan's labor-intensive traditional exports, such as textiles and electrical appliances. In order to retain trade competitiveness Japanese firms, especially the small ones, were compelled to transplant production to other Asian countries where labor costs continued to be lower than at home. The increased buying power of the yen relative to the dollar also gave them a financial incentive, as Japanese firms were able to acquire foreign assets at much lower costs in those Asian countries whose currencies were closely tied to the dollar.

This new surge in the flow of Japan's overseas investment in Asia primarily moved in two directions: one to the export-oriented manufacturing sectors of nearby countries such as South Korea and Taiwan; the other to the less developed but resource-abundant countries such as Indonesia and Malaysia.

In particular, Japan made such a swift advance in South Korea during the early 1970s that she overtook the United States as the largest foreign investor in 1973 in terms of both the number of ventures and the total value of capital invested. In 1967, when South Korea first began to approve private investments from Japan, only 4 projects were granted approval. But by 1973 as many as 320 companies were participating, with a total capital of $205.2 million. As of May 31, 1975 the South Korean government had approved a total of 771 Japanese ventures worth $498.2 million.[40] MAFEZ proved to be the most popular site for Japanese enterprises, particularly those with small-scale and labor-intensive operations. In 1973, for example, of the 115 ventures operating in the zone, 106 were Japanese-owned and accounted for as much as 96 percent of the private investment in the zone.[41]

In the 1970s, the less developed but resource-abundant countries, such as Indonesia and Malaysia, began to attract an increasing amount of Japanese investment. Although Japanese invested in numerous resource-development ventures (iron ore, bauxite, copper ore, tin, and oil), Japanese investment was also attracted by the abundance of low-cost labor and the expanding local markets in these resource-rich countries. As a result, a relatively heavy concentration of Japanese ventures is seen in manufacturing sectors as well (textiles, chemicals, and metal products in Indonesia: and textiles, electrical appliances, and woodchips in Malaysia).

The Philippines is another resource-abundant country that has of late started to host Japanese ventures both in resource-related areas (mining, timber processing, and coconut processing) and manufacturing (textiles, electrical appliances, and automobiles). But Japan's advance into the Philippines is more recent than its foray into Indonesia and Malaysia, and most projects are, still in the early preparatory stages of local operations. (They include one significant project: a sintering plant to be set up by Kawasaki Steel in Mindanao. While it is initially wholly-owned by the Japanese, it will be transferred completely to Filipino ownership in thirty years.) Besides, in the Philippines foreign investment is more strictly controlled. For example, Japanese ventures are forced to accept minority ownership, a share usually ranging from 30 percent to 40 percent, with the exception of only two wholly Japanese-owned ventures set up in Bataan Export Processing Zone.[42]

Indonesia

In Indonesia Japanese investment expanded with an astonishing swiftness in the early 1970s, and a new form of "economic cooperation" embodied in the so-called Asahan project has emerged. This enterprise has become a model for similar projects in other developing countries. Therefore Indonesia is the primary example of a new trend in Japan's overseas investment.

Until 1973 Japanese investment had lagged behind that of the United States in both manufacturing and extractive sectors. But, as shown in table 3.5, as a result of sudden Japanese in-

Table 3.5

Japanese Investment in Indonesia Compared to All Foreign
Countries, 1971-1974
(in millions of U.S. dollars)

Country	1971	1972	1973	1974
Japan	108.5 (26)[a]	67.5 (21)	250.7 (47)	450.3 (32)
All foreign countries	376.1 (113)	497.8 (95)	502.6 (133)	1,050.0 (92)

Source: Indonesian Investment Coordinating Board, as quoted in McDonald, "Indonesia," p. 70.
[a] The figures in parentheses indicate number of ventures.

vestment in Indonesia in the early 1970s Japan became the leading investor. In 1973 and 1974 approximately half the direct foreign capital that Indonesia received came from Japan. At the end of 1974, Japan's share of the total cumulative value of foreign investment approved by the Foreign Investment Board of Indonesia amounted to 27.9 percent, as against the U.S. share of 25.1 percent.[43]

In fact, as shown in table 3.6, among the "top fifteen" multi-national corporations operating in Indonesia (ranked in terms of the value of investments approved by the Indonesian government from 1967 to 1973) nine Japanese firms were listed among the "top ten." Only fourth place was yielded to a U.S. firm. The table also reveals a typical pattern of overseas investments by Japanese industry in developing countries; there is a heavy representation of textiles and general trading companies as organizers of overseas ventures.

The value of Japanese investments stood at $922 million, with 431 ventures, at the end of March 1975.[44] When the production of timber and pulp is included in the primary sector, the largest number of Japanese ventures is seen in agriculture, fishery, forestry, and mining, totaling 114 (forty-one in timber and pulp alone) and accounting for one-fourth of the Japanese ventures in Indonesia. As far as manufacturing is concerned, the heaviest concentration is observable in textiles with seventy-one ventures, followed by chemicals with thirty-eight ventures and then by ferrous and nonferrous metals with thirty ventures.[45] Indonesia successfully induced Japan's synthetic-fiber textile industry to set up, within an unusually short period of time, a completely integrated industry capable of locally producing finished articles from raw materials. From 1970 to 1971 Japan's Toray Industries moved to establish four new joint ventures covering each of the processing stages of fiber production, spinning, weaving, dyeing, and apparel-making. This "all-at-once" approach was a departure from the usual pattern of Japan's textile industry to shift its investment gradually from the intermediate stages of production upstream to the production of raw materials.[46]

Concurrent with the advance of Japanese industry has been the expansion of foreign economic aid given Indonesia by the Japanese government. Japanese aid includes a proportionately (and often absolutely) larger amount of long-term official loans than any other industrial country's. In 1974, for example,

Table 3.6 Top Fifteen Multinational Corporations in Indonesia, 1967-1973

Ranking	Corporation	Average foreign ownership (%)	Planned investment U.S. $,000[b]	Projects	Nationality	Principal activity
1	Mitsui[a]	80	$90,806	15	Japan	Textiles, forestry, beverages, plastics, tires
2	Marubeni Corp.[a]	60	76,721	10	Japan	Iron sheet, textiles, contractors
3	Toray	85	66,515	5	Japan	Textiles, contractors
4	Goodyear	100	23,460	2	United States	Tires, rubber plantations
5	Nisho Iwai[a]	70	22,300	5	Japan	Textiles, metal products, fisheries
6	Mitsubishi[a]	80	15,864	6	Japan	Fisheries, forestry, air transport
7	Ataka[a]	75	13,000	7	Japan	Forestry, metal products, textiles
8	C. Itoh[a]	80	11,818	9	Japan	Textiles, metal products, real estate
9	Toyo Menka Kaisha[a]	75	10,974	6	Japan	Textiles, forestry, fisheries
10	Teijin	85	9,432	1	Japan	Textiles
11	Philips Gloeilampen	66	6,849	1	The Netherlands	Textiles
12	Sumitomo Shoji Kaisha[a]	60	5,600	5	Japan	Agriculture, machinery, forestry
13	Union Carbide	100	2,700	1	United States	Batteries
14	Farbwerk Hoechst	80	1,625	1	West Germany	Pharmaceuticals
15	Unilever	100	1,500	1	The Netherlands	Soap, cosmetics

Source: J. Panglaykim, *Business Relations between Indonesia and Japan*, CSIS 1974, quoted in Panglaykim, "Setting it up," p. 23.

[a] Japan's general trading companies.
[b] Approved by the Indonesian government.

Japan provided Indonesia with $204 million of official loans, compared to $63 million offered by the United States and $38.5 million by West Germany. As a result, Japan's total economic aid, when loans are included, amounted to $221 million, the highest sum among the DAC member countries of OECD and far exceeding the corresponding U.S. and West German figures of $82 million and $57 million, respectively.[47] The heavy involvement of the Japanese government in Indonesia's economic development program is no doubt highly complementary with the advance of Japanese industry.[48]

A case of a more direct involvement of the Japanese government is clearly illustrated by the Asahan project, the most significant venture so far undertaken by Japanese industry in Indonesia with a full financial backing, both directly and indirectly, from the Japanese government for the capital share of the Japanese investors. Because the project has many characteristics of economic development assistance, it has already begun to have important repercussions on the form of Japanese investment in other developing countries. The project involves the construction of a large dam and a hydroelectric power station on the Asahan river, an aluminum refinery that uses the power generated, and related infrastructural facilities.[49] Even before the final agreement was signed between the two countries in July 1975, it had long been publicized as "the TVA of the Suharto Government." The Asahan project is perhaps the first most significant "show case" venture of Japan's resources diplomacy undertaken by both her government and industry in developing countries.[50]

There are many interesting features in the terms of contract and in the process through which the final agreement was worked out. In the first place, Japan was the only country that had cooperated fully in bringing the project to reality and thereby saving the face of the Suharto administration. Several big Western aluminum companies that had initially participated in an international bidding withdrew when they learned of the desire of the Indonesian government to seek a comprehensive project that included a power station, an aluminum refinery, and all the related infrastructural facilities (port and land transportation). For a while, the project seemed likely to become a joint venture with the Aluminum Company of America (Alcoa) and the Kaiser Aluminum & Chemical Co., as they both expressed interest in joining the project, but these American firms decided not to participate as the estimated project costs soared from the initial $400 million to $800 million and as world demand for aluminum precipitously declined in 1974. Thus it became a mammoth project that Japanese industry was left to undertake alone.

Moreover, on the occasion of former Prime Minister Tanaka's visit to Djakarta in January 1974, he turned the tentative undertaking into an official commitment by promising a financial support from the Japanese government. Thus it took on the characteristics of a nationally and politically committed project on both sides: for Japan as a form of economic cooperation, and for the Suharto government as a pivotal regional economic development program. Once Tanaka had made an official commitment, it is said that "the Indonesian regarded political pressure as crucial, and did not rely on conventional channels," and acted "in the belief that the Tanaka and (Deputy Premier Takeo) Fukuda factions of the LDP (Liberal Democratic Party) had the influence to ensure agreement."[51] No doubt in the end political calculation, international as well as domestic on each side, played a decisive role in bringing about a final agreement.

The refinery is initially 90 percent owned by Japanese interests (controlled by five industrial groups, each of them holding 20 percent of the Japanese shares and involving a total of twelve Japanese companies),[52] but in ten years 25 percent of the total shares will be transferred to the Indonesian government. The hydroelectric power station, with a capacity of

430,000 kilowatts, will be turned over to the Indonesian government after thirty years of operation.

Thus, capital investment on the Japanese side is fully backed with credit from both official and private sources. The official sources cover 70 percent of the total cost of the project (loans for the aluminum refinery from the Export-Import Bank; for the power station from the OECF; and for port, highway and other overhead facilities from the JICA), while 20 percent are loans from Japanese commercial banks. The balance of 10 percent, the initial Indonesian share, is financed by the Indonesian government.

One interesting provision in the agreement is that, although the output is primarily intended to be shipped to Japan, up to one-third of it may be supplied to local users if there is demand. The aluminum thus earmarked for local use is expected and purposely designed to stimulate the production of a variety of aluminum-based products such as building materials, and the Japanese themselves are most likely to invest in these linkage-induced manufacturing ventures in the future.

It should be noted that in 1977 the Asahan formula of finance (capital participation of the Japanese government by way of its governmental agencies in a large-scale overseas project initiated by Japanese industry) also has been applied to a huge petro-chemical project in Indonesia's neighbor, Singapore.[53] Again this project, which produces ethylene and other basic chemicals, is expected to encourage the downstream production of plastics and other products—linkages that may invite more Japanese participation.

The Generalized System of Preferences (GSP)

In this section, the generalized system of preferences accorded by Japan for imports from the developing countries is described. The tariff concessions that encourage manufactured imports into Japan from the developing countries naturally have significant implications for Japan's manufacturing investment in the countries that enjoy the tariff privilege.

Despite Japan's modernization efforts, her industrial structure still remains a labyrinth with huge enterprises (even by Western standards) coexisting with primitively small enterprises. Because it is the light manufacturing industries that the developing countries opt to build in the early stages of industrialization and whose products they strive to export, there is an unavoidable friction between these countries and Japan's traditional sector as it struggles to remain competitive. Fully aware of the inevitability of the "chasing-up" competition, the Japanese government succeeded in encouraging the development of heavy and chemical industries, but failed to force the traditional sector to contract as rapidly as desired.

Not unexpectedly, therefore, when Japan's program of preferential tariffs for developing countries was introduced on August 1, 1971, it was largely a political gesture to "lend ears to" the aspirations of the developing countries to earn foreign exchange through "trade, not aid," the aspirations supported by the United Nations Conference on Trade and Development (UNCTAD). The original program is illustrated in table 3.7. It is built upon the so-called ceiling formula, which sets an upper limit on the value or quantity of imports for each group of products each year.

The tariff cuts, initially applied to 96 countries, were further extended to 124 countries on April 1, 1972, including Hong Kong, which had been previously excluded because of her status as a protectorate of the United Kingdom. Those countries which maintained discriminatory trade practices against Japan under Article 35 of the General Agreement on Tariffs and Trade (GATT) were to lose their beneficiary status unless they repealed such practices before August 1, 1974.[54]

Many items were either excluded completely or given special treatment from the application of tariff preferences. For exam-

Table 3.7 Japan's Preferential Tariff System, 1971

BTN[a] classification	No. of items	Tariff reduction	Ceilings	Conditions for enforcement
1-24 (agricultural processed products)	59 "positive items"	20%-100% of the present level	none	Application of escape clause
25-99 (manufacturing and mining products)	780	No tariffs	10% of the imports in the base year (1968)	If a certain developing nation accounts for 50 percent of the import ceiling, Japan will stop giving preferential treatments to that country (applicable to all import commodities).
	57 "sensitive items"	50% of the present level		
	10 "exceptional items"	present level		

Source: Adopted, with modifications, from a table shown in "Foreign Trade," p. 36.
[a] Brussels Tariff Nomenclature.

ple, seven manufactured items (raw silk, silk fabrics, plywood, glue-gelatin, rubber and plastic footwear, footwear parts, and leather garments), together with three petroleum products, were completely excluded and designated as "exceptional items." Fifty-seven other manufactured products were classified as "sensitive items," receiving the maximum 50 percent tariff cuts from the existing levels. These items included seven items of leather products and twenty-seven items of textiles and apparel, all of which are labor-intensive products manufactured mostly by small- and medium-sized firms.[55]

These exceptions were severely criticized, particularly by South Korea and Taiwan. In 1970, South Korea, for example, ranked first as a supply country for Japan's imports of four "exceptional items" (plywood, raw silk, silk fabrics, and rubber and plastic footwear). It also ranked either first or second in Japan's imports of cotton fabrics, apparel, batteries, and other products classified as "sensitive items." Similarly, Taiwan was and still is a major exporter to Japan of both "exceptional items" (leather garments and footwear parts) and "sensitive items" (refined oil, cotton fabrics, apparel, electronics components, and batteries).[56]

Because of these exceptions, the benefits of Japan's tariff preferences for developing countries seemed disappointingly small. Moreover, the actual benefits were further reduced by the extremely low ceilings set by the 1968 levels of imports plus 10 percent. Within twenty-four hours after the implementation of preferential tariffs, two items (men's underwear and nonleather shoes) imported from Taiwan had reached their ceilings, and within two months twenty-six items had exhausted the over-all quotas.[57] That the Japanese government set extremely restrictive ceilings was also reflected in the inactive use of the funds earmarked by the Preferential Tariff Countermeasures Emergency Act of April 1971, supposedly for aid to import-injured firms as a result of the preferential tariffs.[58]

Some minor revisions were made, effective on April 1, 1972,

by increasing the number of beneficiaries by twenty-eight countries and by changing the restriction date on ceiling controls for twenty-seven items from a daily to a monthly basis (that is, even if the ceiling for a particular product was reached in the middle of the month, its import would not be restricted until the end of the month, thus expanding the ceiling in real terms).[59] These modifications allayed to some extent the dissatisfaction voiced by developing countries.

But Japan did not move to liberalize the program substantially. The imports of light manufactures from the developing Asian countries recorded a significant rise, as much as 113.2 percent, from 1971 to 1973 as compared to one of 28.5 percent from 1969 to 1971.[60] This import surge might have demonstrated in part the benefits of Japan's GSP, but it was probably due more to the spillover of Japan's increased domestic demand and the government's effort to reduce its embarrassingly large foreign reserves by momentarily encouraging imports.

While remaining slow to open up domestic markets, for the obvious reason of minimizing injuries to the declining domestic industries, the government encouraged those small- and medium-sized enterprises threatened by imports as a result of the GSP to migrate to developing countries. The government-affiliated banks specifically established to assist financially the small- and medium-sized enterprises, extended guidance and loans to those firms interested in overseas ventures. The Japan Chamber of Commerce also set up in major cities a free consultation program and technical assistance for overseas investment at the urging of the MITI. The Institute of Developing Economies (formerly, the Institute of Asian Economic Affairs) began to provide information on investment environments in developing countries. Japan Export-Import Bank and the OECF also instituted consultations on overseas investment. All these positive "official" acts of encouragement provided an additional incentive to the migration of small- and medium-sized Japanese firms, already troubled by labor shortages and rising wages at home, to the developing countries in Asia and Latin America (notably Brazil). This is an interesting (and perhaps efficient) brand of adjustment assistance to import-threatened firms. For the Japanese companies thus assisted to migrate overseas would be in a position to partake of the benefits of the tariff concessions conferred on the developing countries, the very source of the threat from which they first had to escape.

However, once these firms actively took advantage of GSP, a complicated problem developed. In 1973, for example, Japan's textile imports reached $3.9 billion, more than double the level of the previous year and exceeding her textile exports of $3.2 billion.[61] Japan thus became a net importer of textiles for the first time in her modern industrial history. Textiles are now heavily imported from other Asian countries, and Japan's textile industry itself is in no small part responsible for the rapid development of its counterparts in Asian countries.[62] Thus Japan was confronted with a problem: should she impose restrictions on textile imports (that is, should she protect the domestic textile manufacturers and thereby penalize her overseas textile ventures, the very enterprises the government has assisted to settle overseas?). Although Japan finally succeeded in persuading other Asian countries to adopt an "orderly export" policy in order to avoid the disruption of Japan's textile market, the friction between Japan's domestic and overseas interests developed.

Conclusions

Thus Japanese industry is capitalizing on differences in economic environment between its own economy (which is perhaps over-industrialized in terms of its physical resources and in which the marginal social benefit of industrialization has quickly diminished, while the marginal social cost has soared) and those of the developing host countries (which are still in the early stages of development and in which therefore the opposite pattern of the appraisal of social benefit and cost prevails). Out of this process have emerged two significant trends of Japan's overseas investment in Asia: one is a rapid spread of the labor-intensive and low-value-added end of Japan's dual industrial structure across national borders into neighboring countries, notably South Korea and Taiwan; the other, the expanding role of the Japanese government in assisting Japanese industry to carry out large-scale economic development ventures in developing countries.

The first trend has been generated as a result of a fortuitous convergence of complementary forces at home and abroad—the "push" effect in Japan (particularly labor shortages) and the "pull" effect in neighboring developing countries (their emphasis on the utilization of labor, their most abundant factor of production, with the help of foreign capital and technology, as exemplified by the establishment of tax-free export processing zones). Japan's generalized system of preferences is also serving as a part of the national scheme to help her own small- and medium-sized firms to produce goods in developing countries and to retain control over their domestic markets. Concurrently, however, there has arisen some conflict with local interests, a problem peculiar to Japan's labor-resource-oriented investment in developing countries.

The second trend so far has culminated in an established pattern of government involvement, the Asahan formula of finance. In the following chapter, it will be shown that this formula seems to have become a set pattern of Japan's resources diplomacy in other regions as well.

In short, Japan's needs for low-cost labor, industrial sites, and natural resources and her neighboring countries' need for industrialization coincided with each other, and a closer and ever-deepening economic interdependence has developed between Japan and each of those Asian countries that adopted an outward-looking strategy for economic development. Of course, Japan clearly has a great stake in the economic prosperity and political stability of these market economies, because they are situated along the sea-lane through which pass the giant tankers carrying the vital supply of oil needed to keep her mammoth industrial wheel moving.[63]

Chapter 4

Direct Investment in Far Away Lands

OUTSIDE Asia, the main sphere of Japanese influence, Japan's overseas investments are no longer so intensively oriented to labor resources in the host countries. In other regions, with both geographical and cultural distances the "cost of being alien" quickly rises. As might be expected, the Japanese manufacturers investing in other regions, particularly in advanced Western markets, are those that possess some type of firm-specific advantage or that endeavor to develop technological and marketing advantages by utilizing, through direct investment, the technology resources of Western economies. In developing regions, such as Latin America and the Middle East, the Japanese government and the industrial groups led by their respective trading companies are seen more active in group-oriented and multi-firm investment activities than in Asia, because they are increasingly engaged in large-scale "regional development" projects. This chapter surveys the investment behavior of Japanese industry in other regions outside Asia.

North America

North America has attracted the largest share of Japanese investment in the commerce and service sector. Since the end of World War II Japan's export drive to capture the world's most affluent consumer markets, the United States and Canada, has resulted in the establishment of well-built channels of marketing and distribution in North America by Japan's major trading and manufacturing companies. As might be expected, the United States has attracted much more investment of this type than has Canada, because the former is not only a much bigger market but also it can serve as a distribution center for the latter because of their geographical proximity. Both countries are also key suppliers of vital industrial materials for the Japanese economy, but Canada, in particular, has attracted a relatively large amount of Japanese capital for resource-development ventures. These dissimilar characteristics are exhibited in table 4.1. About 77 percent of Japanese investments in the United States are in commerce, banking, insurance, and other service sectors, while the corresponding figure for Canada is 18 percent. On the other hand, the primary host sectors in Canada are timber and pulp (52.4 percent) and mining (24.9

Table 4.1   Japan's Direct Foreign Investment (DFI) in the United States and Canada at the End of March 1973
(in millions of U.S. dollars)

Industry	U.S.		Canada	
	Value	%	Value	%
Manufacturing	$176.0	13.8	$118.7	55.2
Timber and pulp	90.3	7.1	112.7	52.4
Textiles	7.1	0.6	2.5	1.2
Food processing	10.9	0.9	1.2	0.6
Ferrous and nonferrous metals	.8	0.1	.9	0.4
Chemicals	13.0	1.0 ⎫		
Nonelectrical machinery	19.3	1.5 ⎬ Others	1.4	0.7
Electrical machinery	27.5	2.2		
Others	7.1	0.6 ⎭		
Agriculture and forestry	3.9	0.3	2.2	1.0
Fishery	1.9	0.2	.8	0.4
Mining	106.4	8.4	53.6	24.9
Construction	7.3	0.6	1.1	0.5
Commerce, banking, insurance and other services	977.6	76.8	38.6	18.0
Total	$1,273.3	100.0	$214.9	100.0

Sources: The U.S. data are compiled from *Zaisei Kinyu Tokei Geppo* (Monthly Report on Fiscal and Monetary Statistics), September 1973, quoted in JETRO, *Kaigaishijo Hakusho*, p. 53. The data for Canada are compiled from *Nikkei Business*, September 16, 1974, p. 115.

percent).[1] Japan's manufacturing investments in Canada, when timber and pulp are excepted, are thus minuscule. In addition, the United States hosts Japanese investments about six times as large as those in Canada. The discussion that follows focuses on the investment activities of Japanese ventures in the United States.

Investment by Trading Companies

In the early days of Japan's postwar overseas investment, general trading companies spearheaded her overseas investment by setting up branch offices in the key commercial centers of the world. In the United States, they strove to promote Japan's manufactured exports as well as to secure vital imports such as capital goods, foodstuffs, coal, lumber, and pulp. Trading companies served as both sales and procurement agents for many Japanese manufacturing firms whose exports or imports had not yet become significant enough in volume or who were not yet experienced enough in international transactions to be directly engaged in overseas business operations. Thus the commerce-oriented investment made by trading companies in the United States was designed to strengthen their traditional role as brokerage agents for their closely related Japanese manufacturers.

Yet with the rapid sophistication of Japanese manufactured exports—as seen in a change in the composition of exports from the textile-and-sundries-dominated pattern of the early 1950s to the more diversified pattern of the 1960s with the appearance of technology-based new exports such as cameras, motor cycles, pianos, and automobiles—exporting manufacturers themselves began to set up their own sales and customer-service offices in the United States. They also succeeded in cultivating their brand names overseas. Despite this new trend, which appeared to undermine the role of trading companies as an export-sales agent, their position was not immediately eroded. For Japan's exports of traditional light manufactures such as plywood, sporting goods, footwear, textiles, toys, and Christmas decorations, mostly produced by small enterprises and intermediated by trading companies, still continued to expand in the United States. In fact, it was in joint ventures with these small- and medium-sized firms that trading companies started to establish separate sales companies in the United States, although this type of investment was insignificant as compared to those set up independently by large manufacturers.

As labor shortages began to appear in Japan in the mid-1960s, however, small enterprises experienced difficulties in supplying labor-intensive light manufactures on as competitive terms as before. At the same time, there was rising competition in labor-intensive products from other Asian countries such as Hong Kong and Taiwan. Large U.S. merchandisers and retail chain stores such as Sears Roebuck, J. C. Penney, and F. W. Woolworth started to increase their purchases of labor-intensive merchandise from other Asian countries.[2] When a large number of Japan's small- and medium-sized enterprises rushed to set up factories in neighboring countries, it was no surprise that trading companies themselves invested in many of these ventures as partners, offering managerial and financial expertise. Therefore, so far as their multinationalism in manufacturing is concerned, trading companies' experience originated in light manufacturing ventures, notably textiles. As explained before, they organized these investments in joint ventures with those Japanese small- and medium-sized enterprises that were unable to advance overseas on their own. At the same time, local firms were often involved as additional partners. The low-labor-cost countries in Asia were a logical choice as a location for these labor-oriented ventures. Japanese exports of labor-intensive manufactures to the United States thus began to disguise themselves as products made in Taiwan, South Korea, and other Asian countries.

Rising competition from the developing countries also served as an incentive for Japan's small- and medium-sized enterprises to upgrade products in both design and quality. As some of the firms succeeded in this endeavor, the United States itself became a possible site for their manufacturing ventures, particularly when the United States was (or was expected to be) their main market. With this new development, trading companies began to assist these relatively small enterprises to set up shop in the United States. In some of these ventures they also became partners, but again, this type of joint venture is limited in number.

The interest of trading companies in investing in overseas mining ventures was evident much earlier than it was in manufacturing ventures. Their traditional role of being an import-procurement agent for their respective industrial groups was an important motivation for participating in new extractive ventures to secure stable supplies of vital industrial resources.

Thus the traditional *export-agent* role of trading companies induced them to participate in labor-intensive manufacturing investments overseas on a rather limited scale, while their *procurement-agent* role enticed them to invest in extractive ventures and on a relatively large scale. Naturally, the amount of capital they invested in extractive ventures is on the whole much greater than that invested in manufacturing ventures because of the former's much larger scale of operations. Besides, their greater interest in extractive investment is compatible with the greater role that they have been playing in being procurement agents than in being export agents. Throughout the 1960s, for example, the share of the top ten trading companies in Japan's foreign trade was between 40 and 50 percent in the value of exports and between 60 and 70 percent in the value of imports. Indeed, this tendency is even more pronounced in the business of their U.S. subsidiaries. For instance, it is said that about 60 percent of annual sales of Mitsui (U.S.) come from the procurement (export to Japan) of foodstuffs, industrial raw materials, and machinery for Japanese firms, while only about 20 percent is related to Japanese goods imported into the United

States, the balance being taken up by third-country trade. A similar pattern applies to other trading companies' operations in the United States.

In fact, it is in their procurement-agent-originated investments rather than in their export-agent-originated investments that Japan's major trading companies have a lasting role to play as participants in Japan's future multinationalism. Their export-agent-originated investments in those light manufacturing ventures that can compete mainly on a price basis or on a relatively "thin" technological advantage are limited in scope and future opportunities, although they may be profitable at the moment. The large Japanese manufacturers whose competitiveness is based on a truly superior technology and on a well-established brand name normally do not require the help of general trading companies when it comes to their overseas sales or manufacturing ventures. In general, the more technologically sophisticated (requiring specialized direct customer services) and the more differentiated a product is, the less room is left for trading companies to serve as a sales agent and as a potential participant in overseas production. Because Japanese exports to the United States and Japan's manufacturing investments in the United States are now increasingly made in technology-based industries, fewer and fewer opportunities are open to trading companies to serve as investment partners. (When Sony first produced transistor radios, it turned to Mitsui for help in exporting them. Unimpressed by the then unknown small company's product Mitsui declined the request, a decision that compelled Sony to start its own exporting business.)

On the other hand, with increasing instability in the supplies of industrial raw materials, energy resources, and foodstuffs, the establishment of secure sources of these supplies have become especially important to Japanese industry, and the role of trading companies as the traditional procurement agents of these supplies has compelled them, as mentioned earlier, to invest directly in resource-development ventures overseas. In contrast to their interest in the overseas production of differentiated end-products, big manufacturers of sophisticated products are usually less interested in, or incapable of investing in, the upward-stream stages of their production. The more sophisticated the product is (that is, the higher the value-added component of a product is), the less quantitatively important its raw-material content. Hence, most manufacturers are largely dependent on the supplies of their imported inputs handled by the trading companies. Furthermore, small- and medium-sized manufacturers are much more dependent on trading companies for the supplies of input materials (not only imported ones but also in many cases domestic ones). Consequently, trading companies are more bent on organizing resource-development or resource-processing ventures, the former in collaboration with the firms in the primary extractive industries (for example, mining companies) and the latter with the firms in the resource-processing industries (for example, ore smelters). For the preceding reasons, aside from investments to strengthen their own sales networks, general trading companies' direct investments in the United States and Canada as joint investors are more significant in value and sales in resource-related ventures than in manufacturing ventures.

Investment by Manufacturers

In addition to investment by trading companies, Japanese manufacturers themselves took the initiative to invest directly in the United States. Some of the manufacturers who succeeded in capuring a sizable share of the U.S. market through exports (via their own marketing channels instead of through trading companies) and who, as a result, were soon faced with rising protectionism moved to set up shop in the United States. The prime example is Sony's investment in a plant in San Diego, California, that produces color televisions. Sony, an active user of U.S. technologies in its early days, succeeded in developing its own differentiated products by means of both adaptive and original R & D and aggressive marketing strategies. The U.S. market has been of the utmost importance to the firm not only as an outlet for its products but also as a *technological laboratory* from which to acquire new ideas and the latest technologies and in which to test and introduce new products. Its move to local production in this high-labor-cost country was encouraged by the fact that the assembly operation of color-TV receivers with solid state components had already been highly automated and that it could no longer depend on relatively cheap labor at home, labor that had become quite costly in the wake of sharp wage hikes in the recent past.[3]

Other firms, such as Toyo Bearings, Yoshida Kogyo (zipper maker), Nippon Miniature Bearing, and Hitachi Metals were similarly motivated to produce directly in the United States. All these firms are technology-based enterprises. In addition to retaining control over their former export market, they were enticed to manufacture directly in the United States because the U.S. market offers an innovation-conducive environment and an abundant supply of technology resources and information for the development of new products.[4]

Among other investments specifically aimed at cultivating the favorable U.S. technological environment are Omron R & D, Mountain View, California (a subsidiary of Omron Tateishi Electronics, which was set up to tap U.S. research brain-power by employing many American scientists and engineers laid off from the U.S. space program) and Kyocera International (a subsidiary of Kyoto Ceramic, a leading maker of IC ceramic packages, which purchased a ceramic plant from Fairchild) located in the so-called silicon valley of California. As shown in chapter 2 in connection with the product-cycle theory of trade, all these Japanese manufacturers are former interceptors of U.S. innovations, and they have thus moved right into the technology center of the U.S. market in search of new ideas for their continued technological improvement. They are the follower-turned-innovators who are now in the post-product-cycle stage of innovation, utilizing the very same technology resources that U.S. entrepreneurs alone were once able to exploit in order to develop trade competitiveness in technology-based industries, but access to which is now open equally to innovation-seeking foreign entrepreneurs through direct investment.

Another group of manufacturing investors was equally daring. They are manufacturers of Japanese foods (Kikkoman's soy-sauce factory in Walworth, Wisconsin, and Nissin Foods' instant noodles factory in Los Angeles). Originally catering to a relatively small ethnic market in the United States, they are both now striving to enlarge their market by "educating" the American public's culinary tastes to their respective "gourmet" foods. These foods are increasingly being placed on the shelves of U.S. supermarkets.

Because the United States is both the major supplier of raw materials and the most important export market for some Japanese industries, it has attracted several Japanese firms that are eager to be near the source of supply as well as the market. Kikkoman's investment in Wisconsin also reflects this need, because it depends on the supply of American soybeans as a raw material for the sauce. Other examples include Japan's steel concerns, which rely heavily on scrap iron, and the textile firms, which import American cotton. Both formidably compete with their U.S. counterparts in the end-product market. The first Japanese-owned steel mill to produce construction-related bars is already in operation in Auburn, New York. Other steel-making ventures are reportedly under negotiation. In addition to stable scrap supplies and access to the market, land and electric power, inexpensive by Japanese standards, are major attractions. As might be expected, Japanese textile ventures in the United States (ten ventures at the end of March 1973) are concentrated in the Southern states such as Georgia and South Carolina, the center of the U.S. textile industry.[5] One large cotton-spinning company decided to set up a mill in Levelland, Texas—no surprise, because Japan is the largest importer of

Texas cotton. Moreover, the company was reportedly able to acquire "the land and water rights it needed for a paltry $10," since Levelland was eager to win over several other Texas communities in inviting the company.[6]

Another group of Japanese firms attracted to the low-cost supply of industrial materials in the United States is the manufacturers of chemical products such as paint, printing ink, pesticide, and other chemicals. One interesting strategy adopted by them is to purchase existing U.S. plants instead of building new ones. Denki Kagaku Kogyo, Dainippon Ink & Chemicals, Asahipen, Shin-etsu Chemical Industry, and Sekisui Chemical, have recently chosen this route of entry into the U.S. market.[7] A major motive behind their move was to secure established sales networks, thereby saving time for plant construction and development of new marketing channels—to avoid a newcomer's disadvantage of starting from scratch. Besides, acquisition of existing plants also reduces their visibility as "alien" producers and enables them to fade into the American industrial scene without disrupting the prevailing supply patterns. In addition, their U.S. plants serve as a center to gather information about U.S. and often global market conditions.

The recent advances made by Japan's manufacturers of color televisions (other than Sony whose U.S. venture has already been described earlier) are another recent phenomenon worth noting. Matsushita Electric and Sanyo Electric have already started local production, while Mitsubishi Electric and Tokyo Shibaura Electric are in their preparatory stages. They were forced to choose local production mainly because of a rising clamor against imported televisions, a clamor that resulted in a "voluntary" export control agreement in 1977 with the export ceiling of 1.75 million sets—far below the export level of 2.96 million sets attained in 1976.[8] Their local production is basically assembly operations. The profitability of their U.S. plants crucially rests on the use of parts and components imported from Japan, an advantage these Japanese investors are allowed to enjoy, for the time being, over local U.S. manufacturers. The real test of their competitiveness as true multinationals comes when they are compelled to procure locally produced parts and components, moving toward a more locally integrated production.

In addition to these relatively well-publicized Japanese investments mentioned above, there are many other small-scale manufacturing ventures, ventures engaged in producing sausages, canned oyster stew, fishing tackles, concrete piles and poles, and other miscellaneous goods. Many of these ventures are located in California. In March 1974, 36 out of a total of 91 Japanese manufacturing plants in the United States were found in that state.[9]

Other Investments

Japan's direct investments in the U.S. service sector include leisure-oriented investments (hotels and golf courses) intended to cater not so much to U.S. tourists as to the Japanese themselves, a controversial type of overseas investment made mostly in Hawaii and on the West Coast. In 1974 this type of investment in Hawaii was estimated to have a value between $200 million and $250 million and to control ten hotels with about 5,000 rooms (an equivalent of 15 percent of the total number of hotel rooms on the islands) and four golf courses. In California and other states, the Japanese also invested in hotels and golf courses and in the development of industrial parks and residential housing projects—the total reportedly reaching $750 million in 1974.[10]

Latin America

Roughly 20 percent of Japanese overseas investments, measured in terms of their value, are located in Latin American countries. The average value of investment in the region is higher than in any other regions except the Middle East. This indicates a relatively large scale of ventures necessitated by resource-development projects. Brazil and Mexico are the only two countries that have so far attracted a significant number of Japanese manufacturing ventures as well. Japan's investments in other major host countries such as Peru, Chile, and Colombia are practically all resource-development ventures centered in the mining industries.

About half of the Japanese investments in Latin America are located in Brazil, and it is in this largest resource-rich country in the region that Japanese industry has made a most impressive advance and attained a predominant position as an investor vis-à-vis other industrial countries. The following sections will describe how Japanese industry succeeded in gaining a strong foothold.

Brazil

Japan's industrial advance in Brazil has been faster than any other country's in the recent past. As shown in table 4.2, Japan's direct investment share rose from 3.2 percent in 1969 to 11.2 percent in 1976, while that of the leading investor, the United States, declined from 47.7 percent to 32.2 percent over the same period. Although Japan currently ranks third behind the United States and West Germany as measured by the cumulative value of investment, she is expected to overtake West Germany. From 1975 to 1985 Japan is reportedly planning to make investments worth at least $9.5 billion in Brazil, roughly corresponding to 10 percent of the total Japanese investments abroad.[11]

Sensing this rapid Japanese advance and the declining U.S. position, a 1973 report prepared by the U.S. Embassy in Rio de Janeiro warned U.S. businessmen of the rising competition from Japan: "Brazil should not be regarded as any easy market for American exporters and investors. Other countries, aware of Brazil's potential, are striving to strengthen their presence. The Japanese are noteworthy in this respect. They vigorously pro-

Table 4.2

Direct Foreign Investment (DFI)
and Reinvestment in
Brazil, 1969 and 1976
(in millions of U.S. dollars)

	1969			1976		
	Value[a]	%	Rank	Value[a]	%	Rank
United States	816	47.7	(1)	2,901	32.2	(1)
West Germany	177	10.4	(2)	1,118	12.4	(2)
Japan	55	3.2	(7)	1,006	11.2	(3)
Switzerland	105	6.1	(5)	981	10.9	(4)
Canada	168	9.8	(3)	482	5.4	(5)
United Kingdom	109	6.4	(4)	421	4.7	(6)
France	35	2.1	(9)	326	3.6	(7)
Panama	49	2.9	(8)	275	3.1	(8)
Netherland Antilles	62	3.6	(6)	192	2.1	(9)
Other	134	7.8		1,303	14.5	
Total	1,710	100.0		9,005	100.0	

Source: Computed from data in the Central Bank of Brazil, Boletim, May 1975 and June 1977. Statistics shown refer to direct foreign investment registered by the Central Bank. Loans are not included.
[a] These are cumulative values at the end of the year.

mote not only their Brazilian export outlets, but also their investment in and imports from Brazil. Some of these investments, it should be noted, are joint ventures with Brazilian and/or third country nationals."[12]

First Wave of Investments of the 1950s
Initially Japanese industry started out investing mainly in the commercial and manufacturing sectors, although it is now more active in assisting the Brazilian economy to develop large-scale resources-related industries. It was in the mid-1950s that Japanese industry was able to re-establish its economic ties directly with Brazil through overseas investments. The first Japanese firms to invest in Brazil were general trading companies which intermediated most of the trade between Japan and Brazil.

Over a short period of three years, from 1955 to 1957, all major trading firms quickly opened offices in São Paulo. This rapid and concurrent advance of Japanese trading companies was not confined to Brazil. Throughout the 1950s, as pointed out in chapter 1, these companies were involved in re-establishing and expanding the worldwide marketing networks they had developed in the prewar days. This activity was encouraged by the Japanese government, which allocated scarce international reserves for their use in an effort to promote exports.

At the same time, several Japanese manufacturers also moved in to set up plants. Major Japanese manufacturing ventures in the 1950s are shown in table 4.3. The first wave of these manufacturing investments exhibited two features looked upon at that time as unique. First, their scales were of substantial size by then-prevailing Japanese standards; second, they were wholly- or majority-owned by the Japanese. At that time the Japanese economy had barely recovered from the destruction of war and was struggling to build up its own productive capacities. It also had a chronic balance-of-payments problem and possessed only a meager reserve of foreign exchange. Moreover, the economy after the Korean War stagnated and operated with idle capacity. Why, then, were the Japanese so much interested in setting up shop in such a distant country as Brazil and on such a large scale? Moreover, why did they opt for wholly- or majority-owned investments instead of conserving their capital by enlisting local participation?

There are several explanations. At that time Brazil already had become an important export market for Japanese manufactures, notably cotton textiles (which were Japan's top export item in the early 1950s) and other light manufactures, and the future of Brazil looked particularly promising because of a rich endowment of natural resources. Therefore Japanese industry was bound to be interested sooner or later in making investments there once it acquired surplus capital. But the decisive factor encouraging the Japanese to advance into Brazil at a

Table 4.3 Japan's Major Investments in Brazil, 1955-1960

Japanese firms	Ventures in Brazil	Product	Initial Japanese capital invested (U.S. $ X1,000)	Ownership %	Year
Toyo Bohseki	Toyobo do Brasil	Cotton textiles	2,420	100	1955
Ajinomoto	Ajinomoto do Brasil	Monosodium glutamate	100	50	1956
Ishikawajima-Harima	Ishikawajima do Brasil	Ships and machinery	14,296	90.6	1956
Kanegafuchi Bohseki	Kanebo Brasil	Cotton textiles	2,000	72.7	1956
Yanmar Diesel	Yanmar Diesel Motors Brasil	Motors	2,500	95	1957
Nippon Usiminas	Usinas Siderurgicas de Minas Gerais (USIMINAS)	Steel	—	20.9	1957
Kubota-Tekko Mitsubishi International	Kubota-Tekko do Brasil	Farm equipment	1,979	100	1957
Toyota Motors	Toyota do Brasil	Utility vehicles	5,000	100	1958
Howa Kogyo, Toyobo, Nippon Spindle	Industria Mecanica Howa do Brasil	Textile machinery	2,020	96	1958
Kurashiki Bohseki, Tohmen, Kanematsu	Lanificio Kurabo do Brasil	Woolen textiles	1,235	97.9	1959
Tsuzuki Bohseki	Industria Textile Tsuzuki	Cotton textiles	2,678	100	1960

Source: Compiled from Jukagaku Kogyo Tsushinsha, *Kaigai Toshi Gijutsu Yushutsu* (Japan's Overseas Investment and Technology Export), Tokyo, 1970, as presented in Ozawa, Pluciennik, and Rao, "Japanese Direct Investment in Brazil," p. 109.

time when Japan was still preoccupied with the rebuilding of her own domestic industry was the new industrialization policy of Brazil implemented in the mid-1950s. This policy emphasized import substitution under the so-called law of similars. Under this law, once a particular item was produced in "sufficient quality and quantity," and registered with the government as a product similar to its imported counterpart, it would be protected from imports.

Consequently, many foreign firms quickly moved in to set up local production to produce "similars" and to be qualified for import protection. Japanese manufacturers, who had only recently developed a profitable export business in Brazil, had no choice but to follow suit lest they lose their market. Fortunately, their meager capital did not hinder this move, because in 1955 Brazil introduced a timely measure, called Superintendency of Money and Credit (SUMOC) Instruction 113, which provided numerous incentives to foreign enterprises.[13] In particular, the measure allowed foreign investors in priority industries to import equipment for their ventures and to acquire as payment a cruzeiro capital ownership. In computing their capital contribution equivalent to the value of imported equipment, they were permitted to convert the value of machinery in foreign currency into that in cruzeiros at special rates that purposely kept the cruzeiro overly depreciated under Brazil's multiple rate system. Their investments were thus indirectly subsidized, because they were able to capitalize their assets at a much more favorable exchange rate than the market rate.

The measure benefited all foreign investors, but it was particularly a boon to capital-short Japanese industry. For under SUMOC Instruction 113 the foreign investor was permitted to ship out used machinery as well, and this provision was most suitable for Japan's textile makers, who were, at that time, operating with idle machinery at home. They transferred used machinery from Japan and installed it in their mostly wholly-owned Brazilian subsidiaries to manufacture cotton textiles.

This equipment transfer proved beneficial in the short run and also provided long-run advantages. It immediately enabled major Japanese textile manufacturers to reduce excess capacity in cotton textiles and facilitated their expansion into the production of synthetic textiles then emerging as a new growth sector. Japanese machinery manufacturers, such as Ishikawajima-Harima, were equally eager to invest on a large scale, because their ventures were essentially tantamount to plant exports, exports converted into capital investment at an extremely attractive exchange rate. Under these circumstances, there was not much incentive for them to invite local capital participation. Besides, the valuation of machinery as an investment asset would create some friction in their relationship with the local interests unable to capitalize on such a privilege. As a result, the Japanese opted for sole ownership unless they found it particularly desirable to have a local partner.

In addition to the favorable incentives given by the Brazilian government, the presence of a large number of Japanese immigrants and their descendants (currently estimated to be upward of 700,000) served as a powerful magnet for Japan's investment. That Japanese immigrants were welcomed and well treated in Brazil—both in the prewar and particularly in the postwar period—provided a basis for psychological security for the Japanese. Japanese immigrants, who first arrived back in 1908 as wage workers, came to develop profitable commercial farming, concentrating first in the state of São Paulo and then spreading to other regions.[14] These thriving Japanese farm communities have attracted investments such as Kubota-Tekko's venture to produce "micro" tractors and Mitsui's fertilizer plant.[15] Today, many Japanese-Brazilians work for Japanese multinational companies as business partners as well as employees. Observing a close relationship between Japan's overseas investments and her immigrants in Latin America, the Economist Intelligence Unit's special report commented: "It will be found that the proportion of Japanese investment in any country roughly corresponds to the distribution of Japanese immigrants in Latin America."[16]

A Lull and a Surge in the 1960s

Brazil's import substitution policy resulted in an unprecedented inflow of foreign investments, mostly from the United States and Europe, but Japan too had invested on a small scale in the late 1950s. This rush of foreign capital quickly exhausted the available investment opportunities. Furthermore, runaway inflation, political chaos, and a decline in industrial activities (for example, a negative growth of industrial output occurred from 1962 to 1963) discouraged foreign investment. As a result, Japanese direct foreign investment also waned throughout the first half of the 1960s, with only a few sporadic investments.

With the return of political stability and the subsequent positive economic measures of the Brazilian government, such as "indexation," taken to keep the economy on even keel, Brazilian industry once again started to grow at a rapid pace after the mid-1960s. By then, the Japanese economy had rehabilitated itself completely from the effects of World War II and was in a stage of vigorous expansion. Japan's overseas investment itself, supported by fast-accumulating reserves of foreign exchange, was becoming large enough for Japan to be identified as a leading participant in the global game of multinationalism. This situation was in sharp contrast to her position in the late 1950s when Japanese manufacturers barely had managed to set up ventures in Brazil because of their limited capital; they were able to do so only because of Brazil's favorable investment incentives program. Now Japanese industry had surplus capital to invest, and after the mid-1960s a rush to Brazil ensued, a phenomenon commonly called the "Brazil boom."

However, there was another important force pushing Japanese industry outward to Brazil. Labor shortages in the Japanese economy experienced during the second half of the 1960s forced small- and medium-sized enterprises to transfer their production to Japan's neighboring countries where the supply of low-cost labor was abundant. The sudden presence of Japanese industry, however, stirred up local antagonism, touching off anti-Japanese demonstrations in some countries. Consequently, the Japanese were quickly attracted to Brazil. For Brazil appeared to be a more friendly host country than the Asian countries with not only an ample labor supply but also a fast-growing domestic market. Japan's small- and medium-sized firms quickly moved into Brazil in large numbers, setting up relatively small-scale ventures in diverse fields. Some firms even considered the possibility of transferring their entire corporate operations into Brazil, giving birth to a new phrase, *kigyo iju* (enterprise immigration), popularly used in the Japanese business community.

Increased Cooperation wtih the Brazilian Government: The 1970s

The rankings of major Japanese ventures in Brazil's various industries in 1974 are shown in table 4.4. A large number of Japanese ventures operate in the textiles and light machinery sectors, but the two most significant and successful ventures are found in heavy industry sectors, shipbuilding and iron and steel.

Ishikawajima do Brasil is a majority-Japanese-owned shipbuilding company with the Brazilian government as its local partner. The latter financed 30 percent of the plant-equipment expenditures of the venture and placed construction orders for vessels for the Brazilian navy. The company is the largest shipbuilder in Brazil and in Latin America. In addition to a shipbuilding yard and a repair dock it has a machinery division that produces Sulzer diesel engines, cranes, and allied steel structures.[17] The company has been steadily expanding. In 1974, for example, its expansion plan of about $15 million, approved by Brazil's Industrial Development Council for spe-

Table 4.4 Ranking by Invested Capital of Major Japanese Ventures in Brazil's Industry, 1974

Industry	Ranking	Local Company	Capital (U.S. $ X1,000)	Ownership
I. Textiles:				
(a) yarns and fabrics, natural and synthetic	1st	Fisiba	23,235	Joint venture of Mitsubishi Rayon with Techem-Tecnologia e Emprendimentos Techint-Cia, Tecnica International, and BNDE
polyester yarn and fibers	6th	Safron-Teijin	15,783	Joint venture of Teijin, Marubeni, with Grupo Safra, Sudene Arts
textiles	14th	Nisshinbo	8,768	Nisshin Boseki
textiles	38th	Toyobo	3,653	Joint venture of Toyobo, Sumitomo Brasileiro, Mitsubishi Brasileiro, Brasileiro de Descontos
textiles	54th	Unitika	2,923	Unitika
cotton spinning	56th	Kanebo	2,923	Kanegafuchi Boseki
(b) semi-finished	19th	Brasiliana	3,800	Toyobo, Mitsubishi Rayon
II. Electric—electronics machinery:				
(a) motors, lamps, and misc. electrical material	11th	Hitachi Line	4,384	Hitachi
(b) communication equipment	4th	Nec do Brasil	9,060	Nippon Electric
(c) Home appliances	24th	Toshiba	3,653	Toshiba
	26th	Sharp	3,215	Sharp

III. Nonelectrical machinery:				
(a) heavy equipment—boilers, hydraulic turbines, generators, rolling mills	16th	Yanmar	5,407	Yanmar Diesel
	20th	CBC	5,115	Mitsubishi Heavy Industries
roller and ball bearings	21st	NSK	5,115	Nippon Seiko
mechanical engineering	42d	Howa	3,653	Howa Kogyo
(b) tractors and earth-moving equipment	5th	Hatsuta	7,745	Hatsuta
	7th	Komatsu	5,115	Joint venture of Komatsu Seisaku with Brascan
IV. Shipbuilding*	1st	Ishikawajima do Brasil Estaleiros	44,863	Joint venture of Harima-Ishikawajima with Brazilian government
V. Iron and steel*	3d	Usinas Sid. M. Gerais, S.A. Ushiminas	241,561	Joint venture of Nippon Usiminas with the Brazilian government
VI. Automobiles*	8th	Toyota	3,800	Toyota

Sources: Editora Banas, S.A., *Brasil Industrial 1975*, and *Quem e Quem Economia Brasiliera*, VISAO, 1974. Statistics with an asterisk are from the latter. Cruzeiro capital values are converted to the U.S. dollar values at the 1974 "period average" exchange rate of Cr.$6.843 per dollar, as shown in Ozawa, Pluciennik, and Rao, "Japanese Direct Investment in Brazil," p. 112.

cial investment tax credit, was the largest among the Japanese ventures—an indication of continued strong support by the Brazilian government.

Shipbuilding is an exceptional heavy-machinery sector in which overseas investment has been pushed strongly by Japanese firms. In fact, it is perhaps the sole sector in which Japan's heavy machinery industry has been able to invest on the basis of their technological advantages accumulated through building and exporting vessels for the world market. The export competitiveness of Japan's shipbuilding industry was based on a relatively abundant supply of skilled workers who had previously had experience working for the former Japanese naval shipyards. The Japanese were also quick to use block construction techniques and computerized inventory- and material-handling. The undervalued yen was no doubt another source of competitiveness. When the Brazilian shipyard was set up by Ishikawajima-Harima, it was regarded as a reckless gamble, because Brazil lacked a supply of such skilled labor. Furthermore, there were ample domestic capacities to expand production, if necessary. Yet as Japanese shipbuilding firms began to emphasize the export activity of their heavy-machinery division (in which they had scarcely developed their own technologies to a point that would compare with their reputed shipbuilding technologies), they realized that helping other countries to build shipyards was an effecive way of generating demands for plant exports. A sharp appreciation of the yen also eliminated export competitiveness and made overseas production more attractive than before. In time, Ishikawajima-Harima's Brazil venture came to be looked upon as a foresighted endeavor and induced other major shipbuilding firms with heavy-machinery divisions to follow suit.

The other major Japanese venture that has served as a milestone for Japan's advance into Brazil is Usinas Siderurgicas de Minas Gerais (USIMINAS), a Brazilian and Japanese steelmaking firm established in 1958. The Japanese partner is a semi-governmental holding company called the Nippon Usi-minas K.K. owned jointly by the OECF, Nippon Steel, Ishika-wajima-Harima, and twenty-nine other manufacturing and trading companies. The Japanese group owns 20.9 percent of the common stock and 16.6 percent of the preferred. It currently ranks third in Brazil's iron and steel industry in terms of capital but enjoys a virtual monopoly in such product lines as heavy shipbuilding plate (note Ishikawajima-Harima's participation in the Japanese group) and deep drawing sheet steel for auto bodies.[18]

These two ventures are quite successful not only in business operations (both now pay dividends of 10 to 15 percent) but also in consolidating close economic relations between Japanese industry and the Brazilian government. In further collaboration with the host government, Japanese industry is now advancing into Brazil's basic industries such as petro-chemicals, aluminum, pulp and paper, and fertilizer—industries whose development is stressed in Brazil's second five-year plan for national development (1975-1979). The Japanese are investing in joint ventures with the state-owned enterprises of the host country, willingly accepting the condition of minority ownership imposed by the host government. One such example is the recent move of Japanese companies to participate in Brazil's plan to develop a petro-chemical complex in northeastern Brazil. As shown in table 4.5, different groups of Japanese firms (normally consisting of a major chemical company and a general trading company) are setting up joint ventures with a state-owned enterprise, Petroquisa, and in all cases accepting a minority ownership of 25 to 40 percent. It is said that Brazil's Industrial Development Council, presided over by President Ernesto Geisel, has given this project one of the highest priorities as an urgently needed regional development program. This new form of cooperation is especially significant in the current advance of Japanese multinationals, since several American petro-chemical corporations, well established in Brazil, have

Table 4.5 Japan's Participation in Brazil's Petro-chemical Combine at the End of February 1975

Ventures	Japanese companies	Brazilian partners	Japanese share %
High pressure polyethylene	Sumitomo Chemical C. Itoh	Petroquisa	30
Low and medium pressure polyethylene	Mitsubishi Chemical Industries Nissho-Iwai	Petroquisa Banco de Economia	33
Polyvinyl chloride	Mitsubishi Chemical Industries Nissho-Iwai	Petroquisa Camargo	33
Phthalic anhydride	Mitsubishi Chemical Industries Nissho-Iwai	Ciquine Petroquimica	26.7
Acrylonitrile (AN)	Mitsubishi Rayon Mitsubishi	Petroquisa	33
Polyisoprene rubber	Kuraray Mitsubishi	Petroquisa	30
Chloroprene rubber	Toyo Soda	Petroquisa	Under negotiation
Linear acrylic benzene	Nippon Petro-chemical Nissho-Iwai	Under negotiation	Scheduled to be 25
Formalin	Mitsubishi Gas Chemical Marubeni-Iida	Pasquin	40
Urea	Mitsui Toatsu Chemical	—	Technological export

Source: *Technocrat*, no. 2, February 1975, p. 4.

shown a disinclination to participate in the project unless they are allowed to invest on a majority or complete ownership basis.[19] As a result, the Japanese have emerged as the major participant in Brazil's development of a petro-chemical complex in the northeast.

Another example of close cooperation offered by both Japanese government and Japanese industry in connection with Brazil's regional development is an electric power and aluminum project in the Amazon basin in the state of Para, a scheme very similar to the Asahan project. The project involves construction of a hydropower plant and a smeltery with an annual production capacity ultimately reaching 340,000 tons. Forty-nine percent of the ownership will be taken up by the Japanese and the rest by Brazil's state-owned mining company, Companhia Vale do Rio Doce. The Japanese group, consisting initially of five major smelters, will be expanded into another semi-governmental investing company with capital participation of the OECF and approximately thirty-two private corporations. Although the Japanese multinationals are the actual participants, negotiations basically were carried out between the two governments. When Japan's former Prime Minister Tanaka visited Brazil in September 1974, he signed a declaration with President Geisel promising Japan's cooperation in the project. Japan's pledge was then reaffirmed when then Deputy Prime Minister Fukuda visited Brazil in August 1975. During a visit of Brazil's Mining and Energy Minister Ueki to Tokyo in January 1976, the Brazilian and Japanese parties signed an agreement to set up a joint venture to undertake a feasibility study. When the prolonged recent recession of the Japanese economy delayed the Japanese in making a firm commitment, Brazil approached European nations and succeeded in securing a promise from France for extension of a loan to be used for the hydropower plant project. Fearful of losing to her European competitors, Japanese government and industry made all the necessary arrangements for a final commitment. Minister of International

Trade and Industry Komoto was dispatched to Brazil in July 1976 to work out details with the Brazilian government. Japan's industrial community as represented by *Keidanren* (Japan's Federation of Economic Organizations) announced its all-out support for the project and urged the Japanese government to provide financial assistance equally as strong as that given to the successful USIMINAS steel project. The final contract was signed by the two countries on the occasion of Brazilian President Geisel's visit to Tokyo in September 1976.

Another huge project to which Japanese government and industry also have recently committed themselves is a steelmaking venture at Tubarao in Espirito Santo State. It is an international consortium with the participation of Brazil's state enterprise, Siderbras (51 percent), Italy's Finsider (24.5 percent), and Japan's Kawasaki Steel (24.5 percent). The plant is expected to be completed in 1980. For this steelmaking venture and the Amazon aluminum project, the Japanese government is extending loans of $693 million and $630 million, respectively, in the form of capital financing and deferred payment.[20]

Many similar projects are planned in connection with Brazil's Second Development Plan:

· Companhia Vale do Rio Doce (CVRD) and a group of Japanese concerns led by Oji Paper Co. have set up a joint venture, Cinebra, to produce pulp in the state of Minas Gerais;

· CVRD and a group of six Japanese steelmakers are to establish a company to build an iron pellet plant near Tubarao;

· Petrobras Quimica and two companies of the Mitsui Group of Japan are to set up a new company, Amonio Fosfato do Nordeste, to manufacture granulated fertilizers; and

· Sumitomo Chemicals and Ataka of Japan and a local concern are planning to open a plant in Recife to manufacture a million tons of compound fertilizer a year after 1978.[21]

Indeed, CVRD recently announced that the above-mentioned pulp and iron pellet ventures would involve fifteen-year supply contracts with the Japanese concerns valued at the equivalent of more than $8 billion.[22]

New Brand of Multinationalism

Viewed from the above perspective, Japan's latest advance in Brazil's resource-related industries has begun to exhibit some new features. Major Japanese multinationals have begun to behave as if they were "subcontractors" of their government in implementing the economic cooperation agreements with the Brazilian government. Their ventures are mostly set up in collaboration with Brazil's state-owned enterprises. And financial backing has come or is expected to come from Japan's OECF and her Export-Import Bank.

This approach is certainly a new brand of multinationalism. The multinational corporation has been criticized lately for its insensitivity to economic needs in less-developed countries, and the resource-rich countries are now demanding local control over their resource-related basic industries. The options for multinational corporations are limited to joint ventures with local interests and the acceptance of minority ownership. Multinationals that insist on retention of complete or majority ownership simply have to forego opportunities. Japanese multinationals probably have shown a greater willingness to cooperate under these new requirements than those of other countries.

There are good reasons for their high propensity to cooperate. With a phenomenal domestic economic growth, Japan's dependence on overseas resources has risen enormously. Japanese industry must secure vital supplies of industrial resources abroad. At the same time it is quite willing to transfer overseas resource-processing activities (such as aluminum smelting, steelmaking, and oil refining) whose further growth in Japan is no longer as strongly desired as in the past or simply impractical because of import and environmental constraints. Overseas investments in resource-processing industries are viewed as one important instrument to facilitate industrial restructuring of the Japanese economy toward a less energy-consuming and bulk-resource-dependent entity, while still enabling it to retain the necessary supply sources of processed materials. Moreover, as long as Japan remains the major buyer of the resources developed and processed by her overseas ventures, she can still enjoy a monopsony advantage (an advantage that enables the buyer to control indirectly the volume of output even if he does not have any ownership interest in his supplier). In addition to assuring the supply sources of vital resources, overseas ventures in resource-processing industries also create opportunities to export a large volume of capital goods, the fact that justifies the loans from Japan's Export-Import Bank.

The motivation of Japanese multinationals to take part in Brazil's resource-proccessing industries as minority shareholders essentially derives from considerations of the macroeconomic requirements of their home economy rather than from considerations of rivalry relationships with other countries' multinationals, the primary oligopolistic motif of Western corporations. This perspective, as emphasized in chapter 2, explains why the Japanese government is paving the way for the advance of Japanese industry by concluding economic cooperation agreements with the host country. There has emerged a peculiar match of interests between Brazil (and for that matter other resource-abundant developing countries), which is eager to process her resources before exporting as part of her industrialization efforts, and Japan, which is equally eager to have this particular stage of production performed overseas. Japanese industry, by establishing a pattern of behavior considered desirable both for its economy and for the host country, may well succeed in carving out its share of many overseas markets previously dominated by U.S. and European enterprises.

Brazil, moreover, seems to have some additional reasons to favor Japan as a supplier of industrial technology and capital.

First, Brazil is endeavoring to diversify the sources of foreign capital and technology as much as possible in order to avoid dependence on a particular foreign country. This diversification strategy is designed to alleviate a fear of "selling out" to foreign interests. Although Brazil is becoming increasingly dependent on foreign capital, her bargaining power can be strengthened by taking advantage of rivalries among different investor countries, and Japan has proved to be a good alternative investor in many key investment projects.

Second, because of its cohesiveness and its close liaison and collaboration with the Japanese government, Japan's industry is perhaps much easier for the Brazilian government to approach in seeking the capital and technology required for investment projects it plans than any other country's. The Brazilian government officials can negotiate directly with their Japanese counterparts, who are usually in a position to make decisions and to promise industry's cooperation for specific investment projects. Furthermore, the Japanese government would, if necessary, certainly exert administrative pressure to induce industry's cooperation. As the role of state-owned enterprises expands in Brazil's industrialization program, more and more negotiations are carried out at the government level than at the industry level. Japanese industry is certainly more accustomed to this type of approach than U.S. industry, for example.

Third, there is a fairly high degree of complementarity between the immediate needs of the Brazilian economy and the current pattern of Japanese investments. In addition to the willingness of Japanese industry to accept minority ownership (hence, its political palatability to the host government), Japanese investments in resource-developing ventures are sure to contribute immediately and significantly to an improvement in the host country's balance of payments, because Japanese industry itself (or the Japanese partners themselves in most cases) is the major buyer of the developed resources under a long-term contract. In addition, many Japanese manufacturing investments are relatively labor-using and "intermediate" in the level of technology, because they are clustered around textiles and light machinery. Thus, the economic characteristics of many Japanese investments appear, on the whole, more "appropriate" for the host economy than do those of Western investments. For the latter are heavily concentrated in highly differentiated oligopolistic industries or what may be called "high-technology" or "R & D-based" industries such as chemicals, pharmaceuticals, transport machinery, and scientific equipment —capital-intensive industries in which the investing companies tend to show a strong desire to control firmly the ownership and operations of their local investments.

These Western ventures in Brazil are also inevitably dependent to a much greater extent on the importation of parts and components and other intermediate material from their parent corporations simply because local supplies are nonexistent or because the investing companies' operations are often globally integrated and so they are not interested in producing intermediate inputs locally in each host country. Thus, when forced by the host government to substitute local production for imports, Japanese manufacturing ventures are largely in a better position to do so than Western ones. Besides, Japanese ventures, even though they are competitors to each other in the same local market, seem to have a greater propensity to cooperate in jointly establishing and patronizing a local supplier to avoid the diseconomies of small-scale operations. Because Japan is striving to upgrade her industrial structure, the labor-intensive and low-technology type of industries dominated by small- and medium-sized enterprises will continue to be transferred from Japan to Brazil.

Middle East

Because Japan is dependent on the Middle East for about 85 percent of her imported oil supply, her stake in that region is extraordinary. Japan's direct foreign investment, initially concentrated in oil extraction but now extended to manufacturing and service ventures, has increased swiftly of late as the oil-producing countries strive to acheive "instant industrialization" with the help of foreign capital and technology. At the end of March 1975, Japan's government-approved investments in the Middle East amounted to $780 million (ninety-six ventures) an equivalent of 6.16 percent in terms of the value (or 0.84 percent in terms of the number of ventures) of her global investments. One-half of the total value is absorbed in oil extraction; and manufacturing ventures, although as numerous as thirty-six ventures, account for only about 14 percent of the total value. So far as equity capital investment is concerned, Iran is the largest host country for Japanese investments ($6.42 million and 48 ventures).[23]

One important feature of Japanese business activities in the region is that although private investments in the form of equity capital are relatively insignificant, both Japan's government and industry are most active in extending long-term loans for a variety of investment projects planned by local governments, an activity begun as a reaction to the 1973 oil crisis and pursued ever since. Although Japan was greatly dependent on oil from Saudi Arabia, Kuwait, Abu Dhabi, and other Arab countries, she had scarcely had, prior to the oil crisis, any significant economic relations with the Arab countries in fields other than oil, which was, after all, imported mainly through the major international oil companies. In a very short span of time, however, Japan made an astonishingly swift and successful advance into the market in the Middle East, taking advantage of the rapidly changing political and economic climates of the region. In what follows, we examine how Japan, initially badly shaken by the oil embargo, has become a major participant in investment projects in the Middle East.

Oil Diplomacy: From Initial Panic to Opportunism

When the Arab oil embargo was announced in October 1973, the Japanese reacted emotionally to the prospect of a sudden halt of their industry. During the next month, the Economic Planning Agency made some gloomy predictions; it said, for example, that if the 10 percent cutback of oil shipments continued until September 1974, the real growth rate of GNP for fiscal 1974 would be a mere 1.7 percent. Further, the real growth rate would become negative by as much as 5.5 percent in the event the oil cutback continued throughout 1974.[24] Abruptly, the outlook for the Japanese economy became clouded; it was possible that the worst recession in Japan's postwar history might occur. Expected reductions in industrial output and higher fuel costs also would mean aggravation of supply shortages and inflation, which had already reached serious levels. Many Japanese consumers turned to the hoarding of daily necessities such as sugar, soap, light bulbs, and toilet paper, creating hysterical scenes at supermarkets. A local bank had a run on deposits because of a groundless rumor. The panic-prone mentality of the Japanese clearly reflected their deep-seated feeling of insecurity and the fragility of their confidence in their resource-scarce economy.

However, as in similar situations in the past, the emotional frustration and anxiety of the Japanese was soon replaced by realistic and aggressive actions in self-defense. Business leaders, in particular, quickly saw the need to take a pro-Arab stance and to seek openly an assured supply of oil. They urged the government to send a special envoy to the Middle East. Japan had therefore maintained a politically neutral policy on the Arab-Israeli conflict.

Even before the outbreak of the October War the tentacles of Japanese industry were reaching purposefully toward the oil-producing nations in the Middle East. The Japan-Iran Investment Council, designed to assist Iran's economic development, had already been formed, and a plan had also been under way to set up a similar organization for Saudi Arabia. But the oil embargo provided a decisive impetus to these movements. The Japan-Saudi Arabia Cooperative Association formally came into existence in October 1973, with Ataru Kobayashi, chairman of Arabian Oil, as its head. The formation of similar organizations to extend economic cooperation on a bilateral basis with each of the oil-producing countries in the Middle East rapidly came under consideration.

In November 1973, the MITI announced a policy to increase gradually Japan's import of crude oil directly from oil-producing nations. Japan had been purchasing the bulk of her oil through major international oil companies. In 1972, for example, a mere 2 percent of the total crude oil imported was obtained directly from oil-producing countries. The MITI's new policy was aimed at raising the ratio to a level of 40 percent by the end of this decade.[25]

As a first step toward achieving this goal the MITI worked out a plan to expand the role of the Japan Petroleum Development Corporation (JPDC), a government-created institution whose function, under the original setup, was confined to a supportive role in assisting industry to explore oil and natural gas resources abroad. This institution extended or guaranteed exploration loans, leased drilling equipment, offered technical assistance, and served as an information center. The MITI moved to revise the existing laws to assign much more active capacities to the JPDC, enabling it to acquire concessions directly, to participate in investments in oil-producing countries, and to stockpile crude oil.[26]

Understandably, Japan's rush for direct bilateral agreements disturbed not only the major Western international oil companies but also their governments, particularly the government of the United States, which advocated a solid front for the oil-consuming industrial countries against the price-hike demands of the oil-producing countries. Their startled reaction was clearly reflected in Western reporters' descriptions of Japan's move as "a blatant surrender" or "an unabashed effort." Yet Japan, reassured in part by the recalcitrant attitude displayed by France toward U.S. leadership, pushed her oil diplomacy vigorously during the oil cutbacks.

The Tanaka Administration, then in power, dispatched special envoys, one after another, to the Middle East. First, Vice Prime Minister Takeo Miki visited eight Arab nations, including Saudi Arabia, Kuwait, and Egypt, in December 1973. A month later, his visit was followed in quick succession by those of Minister of International Trade and Industry Yasuhiro Nakasone, former Foreign Minister Zentaro Kosaka, and Speaker of the House of Representatives Shigesaburo Maeo. Their missions were not defined exactly; they were sent for the purpose of "explaining Japan's position on the Mideast." Their real intent was, no doubt, to curry the favor of the oil-producing nations for an assurance of oil supplies. In exchange, Japan offered generous financial and technical assistance for the economic development of the region. In fact, the administration was extremely eager to seek favor—so eager that the amount of aid and loans offered by these envoys added up to about $3 billion (including $1 billion each to Iran and Iraq, and $280 million to Egypt), an amount five times as large as the total amount of official Japanese aid (approximately $600 million) appropriated in 1972.[27] Indeed, this phase of diplomacy momentarily left both the Ministry of Finance and the Ministry of Foreign Affairs worried about the consequences.

Japan's diplomatic efforts proved quite effective. Her willingness to extend economic cooperation was soon matched by the eagerness of the countries in the Middle East to request Japan's cooperation in industrialization, and the visits made by Japan's government officials were promptly reciprocated by officials of the Arab world—partly as a calculated gesture to show the West that there were alternative sources of the technical expertise needed by the Arabs for industrialization, but mostly in an earnest search for industrial and technical assistance.

During the visit of the MITI's chief, Iraq promised to provide Japan with 160 million tons of crude oil, liquefied petroleum gas, and petroleum products over the next ten years in return for Japan's economic and technical cooperation, including a $1 billion loan at 5.25 percent per annum.

In January 1974, the oil cutbacks to Japan were removed and Japan was placed on the Arabs' list of "friendly nations." The Japanese were further gratified to learn that the Arabs had, after all, not curtailed oil shipments to Japan as much as originally planned and that Japan's oil reserves had not dwindled as much as feared.

Then in February 1974 Saudi Arabian Oil Minister Sheik Ahmed Zaki Yamani visited Japan; he reached an agreement with Japan on economic and technological cooperation with Saudi Arabia. He reportedly stated that "Japan is in the No. 1 position both to help us and to be the recipient of Saudi Arabian oil on a long term basis."[28] In the same month, Japan also received from Algeria a mission headed by Industry and Energy Minister to Abdussalam Belaid. The Algerians solicited Japan's cooperation for their second four-year industrialization program. This visit resulted in numerous business relations between the two countries. Egypt also secured Japan's commitment to a loan for repair work on the Suez Canal and other projects when Egyptian Vice Prime Minister Muhammed Hatem visited Tokyo.

Trading Companies as Vanguards

The government's favor-seeking diplomacy under the pressure of the oil crisis has been successful and has paved the way for industry to advance. Japan's omnipresent general trading companies are the spearheads. Practically all of Japan's industrial projects in the Middle East are either intermediated by, or participated in by, trading companies. Long before the sudden recent emergence of the Middle East as the world's economic focal point, Japanese traders were laying out their marketing networks and cultivating local businesses. In fact, they had been the only resident Japanese in the desert kingdoms and sheikdoms.[29]

Japan's new advance in Algeria was made in response to the latter's call for assistance in economic development and was led by Japan's trading companies. To carry out various projects for Algeria's second four-year economic plan, five major trading companies (Mitsubishi, Mitsui, Marubeni, C. Itoh, and Sumitomo) signed an agreement with SONATRAC, Algeria's state-owned oil-gas corporation. Twenty other giant Japanese corporations are expected to participate in the assistance program.[30] It was the first time that an assistance program for economic development, normally concluded as an intergovernmental agreement, had been entrusted to a group of trading companies. This unprecedented arrangement marked a new approach to developing countries by Japanese business. Japan's major trading companies perhaps have a unique organizational capacity to provide concerted and comprehensive industrial and technical assistance in a package to developing countries, because each can draw upon its own *keiretsu* group for necessary resources.

In April 1974, SONATRAC also signed a contract with Toyo Engineering and C. Itoh to establish, on a turnkey basis, a huge plant maintenance and repair complex for Algeria's pipeline making, oil refining, petro-chemical, liquefying of natural gas, and mining industries. The Japanese group is expected to "set up a staff of 3,000 technicians at the center for taking over all of the maintenance work hitherto handled by European and U.S. firms and also to train machinery processing and repairing experts."[31]

The ability of Japanese trading companies to organize overseas production is not limited to their closely affiliated compatriot firms alone, however. They are becoming increasingly active in pulling together industrial firms of major countries in a truly multinational setup. The overseas activities of C. Itoh & Co., which in 1974 organized an iron mill venture in Egypt, are clear evidence of this trend. The $200 million mill, to be constructed near Alexandria, is a joint venture among the Egyptian government (50 percent ownership), C. Itoh, Korf-Stahl of West Germany, and Compahia Vale do Rio Doce of

Brazil. Korf-Stahl supplies technology to directly reduce iron ore to sponge iron; the Brazilian partner provides iron ore; and Egypt provides natural gas to fuel the plant.[32]

Thus Japan's trading companies have emerged as organizers eager to arrange projects on a multinational basis whenever such opportunities exist. With an expanded role to play, these companies are making all-out efforts to strengthen their operations in the Middle East by reorganizing their corporate structures, by placing able staffs in the region, and even by enrolling some of their employees at Arab universities to produce regional experts.

Later the Japanese government also stepped up its economic cooperation program to the region, particularly Iraq and Algeria, with an eye to securing oil from as many different sources as possible. In April 1967, the government extended an additional loan of $1 billion requested by Iraq for the construction of seven key projects related to oil refining, petro-chemicals, LPG, fertilizer, aluminum smelting, cement, and a hydropower station. The new loan, as well as the original $1 billion loan, would be used whenever Japanese industry won an international bid to supply industrial plants, a feature clearly designed to promote plant exports. In the same month, Japan's Export-Import Bank decided to provide Algeria with a "buyer's credit" worth approximately 100 billion yen (about $330 million), the largest such credit ever extended by the bank, to finance the export of a gas cycling plant by Japan Gasoline and C. Itoh.[33]

The net result of all these Japanese efforts was the emergence of Japanese industry as a leading participant in the economic development programs of the Middle East. Major projects secured or being negotiated by Japanese industry at the end of June 1974 are shown in table 4.6. These contracts marked a strategically important beginning by providing footholds for the further advance of Japanese industry as well as for the promotion of plant exports. American and Japanese predominance in the region can be explained. Lawrence G. Franko observes:

Table 4.6 Major Japanese Projects in Middle East at the End of June 1974

Country	A. Under Construction		B. Under Negotiation	
	Project	Contractor	Project	Bidder
Abu Dhabi	LNG station	Chiyoda Chemical & Engineering		
	LNG tank	Ishikawajima-Harima		
	Cement plant	Ishikawajima-Harima		
Algeria	2 cement plants	Kawasaki H. I.	Oil refinery	Chiyoda Chemical & Engineering Japan Gasoline Toyo Engineering
	Ethylene plant	Toyo Engineering		
	Repair center	Nippon Steel Toyo Engineering		
	Telecommunications networks	Fujitsu		
	Consulting for economic development planning	The Long-Term Credit Bank of Japan		
Iran	Cement plant	Kawasaki H. I.	Cement	Kawasaki H. I.
	Cement plant	Ishikawajima-Harima		
	Vinyl chloride plasticizer plant	Mitsubishi H. I.	Textiles	Mitsubishi Corp.
	Galvanized steel sheet plant	Kawasaki Steel		
	Plant manufacturing & engineering firm	Chiyoda Chemical & Engineering		

Country	Project	Firm	Project	Firm
Iraq	Fertilizer plant	Mitsubishi H. I.	2 fertilizer plants, LPG plant, Oil refinery	Mitsubishi H. I., Mitsubishi H. I., Sumitomo Shoji, Ishikawajima-Harima, Tokyo Shibaura, Nissho-Iwai
Kuwait	Seawater desalination	Ishikawajima-Harima	Power generation, Prawn fishing & processing, Seawater desalination	Hitachi, Sasakura Engineering
Libya			Lubricator plant, Truck plant	Chiyoda Chemical & Engineering, Nissan Motor
Ras Al Khaimah	Cement plant	Ishikawajima-Harima		
Saudi Arabia	2 oil refineries, 2 cement plants, Steelworks, Steel pipe plant, Agricultural development planning	Chiyoda Chemical & Engineering, Ishikawajima-Harima, Nippon Steel, Nippon Kokan (in joint venture with U.S. and European steel firms), Sumitomo Metal Industries, Sumitomo Shoji, Pacific Consultants		
Sudan				
Syria			Fertilizer Plant, Oil refinery	Toyo Engineering, a group of Japanese firms
Qatar	Steelworks	Kobe Steel		

Source: Compiled from reports published in *Nihon Keizai Shimbun*, as presented in Ozawa, "Japan's Mid-East Economic Diplomacy," p. 44.

American and Japanese MNEs appear to be disproportion-
ately involved in Middle-East industrialization plans. It has
recently become clear that in 1974, the United States and
Japan both had the highest total volume of exports to OPEC
countries and the highest growth rate in exports to OPEC
(after Canada). The U.S. and Japanese exports in 1974 to
OPEC countries totalled perhaps 45 percent of all OECD
exports to OPEC. American and Japanese predominance in
production facilities with foreign ownership in the Middle
Eastern Oil-Producing Countries appears to be considerably
greater, according to the preliminary data. . . .

Precisely why American and Japanese companies should be
pioneering in the Middle East is not intuitively obvious. Japan
as a country is anxious to assure supplies of oil and to continue
to supply its established export markets for intermediate and
finished goods: "oil for industrialization" is one clear bargaining outcome. But why more so for Japan than European countries? The long American political involvement in the Middle
East and the lengthy experience of U.S. oil companies in the
region could help explain U.S. involvement. . . .

An alternative explanation perhaps lies in the possibility that
American and Japanese production processes are more capital
intensive (or at least less management and technical-skill intensive) than European processes—at least in mature products.
Some executives assert that in some industries a similar difference now exists between Japanese and European processes.
The fact that sales-to-employee ratios of many Japanese enterprises substantially exceed those of comparable European (and
even American) firms is consistent with the hypothesis that
Japanese processes are capital intensive. (Such contrasting
ratios could, of course, be the result of factors ranging from
employee motivation to quirks in exchange rates.)

Another possible cause of the American and Japanese predominance may have to do with plant and enterprise scale:
until the oil-price increase, developing countries sought projects and plants from MNEs. Today, the oil exporters are seeking instant economies. The most likely suppliers of instant

economies may be enterprises used to operating on the scale
of the continental United States.[34]

The suggested high-capital-intensity of Japanese enterprises,
if true, is an advantage in the sales of Japanese plants in those
oil-producing countries that are lacking in industrial skills but
abundant in capital. Such capital intensity is no doubt related
to the scale of operations. Japanese industry has attained "the
scale of the continental United States" by virtue of its domestic
economic growth as well as by its emphasis on export expansion. But its ability to supply "instant economies" has to do not
so much with the scale of individual enterprises as with a high
degree of interenterprise cooperation coordinated by industrial
groups, by their powerful trading companies, and by the diplomacy of the Japanese government.

Debacle in "Show-Case" Projects

Japan's oil diplomacy and industrial advance in the Middle
East has not been without snags. Its vigor was somewhat weakened in March 1974, when the Iranian government turned
down Japan's offer to help construct an oil refinery and petro-
chemical complex with financial assistance of $1 billion, and
talks between the two countries on the project were suspended.
Iran's rejection was due perhaps to a combination of economic
and political reasons. Iran, in addition to shipping the products
from the refinery to Japan, wanted some part of the naphtha
output to be used as feedstock for "downstream" petro-chemical
projects. Such an expanded plan would cost Japan another
$1 billion, for which the Japanese government was reluctant to
make a commitment. Iran also appeared to be annoyed by
Japan's rapprochement with Iraq with which she had border
skirmishes. Toyota's proposal to build an automobile assembly
plant also hit a snag. The company had planned to produce
50,000 vehicles a year, while the host country demanded a plant
with the capacity of 500,000 vehicles.[35]

Japan's debacle in the Iranian petroleum project, which had been intended to be a show-case of economic cooperation on a bilateral basis, provided Japan with an opportunity to review her precipitate diplomacy in the Middle East, formulated under the pressure of the oil crisis. Indeed, Japan's impetuous rush for bilateral deals was severely assailed by the United States. With oil in abundant supply again, Japan recovered from her initial fluster and began to mend her relations with Western countries. In April 1974, the Japanese government formally announced its intention to move from the bilateral approach to a multilateral policy, with an emphasis on cooperation with other industrial countries, particularly the United States. The announcement of this policy change proved timely—or perhaps was so designed, because the Arab world, having initially directed its oil weapon against the United States, quickly reversed itself to become pro-American when a temporary agreement with Israel was mediated by the United States. Former President Nixon's triumphant visit to the Middle East climaxed this dramatic shift in the political atmosphere of the region.

By then, most of the industrial projects in the oil-producing countries (hastily proposed right after the oil crisis) had reached the stage where feasibility studies and other preparatory works had been completed and actual implementation was to be decided upon. With oil flowing again in abundance in the Middle East (although at much higher prices than before) and with the world market for most petro-chemical products glutted as before, the enthusiasm of the Japanese government and industry toward the Middle East had cooled considerably. The severe economic recession at home dampened it further. In the meantime, moreover, the costs of plant construction had skyrocketed, so that original estimates were vastly exceeded. As a result, many of Japan's promises of multi-million-dollar projects did not materialize. Understandably, Japan was criticized by the OPEC countries for "lack of cooperation between the Japanese Government and private industry in implementing projects" at the Tokyo meeting of the World Petroleum Congress held in the summer of 1975.[36]

Perhaps the most significant "delay" in Japanese investment projects was the Mitsubishi group's decision to suspend for three years its plan to construct in Saudi Arabia a petro-chemical plant with an annual productive capacity of 300,000 tons of various kinds of ethylene derivatives, a project considered to be a key element in Japan's extension of economic cooperation to Saudi Arabia. The most important reason for postponement is said to be the poor prospects for marketing ethylene, because the supply of this product in the Japanese market alone would exceed the demand by approximately 1 million tons.[37]

Yet with an economic recovery in sight, and more importantly, because of a fear of losing the Saudi Arabian market to other industrial countries the Japanese government finally made a commitment in 1977 to support the project with funds from the OECF and the Export-Import Bank of Japan—again, a financial arrangement of the Asahan formula. The Japanese government is expected soon to revive the suspended petro-chemical project in Iran by extending the required loan.

Other Regions

In major host countries in which Japan's overseas investments have expanded rapidly, Japanese industry (often with the Japanese government as a promoter and a close partner) has exhibited a variety of the unique patterns of behavior which were designed to accommodate both its own economic needs and those of the host countries. The four major regions (Asia, North America, Latin America, and the Middle East) surveyed above account for approximately three-fourths of the total value of Japan's overseas investment. Europe, Oceania, and Africa are the regions constituting the balance of Japanese overseas investment.

Europe

Surprisingly, despite a heavy concentration of the world's industrial and commercial activities, its relatively high degree of openness to factor movement (albeit only within the European Economic Community, Common Market), and the existence of common tariffs against nonmember countries that induced U.S. firms to set up a large number of "tariff factories," Europe has not attracted as much Japanese investment as might have been expected. In 1974, for example, only about 10 percent of the accumulated total of Japan's overseas investment was in Western Europe in contrast to approximately 38 percent of the United States and 60 percent of West Germany.[38] Moreover, most Japanese investments were in the service sectors (commerce, finance, insurance, and branch offices) and those in manufacturing accounted for only 9.8 percent in 1974.[39]

Although classified by the Japanese government as "investments in manufacturing," many of these investments in Europe are merely "ventures set up by manufacturers" that take the form of sales companies rather than manufacturing plants. These enterprises are established primarily as a means of promoting Japanese exports and secondarily as a toehold to develop marketing channels if and when the Japanese later initiate local production. The main motivation of Japanese investments in Europe is, at the moment, clearly to secure a beachhead in the growing markets of industrialized European economies. Japan is not dependent on Europe for natural resources, as she is on North America or on Australia. Hence, practically all Japanese investments in the European community are designed either to promote exports or to reinforce trade competitiveness with partial local manufacturing if necessary. In other words, Japanese industry can still compete successfully in Europe through exports. In this respect, most of Japan's manufacturing investments there are still in the initial stages of transition from export dependence to direct local production.[40]

In fact, the recent fears expressed by Europeans about the imminent onslaught of Japanese investments was based on Japan's trade competitiveness rather than on Japan's competitiveness in local manufacturing. Thus, as far as manufacturing is concerned, Japanese investments have not made any significant inroads in the European market. According to Gene Gregory:

> In 1972, when the hysteria in Europe about an imminent Japanese invasion was at its height, I mustered all the courage I could find and went out to meet the invading forces. After several months of exhaustive search, I managed to find 45 Japanese direct investments in manufacturing operations in Europe, with a total cumulative investment of less than $20 million. . . . With very few exceptions—notably Honda, Brother and Sanyo—Japanese investments were spread over an array of industries in which Japan had almost no market position in Europe to speak of, rather than in sectors which were widely claimed to be sorely pressed by Japanese competition.
>
> While with a little imagination Nisshin's investment in Spain might be considered as a challenge to European steel makers, and Mitsui's stake in acrylic fiber weaving and dyeing in Portugal could conceivably seem like a sneaky flanking action directed against Europe's beleaguered textile industry, it would be pretty difficult to stir up much excitement about forays into production of agar-agar (for the Japanese market), monosodium glutamate, processed cheese or dry-cell batteries. As a matter of fact, the only investment activity that vaguely approached a well-planned European strategy by a Japanese manufacturer was that of Yoshida Kogyo, better known as YKK, which, by dint of better production techniques and overall management was in the process of carving a solid niche for itself in Europe with five separate production facilities.
>
> Things have changed in the past two years, it is true. But at the end of March (1974), total approved direct investments in manufacturing in Western Europe were still only $64 million.[41]

Yet the current spurt of Japanese manufacturing investments in Europe is essentially involuntary in the sense that Japanese manufacturers already have captured a sizable share of the local market and the only way to retain the market is through direct investments. In their transitional attempt to move toward local production, however, Japanese industry has encountered many difficulties. The usual approach of setting up "knock-down" assembly plants met strong opposition by local competitors in many instances. For example, Honda's production plant in Rome, Italy, was foiled because of strong oppositon of the local interests, who argued that components (particularly engines) would be imported from Japan "at dumping prices," enabling Honda to produce motorcycles at low prices. Yoshida Kogyo's fastener production in Britain was criticized as "an export dumping in disguise."[42]

Only those technology-based Japanese manufacturers seem to be able to make smooth entry by setting up a joint venture with equally technology-based local interests in the early stages of the life-cycle of new products. This new trend is exemplified by the recent move of Japan's leading optical manufacturer, Canon, to form a joint venture with ECE, Gmbh of Giessen, West Germany, to manufacture plain paper copiers.[43] There is obviously less friction when Japanese manufacturers move into new product markets than when they invest in conventional products as a replacement of export activities that have already weakened the local market. In this new approach Japanese manufacturers are also benefiting from technological resources in Europe.

Oceania

Australia takes a majority (about 70 percent) of Japan's investment in the region. Roughly half of Japan's direct investments in Australia are concentrated in mining, timber and pulp, agriculture, and fishery, and many of Japan's manufacturing ventures are similarly resource-related (such as food processing and nonferrous metals). Another unique feature is a relatively large proportion of loans (debt capital acquisition) in Japan's total investments in Australia. At the end of March 1975, for example, loans accounted for 53.3 percent, far exceeding the 30 percent average for Japan's entire investment throughout the world.[44] These loans are extended in connection with Japan's D & I ventures in mineral resources, notably iron ore.

Japan's investment in Australia is basically motivated by the essential differences in factor endowments between the two countries. Japan is the biggest importer of Australian products, mostly mineral resources and farm products, and the second largest exporter of manufactured products to Australia. Japan's extractive investments are designed to secure stable supplies of natural resources, and thus can be characterized as "import-augmenting." On the other hand, Japan's manufacturing investments (particularly in automobiles and color televisions, the two major export items from Japan) have been made, rather as a second-best policy, in response to the import-substituting policy of Australia. In this sense, they are "export-substituting." In 1975 this asymmetrical impact of Japanese investments on her exports and imports resulted in a relatively large trade deficit of $2.4 billion for Japan.

Economic relations between the two countries have become closer in recent years as a result of their growing complementarity in commercial needs. In June 1976 the two countries signed the Basic Treaty of Friendship and Cooperation, an act signifying an acknowledgment by both parties of their deepening structural interdependence and their desire to enhance mutual understanding.[45]

Japan's investments in New Zealand are mainly in manufacturing (such as automobile assembly, oil refining, and aluminum refining) and commerce. Japanese participation in Comalco of Australia, which imports alumina from Australia to be processed with the relatively low-cost electricity of New Zealand, is at the moment, the major on-going investment.

4. Direct Investment

Africa

Africa has so far attracted only about 2.5 percent of Japan's overseas investment. Japanese investments are mostly (about 63 percent) in mining. Although manufacturing investments account for 16.5 percent of the total, one-third of them are in textile ventures designed to cater to the local markets. Japan's investments in Africa are concentrated in resource-rich, relatively underpopulated countries such as Nigeria and Zaire or in countries developing with relative rapidity such as Kenya and Tanzania—countries that can be used as production bases to serve neighboring African countries in light manufactures (mostly daily necessities such as apparel, radios, fishing nets, batteries, and matches).[46] Japan, however, is expected to increase her investment in the region as African nations develop more concrete industrialization programs. At present, Africa, on the whole, remains "marginal" to Japan's global investments, chiefly due to the barriers of vast geographical and cultural distances.

Chapter 5

Japan's Resource Dependency
and Overseas Investment

JAPAN'S demand for industrial resources has grown enormously in recent years. Among the non-Communist countries Japan now ranks second behind the United States in the consumption of such basic industrial resources as petroleum, copper, zinc, aluminum, nickel, and crude steel. Indeed, Japan's growth rate of consumption of industrial resources has been the highest in the world. From 1964 to 1968, for example, her demand for petroleum expanded at an average annual rate of 17.6 percent, more than twice the growth rate of the non-Communist countries taken as a whole; her demand for copper increased at an average rate of 11.7 percent, more than seven times that of non-Communist countries as a whole; for zinc, her demand increased at 8.0 percent, about four times the rate of the non-Communist countries; for aluminum, 21.0 percent; for nickel, 25.2 percent; and for crude steel, 20.0 percent—each far exceeding the average rate of the non-Communist countries. Interestingly enough, most of these growth rates were much greater than that of Japan's GNP (10.6 percent per annum from 1964 to 1968); this circumstance reflects a rapid shift of orientation in Japan's industrial structure from light manufacturing to heavy and chemical industries, sectors that are both more resource-intensive and more energy-consuming.[1] This chapter analyzes the problems of Japan's dependence on overseas resources, notes the direction of her recent policy on natural resources, and discusses the new characteristics of her overseas investment in extractive activities.

Increased Dependency on Overseas Resources

Because Japan is poorly endowed with natural resources, she has inevitably grown more dependent on foreign sources, and has become the world's largest importer of many vital resources. For example, her share of trade in coking coal among the OECD member countries had climbed from 15.8 percent in 1964 to 41.6 percent in 1969; in iron ore from 23.7 to 39.3 percent; in timber from 15.4 percent to 29.9 percent; in copper from 9.5 percent to 19.1 percent; and in crude oil from 12.6 percent to 15.6 percent.[2]

A similarly high degree of import dependence has developed in food and forest resources. Until the early 1960s, for example, Japan was relatively self-supportive with respect to food. Her self-sufficiency in principal food grains was as high as 83 percent in 1960, but fell to 43 percent by 1972. If rice—Japan's main food staple and her only surplus grain—is excluded, the decline in self-sufficiency appears to be more pronounced. In 1974 Japan imported about 95 percent of all the wheat she consumed, 96 percent of her soybeans, and 82 percent of her barley.[3] The major supplier, the United States in 1976 provided 92 percent of Japan's import requirements of soybeans, 74 percent of corn, and 56 percent of wheat.[4]

Japan is the world's largest consumer of fish in total as well as in per capita volume of consumption. Yet as a result of industrial pollution and depletion of some fish stocks and marine plants, the yield from coastal fishing, which accounted for about 20 percent of Japan's total catch in 1970, has been steadily on the decline in recent years (by 1.4 percent in 1972 and 2.7 percent in 1973), and this trend is expected to continue.[5] Thus Japan, in the face of an ever-expanding demand, must increasingly depend for her fish supply on catches from offshore and distant ocean fishing as well as on imports. According to a report of FAO (United Nations Food and Agricultural Organization), Japan became the world's leading fishing nation in 1972, accounting for 15.5 percent of the world's total catch.[6] Because Japan's catch is said to have reached a possible maximum in terms of available fishing grounds, the value of imports has expanded at a rapid rate; they increased 53.7 percent in 1973, 10.8 percent in 1974, and 19.4 percent in 1975, although price increases are partly responsible for this trend of acceleration.[7] In 1971 for the first time in her history, Japan, a traditional exporter of marine products, became a net importer with imports soaring to a figure some twenty times the volume of a decade earlier and nearly tripling that of the previous three years.[8] As might be expected, Japan is particularly concerned about the outcome of the U.N. conferences on the Law of the Sea. At the 1974 Caracas meeting Japan was jolted by the consensus that emerged on the extension of territorial waters from the conventional three-mile limit to twelve miles and the establishment of the so-called coastal economic zone of 200 miles.

Japan's self-sufficiency in lumber has declined from about 71 percent in 1965 to 36 percent in 1973, the result again translated into an increase in imports. Lumber has recently ranked second in Japan's total value of imports next to petroleum.[9]

In the wake of feared global shortages of basic raw materials and foodstuffs together with economic nationalism in resource-abundant developing countries, Japan's procurement of overseas resources has been beset suddenly with a host of difficulties. Environmental concern, especially in resource-rich advanced countries such as the United States and Canada, has compounded the problem. Friction is growing in Japan's economic and diplomatic relations both with the resource-exporting countries and with other resource-importing countries. Japan can no longer let her demand for overseas natural resources grow as fast as she has in the recent past. Nor will she be able to secure them in as relatively easy and economical a manner as she has in the past.

International Friction in Resource Acquisition

Now that the Japanese economy has grown so dependent on overseas resources, it is highly vulnerable to any adverse changes in conditions of supply. The U.S. export embargo on soybeans in the summer of 1973 and the Arab cutbacks in oil exports in the fall of the same year gave ample warning to Japan's policymakers. One can easily understand Japan's concern about these supply cutoffs. Japan was then relying on the United States for about 85 percent of her soybean imports and on the Middle East for about 85 percent of her oil imports (in 1972 as much as 76.3 percent of Japan's energy requirements were met by oil, and almost the entire amount of it, 99.7 percent, came from sources abroad).[10]

Japan's dependency on overseas supplies for bauxite, nickel ore, and uranium reaches almost 100 percent; about 90 percent for iron ore; 83 percent for copper; 73 percent for natural gas; and 50 percent for lead and zinc.[11] Not only the possibility that the supply of these resources might be abruptly cut off but also their rising prices pose serious threats to Japanese industry. The emergence of cartels for natural resources, other than the OPEC, such as the Intergovernmental Council of Copper Exporting Countries (CIPEC) and the International Bauxite Association (IBA), is another concern.

Conversely, Japan's increased reliance on overseas supplies has resulted in an equal or even greater dependence upon the Japanese market by some of the major resource-exporting countries, making economic vulnerability a two-way problem of interdependence. In 1971, for example, all of Malaysia's export of bauxite and 96.3 percent of that of Indonesia went to Japan. In the same year, Australia sent 84.6 percent of her iron ore exports to Japan and India 96.3 percent. Canada sold 93.5 percent of her exports of copper ore to Japan, the Philippines 92.7 percent.[12] Thus Japan has become the single major export market for many resource-exporting countries. As a consequence, the national incomes of these exporting countries are often subject, through the familiar trade mechanism, to economic fluctuations generated in Japan. Australia and Canada are acutely concerned about this rising danger of economic dependence upon Japan. The former prime minister of Australia, E. G. Whitlam stated: "Australia shares with Japan a very deep interest in ensuring that the great industrialized nations of the world have secure and steady access to the resources their economies need. We also believe that the resource-producing and exporting nations like Australia are entitled to have secure and steady markets for their exports at fair and reasonable prices."[13] Reportedly the Australian government's standing Interdepartmental Committee on Japan submitted an advisory report urging an ultracautious approach to the deepening of the nation's economic ties with Japan.[14]

In fact, Japan has succeeded in tipping the scale of two-way interdependence much in her favor in the acquisition of several key mineral resources. In a study on the bargaining power between Japan as a buyer of natural resources and primary-exporting countries, Kiyoshi Kojima points out:

If the share of the supplies exported to Japan from a certain supplying country in Japan's total imports . . . amounts to more than 50 percent, it means that the supplying country is the dominant supplier so that it can manifest the bargaining power of "monopoly." However, this rarely occurs in Japan's case, for over three-quarters of Japanese total imports, in most cases, are supplied by three different countries. In other words, these three countries together are the major suppliers. The reason for this is that Japan has been considering the diversification of the suppliers of natural resources as the key to the policy for resource security. It is not, however, a mere diversification having numerous suppliers, but the suppliers have been limited to three or four in order to realise the extensive-scale of development and the economies of scale of bulk transaction. . . .[15]

Closely associated with this export dependence on Japan is the asymmetrical pattern of trade between these major resource-exporting countries and Japan; the former export primary goods to Japan and import manufactured goods from her. This trade pattern is politically irritating, particularly for the major resource-exporting countries such as the United States, Canada, and Australia. They realize that developing countries must export primary goods and import manufactures from Japan by necessity, while industrially advanced Western nations should feel no real need to depend on Japan for manufactured products. More important, some of the resource-exporting countries saw their own independence formalized by cutting off this type of trade dependence with their mother countries, and feel uncomfortable watching their trade relations with Japan evolve into the old colonial pattern. This feeling is clearly expressed by Ivan L. Head, special assistant to Canadian Prime Minister Pierre E. Trudeau:

> It is not much of an exaggeration to say that Japanese governments have looked upon Canada in recent years as a large open-pit mine; as an endless and reliable source of raw materials to satisfy the Japanese industrial appetite. . . .
>
> As a Pacific neighbour, it is in Canada's interest that Japan continue as a dynamic and responsible political and economic actor on the world scene. Canada is willing as a result to contribute to that process. In order to do so, however, it will be necessary for Japan to recognize the quality and the competence of Canada in a variety of economic and non-economic fields; to do more than, as is now the case, regard Canada primarily as an object of its 'Resources Diplomacy.'[16]

However, the cost of dependence is certainly not symmetrical. If trade between one of these major resource-exporting countries and Japan is disrupted, Japan is likely to be the loser. She is much more in need of outside supplies of vital industrial resources than Western resource-exporting nations are in need of her imported manufactures. They can easily manufacture substitutes at home or go to alternative sources for their imports. But alternative sources of supply of natural resources are not easy to come by for Japan, a fact well demonstrated in Japan's recent attempt to diversify them. Manufactured imports from Japan often are regarded by Western countries as the price of enabling Japan to purchase their primary goods. In this respect, an observation made by K. Bieda is interesting:

> If we fear that Japan might suddenly cut imports from Australia in future we must realize that this would hurt Japan at least as much as it would hurt us. If Japan were to put very stiff terms on her exports, she would be hurting herself, because what she sells can be purchased elsewhere. Above all, Australia can always retaliate in such a situation.
>
> One way of making a trade blackmail by Japan less likely is to increase now the potential penalties in future by *increasing* now our imports from Japan. A partial diversion of our import trade to Japan would make Japan as much more dependent on us in the sense that if we decided to retaliate we would wield a much bigger stick. This puts the conventional argument on trade dependence upside down.[17]

This recommendation, however, would make the stick only marginally bigger, and Australia already has enough leverage to deter Japan from resorting to a trade war. Japan is critically dependent on Australia for resource supplies; Australia, in contrast, is far more self-sufficient. A Japanese threat to cut off imports of vital resources would be farcical, and even suicidal. Japan is probably more worried about Australia's resorting to a trade war than vice versa. Thus, given the remote possibility of a trade war, the strategy of increasing Japan's share of manufactured imports into Australia would work mostly in favor of Japan. Such a measure would improve Australia's retaliatory strength only marginally and might, by increased import competition from Japan, probably much fiercer than from anywhere else, retard the growth of Australia's domestic manufacturing sector. Thus, the "marginal" considerations seem far more important for Australia's infant manufacturing industry than for Japan's already vulnerable dependency on Australia's resources.

Another major area of conflict is Japan's scramble for resources in competition with the Western industrial powers. During the Arab oil embargo Japan's unilateral oil diplomacy annoyed the major Western international oil companies as well as their governments, particularly that of the United States, who wanted to present a united front against the Arab oil producers. The major international oil companies were disturbed by Japan's quick move to purchase oil directly from the governments of the oil-producing countries which had begun to nationalize their oil companies. For example, Japan was the willing purchaser of the first cargo of "participation oil" from the Oman government when it nationalized 25 percent of the Shell interest. Japan also made similar moves with Abu Dhabi, Kuwait, Saudi Arabia, and other oil-producing nations. (The oil Japan purchased from Abu Dhabi on a direct-deal basis in 1976 was reportedly cheaper more than 10 cents per barrel than the one imported through the oil majors.)[18]

Japan vexed the United States and the People's Republic of China by her interest in the resources of Siberia. In 1974, when Japan signed a protocol extending $1,050 million in tied loans for the joint development of natural gas at the Yakutsk and of other projects in Siberia at the interest rate of 6.375 percent per annum, the United States reportedly was annoyed, and criticized such loans as "an interest subsidy" on the export of industrial goods such as rails, rolling stock, and other industrial goods that Japan was expected to sell for the project.[19] The United States was unable to offer such favorable terms because of the 7 percent floor on U.S. Export-Import Bank loans.[20] China was irked by proposed Japanese participation in the development of transportation for Tyumen crude on the ground that any improved transportation between Irkutsk and Nakhodka—either highway or railway—would serve to increase the military potential of the Soviets against the Chinese.

Some basic differences have also appeared between Japan's position on the world's future food policy and that of the United States. Concerned over the security of food supplies, Japan is favorably disposed toward some global system of commodity agreements and multinational food reserve policies designed to smooth out the instability of free markets. On the other hand, the United States is skeptical about the formation of strict commodity agreements with specific reserves to stabilize prices as well as a contingency stock. The U.S. opposition to such a scheme is based on the fear that it might exert the same stagnating influence on commercial trade and production incentives as did the former stockpile program. Instead it proposes that adequate commercial stocks be maintained at each nation's own discretion.[21]

In addition to these sources of conflict between Japan's national interest and the interests of other countries over resources, Japan's image has deteriorated considerably in the international economic community. Japanese businessmen have earned such epithets overseas as "economic animals" as a result of their economic drive, hardworking by their own standard but considered aggressive by others. The plaque, "economic miracle," which Japan once proudly displayed, has suddenly lost its power to impress. As dramatized in the Club of Rome's *Limits to Growth*,[22] the process of precipitate economic expansion and its uncontrolled side-effects are seen as a short cut to the self-annihilation of the human race, and the gospel of growth that the world blindly followed after World War II is no longer sacrosanct and now connotes malignancy. Environmentalists, conservationists, and other soothsayers, see Japan as a villain because she is conspicuous for participating, both at home and overseas, in the accelerated destruction of the earth's natural sanctuary through her enormous appetite for resources.

The recent international furor about Japan's whaling activities, although emotionally exaggerated on both sides, reflects this feeling. A ten-year moratorium on whaling was sought at the U.N. Environmental Conference in Stockholm in 1972 and was again demanded by the United States at the International Whaling Commission Meeting in London in 1974. Various conservation groups in both the United States and Europe threatened campaigns to boycott Japanese goods and services and even dispatched delegates to Tokyo to appeal to the Japanese public. Although the U.S. call for a total ban in 1974 was shelved by a compromise to classify species into different categories and to allow whaling of only those species considered safe from extinction, Japan's whaling industry will come to an end. Both government and industry are preparing to phase out commercial whaling, which dates back to the early seventeenth century.[23]

Another environmental problem growing out of Japan's dependence on overseas resources is the risk associated with their transportation on the high seas, a problem illustrated recently by massive oil spills from Japanese tankers in Japan's Inland Sea and in the Malacca Strait. Also, Japan's first nuclear-powered merchant ship leaked radiation on her maiden voyage. These incidents are an ominous forecast of similar and possibly more frequent accidents, for which the Japanese economy will be held responsible by the environment-conscious world community.

Efforts to Reduce External Vulnerability

The Japanese government, seriously concerned by the danger of creating friction and animosity overseas, is taking various measures to thwart criticism. Among the most noteworthy is a basic change in policy adopted by the Miki administration. In his first policy speech to Japan's legislature, Prime Minister Takeo Miki referred to Japan's increased demand for overseas resources:

> I have no intention of viewing the current situation deliberately with pessimism, but I do believe that solutions would be

coming forth from a sense of crisis we all share when we look at the austere reality in the face.

If our Government and economy were allowed to follow their own courses as before, a terrible situation would confront Japan. I fear that the same would happen to the world itself.[24]

He thus indicated that Japan would no longer be able simply to continue drawing upon overseas resources if her economy continued to grow as fast as it had done in the past. Takeo Fukuda, then deputy prime minister and director of the Economic Planning Agency, elaborated upon this view and announced that the government would adopt a strategy based on slow economic growth. "As the world economy has entered a period in which there is a limit to acquiring resources, necessity has arisen to switch to a low economic growth."[25] Although the target of long-term rate of growth was yet to be determined, the new policy was definitely desirable, not only in tempering the rising demand for resources and in curbing domestic inflation but also in placing more emphasis on structural changes in Japanese industry.

In 1971, a far-reaching plan to reorganize Japan's industrial structure was officially announced by the MITI in its white paper on international trade, following recommendations made by its advisory council on industrial structure. It emphasized the need for a reorientation of the economy away from "pollution-prone" and "resource-consuming" sectors toward "clean" and "knowledge-intensive" ones. In 1973, the Arab oil embargo and subsequent increases in the price of oil gave further impetus to the national sense of urgency to reorganize the economy toward a less resource-dependent structure. In 1974 in an economic white paper, entitled "Beyond Growth Economy," the Economic Planning Agency boldly proclaimed that the economy was about to enter a new era of historically significant structural change.

According to a government study, the resource requirements

of Japan's industrial structure in 1970 were the world's highest, despite the fact that Japan is one of the world's most resource-poor countries. As shown in Figure 5.1, Japan, compared with the United States and West Germany, exhibited the highest concentration of industry in the sectors consuming the most resources and the lowest concentration in the sectors consuming the least resources. One may naturally wonder how and why Japan developed into this heavily resource-consuming pattern of industrialization, the major cause of Japan's present economic predicament from which she now struggles to extricate herself.

Myriad forces pushed the Japanese economy into this anomalous direction until very recently. First, the traditional belief that Japan, a small resource-poor island with a large population could not prosper without depending on trade to acquire foreign resources, has succesfully generated a strong drive to build export-oriented manufacturing industries at home and to secure raw materials and energy resources abroad in exchange for manufactures. The manufacturing industries themselves constantly evolved toward more resource-consuming heavy and chemical industries, following the expansion of world demand after the end of World War II. Japan's postwar economic policies strove to protect domestic industries to promote export- and import-competing industries, and to search for overseas resources.

Second, the Japanese industrial strategy, for the most part, was accommodated by fortuitous economic conditions prevailing outside Japan. With the help of the liberal postwar trade policies of Western countries, particularly that of the United States, and the increasingly undervalued status of the yen, Japan was able to capture quickly a substantial share of world trade. Japan was also able to acquire overseas resources in ever-growing amounts at relatively advantageous prices. For example, Japan became more dependent on oil and imported coal than on domestic coal, which had been a major source of energy

Figure 5.1: Mineral and Energy Resource-Consuming Structure of Manufacturing: Japan, West Germany, and the United States, 1970

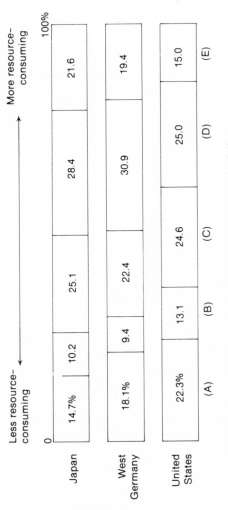

(A) Lumber, wooden products, foodstuffs, leather, and printing
(B) Textiles, apparel, furniture, precision instruments, and rubber products
(C) Transport equipment, nonelectric machinery, other manufactures
(D) Pulp, paper, electric machinery, metal products, chemicals
(E) Stone and glass, steel, nonferrous metals, and petroleum and coal products

Source: MITI, *Tsusho Hakusho,* 1973, p. 236.

until about 1960. (In 1953, no less than 46.8 percent of Japan's national energy requirements was met by domestic coal, only 6.0 percent was accounted for by imported coal, and 17.7 percent by petroleum. Twenty years later, however, the weight of domestic coal declined to a minuscule 3.8 percent, while that of imported coal nearly doubled to 11.7 percent and that of petroleum rose to as much as 77.6 percent.)[26] Indeed, one may even argue that the exiguity of domestic resources turned out to be an unexpected advantage to Japan in comparison with the resource-abundant Western countries, which often had to maintain artificially high prices for domestic resources. An Australian example illustrates this situation. According to K. Bieda:

> Japan is extremely short of raw materials of any kind. Geographers usually consider this a disadvantage, but the fact is that the Japanese have turned this lack of domestic sources (which if available might have been not very economic) to their advantage, because Japanese industry is not compelled to buy expensive and/or inferior domestic materials but can buy from the cheapest source *in the whole world.* . . .
>
> The preceding paradoxical advantage is shown . . . with respect to a country that discovers some natural resource which for reasons of its quality, location or domestic factor costs is not *the* cheapest in the world. For example, this has happened in Australia, where the recent discoveries of oil (which for various reasons will be substantially dearer than the imported oil) will tend to impoverish the country for many years because the oil could be obtained at a lower 'opportunity cost' from abroad, but the government compels the country to use the dearer domestic oil.[27]

The recent phenomenal increases in the price of oil and other commodities have changed the picture entirely; now the blessed are the "have" nations and the cursed are the "have-nots." Nevertheless the meagerness of Japan's domestic resources did allow her to shop around in the world market and secure overseas supplies at the most economical prices, and she thus escaped for a while the burden of supporting a continued production of inefficient and costly domestic supplies. (Actually, the Japanese government initially imposed a tariff on oil and gave domestic coal price subsidies to make it competitive with petroleum. But in the early 1960s, the government moved away from protecting the coal industry and instead acted to mitigate the social and economic dislocations caused by mine closings.)[28]

Third, the postwar industrial transformation of Japanese industry, on the whole, was accomplished by the successful adoption (and adaptation) of foreign technologies, mostly those imported from the United States. Many of these technologies, however, originated in quite a different economic environment: U.S. technologies were developed against a background of relatively abundant domestic supplies of industrial raw materials and energy resources; hence they are resource-intensive. So long as Japan succeeded in acquiring resources overseas as economically as the United States did, the resource-intensive nature of imported technologies posed no serious problem. Japan's industry expanded by leaps and bounds, becoming more and more dependent on overseas resources.

Fourth, Japan's seemingly disadvantageous topography quite unexpectedly turned out to offer extremely favorable conditions for developing the heavy and chemical industries that required a heavy input of raw materials and produced a bulky output. The limited amount of land available forced the Japanese to reclaim coastal areas in order to create many polders, ideal industrial sites for steelworks, smelters, petro-chemical complexes, and paper mills. Helped by the deep coastal waters, they proved to be extremely efficient and convenient in handling the bulky raw materials imported and in transporting the outputs of heavy weight by ocean routes to overseas markets as well as to other parts of Japan. This unexpected advantage, once discovered, was soon actively exploited. Consequently, more and more resource-processing industries were constructed along Japan's coastal regions, notably on the Pacific Ocean. This pattern of development also aggravated the present problems of pollution and ecological decay. Thus, Japan's "economic miracle" has caused serious problems that have matured only in recent years.

To escape from the petroleum entanglement, in 1974 the government initiated a massive research program, dubbed "Project Sunshine," to develop alternative energy resources at home. R & D into solar, geothermal, and nuclear energy and into gasification of coal are being emphasized. Research is also being conducted in cooperation with other industrialized countries. In July 1974, for example, Japan and the United States signed a pact to cooperate on energy research and development. In October 1974 Japan reached an agreement with Australia to undertake a joint research program on the liquefaction and gasification of coal.

Although increased use of domestically available coal and development of geothermal and solar energy will contribute to Japan's energy supply in the short-to-intermediate run, in the long run more nuclear power is expected, although there are many unsolved safety problems associated with the production of nuclear energy and the disposal of waste materials. But with the long-term trend in mind, Japan is simultaneously stepping up her efforts to strengthen R & D to solve these problems and to search out stable supplies of uranium overseas.

The MITI's plan, announced in 1975, aims at developing by 1985 a nuclear generating capacity of 49 million kilowatts, or an equivalent of one-fourth of the total power generated in Japan.[29] One-third of Japan's uranium requirement is to be secured directly from the D & I investments of Japanese enterprises, another one-third by imports from foreign suppliers on a long-term contract basis, and the rest under spot purchase contracts. In 1975, the MITI also initiated an ambitious research project to extract uranium from sea water. The project's goal is to supply about 15 percent of the expected domestic demand for uranium in 1990.[30] In any event, so far as nuclear energy is concerned, Japan must depend on overseas uranium, because her own deposits are insignificant. Nevertheless, because uranium will generate more energy than conventional fuels, Japan's over-all dependence on imported fuels probably will be reduced with the development of atomic energy at home.

Japanese industry, initially in an effort to prevent pollution, began to strive in earnest to recycle industrial wastes. Recycling, however, has become focused more and more on extracting reusable energy and raw materials. As a result, various new technologies are being introduced so that natural resources can be used more economically.

Extractive Investment Abroad

Japan's resource policy, ranging from the strategy of slow economic growth to the resource-saving industrial structural reform and to Project Sunshine, certainly cannot bring about immediately any significant reduction in her over-all dependency.[31] Even if these efforts prove successful, it may take at least a decade or two to produce any noticeable impact. In the meantime, therefore, Japan is pressing ahead with overseas investment aimed at expanding, diversifying, and securing resource supplies. This route is designed to stabilize the over-all supply by reducing the proportion of resources imported through spot-market channels. As shown in table 5.1, by 1969, Japan had succeeded in procuring about 95 percent of her imported iron ore and 78 percent of coal (coking and bituminous) under the D & I arrangement (although mostly under long-term loans and purchase contracts rather than through equity investment). But she is still dependent upon regular import purchases for more than 90 percent of the bauxite and nickel that she needs. Although the proportion of the D & I type of procurement is equally low for lead, zinc, and natural gas, Japan is in a comparatively secure position because domestic supplies of

Table 5.1
Supply Sources of Major Resources, 1969

Resource	Domestic supply %	Develop-and-import (D & I) investment abroad %	Regular import purchase %
Copper	28.3	16.1 (11.6)[a]	55.6
Lead	44.7	6.3	49.0
Zinc	51.1	2.5	46.4
Aluminum (bauxite)	—	9.6	90.4
Nickel	—	6.4	93.6
Iron ore	14.0	82.5 (75.2)[a]	3.5
Coal	22.4	68.6 (61.5)[a]	9.0
Crude oil	0.5	10.5	89.1
Natural gas	95.6	4.4	—
Uranium	—	0	100.0

Source: MITI, *Tsusho Hakusho*, 1971, p. 344.
[a] Percentages in parentheses show those imports developed under long-term loans instead of direct investment.

these materials are relatively significant in terms of the current levels of consumption. Japan also has successfully developed relatively secure supply sources of copper ore, because she initiated extractive overseas investments in that ore much earlier and more extensively than in other nonferrous metals. In fact, in late 1974, as the result of an economic slump, Japan had an excess supply of copper ore. This development was perhaps the most ironical twist of events for the newly formed CIPEC group: Japan asked them to honor their "promise" to cut their ore supplies to Japan. The supply cut was intended by the CIPEC to raise their revenues in a fashion similar to the action of the OPEC.

From 1968 to 1970 Japan's D & I investments expanded at a rapid pace; investments in petroleum, lead, and zinc doubled those made in the preceding years; those in copper and nickel tripled; and those in coal, bauxite, and uranium multiplied from five to eight times. Joint ventures and "loan-cum-purchase" contracts are the predominant forms of these increased investments.[32]

Since the soybean embargo and the Arab oil cutback and price hikes, which occurred in tandem, Japan has been gripped by a sense of the urgency of securing stable supplies of resources. Japan's most vulnerable areas are supplies of bauxite, nickel, crude oil, and uranium. Her D & I efforts are consequently directed toward bauxite (a more important industrial resource than nickel) and uranium (the major future source of energy). Investments for uranium development are all in prospecting, except for one successful ore discovery in Niger by the Overseas Uranium Resources Development Co., a group formed in 1970 by thirty-three Japanese companies from the trading, utilities, nonferrous metals, mining, heavy machinery, and banking industries. Furthermore, the Metal Mining Agency of the MITI is assisting companies undertaking these high-risk ventures with loans that cover 50 to 70 percent of prospecting costs and that need to be repaid only after successful prospecting and development.[33]

New developments are also emerging in Japan's overseas extractive ventures in such industries as aluminum and copper. The smelting segment of these industries is increasingly being transferred to the source of the ore supply in order to use locally available electric power. As exemplified by Japan's recent participation in the Asahan and the Amazon project, where a power supply is not already available, necessary investments in new power plants are made. This type of more vertically integrated extractive investment is in the interest of both Japan and the resource-rich developing countries. Japan will not only secure vital resource supplies at lower transportation costs but also save energy at home and eliminate the pollution costs of smelting. In the developing countries, on the other hand, such investments often serve as a "development-aid-package," constituting vital regional development projects. As a result, Japan's downstream-integrating extractive investments are welcomed in the developing countries.

Develop-And-Import Projects in Food

Japan also has been lulled into a comfortable dependence on imported food. As her industrial output and exports expanded and her foreign exchange reserves rapidly accumulated, Japan increasingly developed the mentality and habit of purchasing foodstuffs and feed grains from overseas, an act rationalized by the principle of comparative advantage. Increased farm imports were considered desirable, because Japan was disadvantaged and inefficient in farm production. Moreover, the United States, to which Japan directed her export drive in manufactured goods, understandably pressured Japan to buy more agricultural products. In addition, an expanded supply of foodstuffs from overseas was complementary with Japan's need for a shift of resources, particularly labor, from the agricultural to the ever-expanding industrial sector throughout the postwar period. Such resource transfers were instrumental for an overall increase in productivity and for high-powered economic growth.

As a result of complacency over food imports, Japan has become the least self-sufficient in food of all the industrialized nations and imports the largest amount of food in world trade. A study by the Ministry of Agriculture and Forestry revealed that in 1972 Japan's wheat imports constituted 8.5 percent of world trade in that commodity; maize 16.3 percent; crude sugar 12.5 percent; and soybeans 24.8 percent.[34]

Japan now contemplates reversing that direction. The worldwide shortages of grains in 1972 and 1973 and the U.N. World Food Conference held in Rome in 1974 gave impetus to a drive for agricultural protectionism, a movement long considered irrational from a global trading standpoint. The recommendations made public in January 1975 by the Agricultural Policy Council, an advisory organ for the Ministry of Agriculture and Forestry, sought over-all self-sufficiency of 75 percent by 1985; this is only a slight improvement over the 1973 level of 71 percent. However, despite the planned over-all decline in import dependency, the demand for imported feed grains is expected to increase due to Japan's rising consumption of meat and dairy products. This projection is based on Japanese dietary trends; tastes have been considerably "Westernized," demand shifting from rice to wheat and from vegetable protein to animal protein. According to a study made by the Economic Planning Agency, for example, the income elasticity of demand for beef is as high as 0.6 (that is, a 1 percent increase in national income results in a 0.6 percent increase in the demand for beef), while that for rice is negative 0.04 (that is, a 1 percent rise in national income leads to a 0.04 percent reduction in rice consumption).[35] Thus rice, Japan's staple food for many centuries, has become an "inferior" good in the recent past.

Some people criticize the Westernization of Japanese dietary tastes. For example, an editorial in *The Japan Times* advocated a reversal of the trend:

[T]he goal of food self-sufficiency rate—75 percent—may be regarded as unduly low. To revise it, however, it would be imperative to change the basic premises, including the people's food habit and way of life in the years to come.

The estimates contained in the reports are merely statistical extensions of the present and recent trends. They reflect only what "is" and not what "ought to be."

The reports speculate, for instance, that per capita meat consumption in Japan would increase by 30 percent to 19 kilograms. On the basis of this figure, it is estimated that the number of head of cattle needed to supply that amount of meat would be 5,870,000 or 1.6 times the present figure. From this is derived the volume of feeds needed and then the amount of feed grains to be imported. . . .

What is important, however, is that estimates for needs should not be based on the naturalistic expectations based on uncontrolled human behavior. If, for instance, we are to reduce our dependency on imported food, then we must first establish a goal for reducing our consumption of imported food. And if, on the basis of such a consideration, certain changes should become a requirement in our food habit, the changes ought to be effected by whatever means necessary—legislation or popular education.

As nutritional experts have been saying, for instance, animal protein is not an essential element of our daily diet. Then a food policy with more emphasis on vegetables and grains instead of meat should be instituted.

Likewise with arable land. For whatever needs may arise in the future, action must be taken to create food-producing land —even by converting golf courses into rice paddies and vegetable gardens.

We hope that the Agricultural Policy Council will produce recommendations including such basic requirements for the future of the people.[36]

It is doubtful, however, that the present Westernization of tastes can be reversed and that a more "original" Japanese way of living can be developed to replace an already highly Westernized mode of life. Even if the demand pattern can be remolded by "whatever means necessary—legislation or popular education," the supply conditions are unfavorable. In 1974 the Ministry of Agriculture and Forestry conducted a mock experiment with Japan's ability to attain self-sufficiency in the complete absence of imports. It was demonstrated that, given sufficient time for necessary adjustments and mobilization of resources (including the conversion of two-thirds of Japan's 1,367 golf courses into farm land for growing sweet potatoes, the "conscripting" of some white-collar and blue-collar workers for farm work, and the transfer of crops from vegetables and fruits to basic grains), Japan would only be able to attain a bare degree of self-sufficiency equivalent to a dietary level that prevailed from 1950 to 1955.[37]

Because arable land is only about 15 percent of the total land and because rising incomes inevitably produce greater demands for meat and fruits, Japan's program to become more self-sufficient in producing food would serve merely to protect inefficient domestic agriculture rather than to cut import needs. As might be expected, the Foreign Trade Council, an organization composed of major trading companies, objected to and criticized the program of the Ministry of Agriculture and Forestry to attain greater self-sufficiency in food production. In a movement similar to that occurring in the extractive industry Japan seems to have no recourse but to emphasize D & I investments in foodstuffs. This emphasis is being pushed by the private sector, particularly by trading companies, which foresee attractive business opportunities in handling the marketing of foodstuffs not only for Japan but for other countries heavily dependent on food imports.

Japan is most actively engaged in D & I investments for large-scale production of soybeans, corn, and beef in Brazil. Japanese investors also favor Australia for overseas ventures in beef production. Other host countries in which similar D & I programs are either underway or under study include Mexico (soybeans, corn, sorghum, and beef), Argentina (corn and sorghum), Indonesia (corn, palm oil, and beef), Thailand (corn), Philippines (corn), and Madagascar (beef).[38]

Despite the rhetoric of Japan's self-sufficiency policy for food, her agricultural ventures overseas will continue to expand rapidly. Her agricultural technology is in great demand, especially in the developing Asian countries. For example, Japan possesses a unique type of advanced technology in the wet paddy cultivation of rice, the mainstay of Asian farming. Unlike those of their Western counterparts, Japanese farming methods generally use more labor and are more compatible with the densely populated conditions of the Asian region. This compatibility is attested to by the establishment of the Asian Rural Development Center, undertaken jointly by FAO at the latter's request for extension of technical assistance from Japan.[39]

The Japanese government itself has been promoting agricultural technical assistance as an essential part of its economic cooperation program and, at various international conferences on economic development held in recent years, has promised to expand such assistance. In 1974, for example, Japan had in operation in Asia 111 officially sponsored agricultural-aid projects worth $76 million, designed to improve local food supplies and feed grain production for export.[40] Because the developing countries, if they are to develop an export-oriented agricultural industry, need not only technology but also capital and market outlets, participation of Japanese business firms is equally desired. Thus Japan's technical cooperation is opening up new opportunities for her overseas ventures.

In addition, a trend is also appearing in the food-processing industry in a fashion analogous to the one that occurred earlier in the extractive industry (that is, to move to the overseas locations of supplies of raw materials). Firms in the confectionery, edible oil, and coffee-processing businesses are transferring the processing segment of their production overseas to secure stable supplies of raw materials.

As might well be expected, similar developments are in the making in the fishery industry. Japan's official cooperation with the developing countries in this industry, however, started rather belatedly with the establishment of a special fund for overseas cooperation, the Overseas Fishery Cooperation Foundation (OFCF) as recently as July 1973.[41] Yet Japan's fishery industry, led by such leading large firms as Taiyo Fishery, Nippon Suisan, Nichiro Fisheries, and others, has long been active in the D & I type of ventures, notably in prawns and shrimp trawling. In almost all cases they are joint ventures with the local interests or with the local government and numbered 164 in 1973.[42]

Now that the "economic zone" of 200 nautical miles is claimed generally by the majority of nations, the only way out for Japan's fishery industry is to promote international cooperation through joint ventures and technical assistance. Because 85 percent of Japan's total catch from distant ocean fishing in 1973, for example, came from waters within 200 miles of all the world's coasts,[43] Japan is naturally eager to offer whatever assistance and collaboration she can to other countries, especially the developing countries that lack the fishing vessels, equipment, and technology necessary to develop rich marine resources in their coastal waters.

Systems-Focused Strategy: Group Investment

The D & I approach to acquiring resources requires a much greater use of diplomatic skills than does the ordinary import transaction, because the former involves direct, although partial, participation in the ownership and extraction of resources in the host countries. The presence of foreign interests in the ownership of natural resources, although officially sanctioned, is still viewed with alarm by the people of many host countries, particularly those which have suffered under colonialism in the past. In fact, Japan attempted to pursue her own brand of imperialism to secure vital resources prior to and during World War II under the banner of the "Greater East Asia Co-Prosperity Sphere." Given this background, how will Japan be able to push her new policy of resources diplomacy without resurrecting the old suspicions and antagonism in resource-rich countries?

To assuage the host countries' fear of Japanese control, rooted in the memory of Japan's military incursions during World War II, and to build a new, more respectable image, Japan appears to be adopting two basic strategies. First, her D & I policy will not be restricted merely to the extraction of a particular resource that she seeks. It also may be designed, as much as is practicable, to assist the host country in its general economic development; for example, Japan may help to set up a necessary infrasructure for the extractive industry and for initiating local downstream industries. This type of approach now is being followed increasingly in such countries as Indonesia and Brazil, where the host country is eager to industrialize. There is, however, nothing altruistic about Japanese motivation. To begin with, assistance with economic development is becoming an implicit condition for foreign interests to participate in the development of natural resources in practically all developing countries. Resource-rich developing countries want foreign investors to process primary products locally as much as possible so that their domestic industries will develop along the path of vertical integration originated in the extractive industry. Developing countries can earn more foreign exchange from the higher value-added production of these related industries, can attain higher employment, and can acquire more skills associated with the processing activities. Japan shows a great willingness—perhaps greater than that of any other industrial country—to transfer processing activities to the host countries, and Japan has reached such a high density of processing industries at home that she no longer desires to expand pollution-prone and energy-intensive processing activities. A new harmony seems to have emerged between the needs of Japanese industry and those of the resource-rich developing countries.

Second, Japanese industry is likely to offer as many concessions as possible to the host country by way of ownership and profit sharing. For example, many observers have noted the relatively high propensity of Japanese firms compared to U.S. firms, for example, to form joint ventures with local interests instead of operating through wholly-owned ventures. Moreover, Japanese industry is even willing to go along with the so-called divestment scheme according to which ownership will be completely transferred to the local partner within a specified period of time. A recent steel venture in Indonesia is a prime example.

A group of sixteen Japanese companies are supplying half the capital needed to build a cold-rolled-steel sheet mill (about $60 million) but will hand over full ownership to its Indonesian partner in fifteen years.

How, then, will the Japanese profit from their new brand of resources diplomacy? Japan's primary goal in making overseas extractive investments is to stabilize her supplies of resources. Profitability of a specific extractive investment is rather a secondary consideration. In fact, many of Japan's extractive ventures overseas, especially in oil and natural gas, are reportedly operating at a deficit.

Yet these seemingly "unprofitable" ventures, when considered as independent projects, may not after all be uneconomic when looked at from a systems-focused point of view. This fact can be analyzed at three different system levels; a company, an industrial group, and the economy. First, at the company-systems level, extractive ventures are often part of the vertically integrated operations of the parent company (or more often a group of companies), and hence the parent company (or a group) may be able to compensate for less profitable overseas operations by its more profitable downstream stages of production. This trend appears to be developing in Japan's steel industry, for example. Japanese companies are moving toward overseas production of crude steel or semi-finished steel that would be shipped back to Japan for further processing into high-technology specialty steels (for instance, high tensile steel plate).[44] Indeed, this type of international division-of-labor strategy increases the company's profitability, because it can concentrate on more technology-intensive and higher value-added stages of production in conformity with the general design of the Japanese economy to upgrade its industrial structure.

Second, even if a particular Japanese company may not profit directly from a given extractive venture itself, some other Japanese companies are likely to capitalize on profitable opportuni-

ties generated by such a venture in related business activities—
new demands for equipment, machinery, plant, technical, financial, and marketing assistance, and so forth. Here, the strategy
of a group investment comes into the picture. Group investment
is essentially a systems-focused strategy pursued by a group of
companies operating in mutually complementary fields. Japanese companies are increasingly investing as a group in extractive ventures in order to share in linkage opportunities. Immediate spillovers or linkages might be newly created demands for
plants and capital equipment to be used for a venture. Some
capital-goods producers in the group will be able to profit from
these exports. Louis Wolf Goodman observes:

> The MNC [Multinational Corporation] activity most fre-
> quently discussed in the social scientific literature is direct for-
> eign investment (DFI). However, DFI is only one of a num-
> ber of business activities carried out by MNCs. In fact, it is
> more sensible to think of DFI as an integrated package of the
> range of business operations available to firms. These opera-
> tions include *importing* and *exporting* raw materials and goods
> in various stages of manufacture; *licensing agreements* which
> authorize the use of patented technologies and trademarks;
> *management contracts*, which provide managerial services and
> "know-how" for a fee; *service contracts*, which provide for the
> maintenance and upgrading of plants, equipment, and proc-
> esses; *equity investment*, entitling the investor to a share of div-
> idends; *capital lending*, wherein the MNC loans funds to the
> firms in the nation; *marketing contracts*, where products of a
> country are sold in international markets by an MNC; and
> even *financial speculation*, where the operations of a corpora-
> tion in a Third World nation allow the MNC to attempt to take
> advantage of fluctuations in international money markets.[45]

Any single Japanese firm may not be quite large or capable
enough to provide all these operations in an "integrated package." Yet each of those Japanese firms forming a group has a
comparative advantage in performing a particular function.

Thus, with the "division of labor" adopted among the participating firms, the efficiency (hence the competitiveness) of operations offered in an integrated package is enhanced. Herein lies a new source of advantage for Japanese industry to implement huge-scale overseas ventures. The relative weakness of Japanese individual firms, therefore, is turned into an advantage in the form of group investment. In addition, the arrangement of group investment itself is uniquely facilitated by the existence of *keiretsu* groups in Japan—oligopolistic industrial groups, mostly originating from the former *zaibatsu* groups, which are functionally conglomerated in a mutually complementary way within their respective group with a major general trading company and a leading bank as their nucleus.[46]

When it comes to overseas investments, each group is normally led by its general trading company. For example, the Mitsui group is led by Mitsui, the Mitsubishi group by Mitsubishi, and so forth. The trading companies are best fitted as organizers of systems-focused ventures and are by far the most active in Japan's resource-development projects overseas. Because they have traditionally acted as intermediaries for the parties of different but mutually complementary interests, they are quick to discern those business opportunities that might be passed up by a single individual company.

With their well-established business connections, they are also able to bring together related interests, especially within their own *keiretsu* group, but if necessary with other groups as well. In fact, the trend of the systems-focused group investment seems to be from the intra-*keiretsu* to the inter-*keiretsu* activity. Although the *keiretsu* groups are known for their fierce competition with each other at home, their interests often converge in overseas investments, especially in large-scale extractive investments. Furthermore, trading companies have been inviting foreign companies as their partners in their multinational ventures.

The formation of an inter-*keiretsu* consortium is often a necessary step in putting political pressure on the Japanese government to help finance a large-scale venture overseas (for example, the Asahan project and other "economic development" ventures that have followed it). It is also worth restating that Western interests withdrew from the Asahan project when they learned of Indonesia's desire to seek an agreement involving not only an aluminium refinery but also a power plant and other infrastructural facilities. Group orientation is clearly weaker in the case of Western interests, whereas Japanese industry welcomes the "comprehensiveness" of a project, because it provides linkages that its industrial groups find most advantageous in such an integrated package deal.

Group investment also plays an important risk-sharing function, because large-scale investments, particularly in resource development, call for huge sums of capital outlay involving extremely high risks. Yet the linkage-sharing function played by group investment appears to be a positive and unique characteristic of Japan's systems-focused strategy for extractive ventures overseas.

Third, at the economy-systems level, the industrialization of resource-rich developing countries is no longer viewed as a threat to Japan's own industries. This change in outlook partly may reflect a realistic appraisal by Japan that developing countries will eventually follow the global path of industrialization sooner or later and that it is thus in her interest to assist them positively and to make the most of their economic development. As has already happened in such low-technology sectors as textiles, Japanese industry must expect rising competition from these countries in both resource markets and product markets. But if Japanese industry succeeds in transforming itself into a resource-economizing and knowledge-intensive industrial structure, potential friction with developing countries can be avoided. Indeed, active industrial transfers will serve as a catalyst to "houseclean" and upgrade Japan's industrial structure while retaining future dividends from her overseas investment. Thus the establishment of complementary relationships is aimed at in Japan's economic diplomacy toward developing countries. Their industrialization in processing and low-technology industrial sectors will be complementary with Japan's overseas investment, and a subsequent rise in their incomes will create export markets for Japan's high-technology products.

The systems-focused strategy also relates to the flow of resources. To stabilize the supplies of vital industrial resources, such as minerals and oil, Japan is emphasizing the ownership and control of the flow of resources to Japan rather than those of the extractive activities themselves (that is, the controlling of logistics). This point is succinctly observed by Norman Macrae in *The Economist*:

> The Japanese will help to build deep-water ports, automated warehouses, roll-on-roll-off facilities for transferring supplies to giant purpose-built bulk vessels (which, like supertankers, will be initially Japanese-built and Japanese-owned), similarly automated facilities at Japan's own ports (which will use less and less labour on the dockside, so that if other islands like Britain continue to use far too much dock labour in its unhappily about-to-be nationalized ports, modern ships simply will not call here—which for other desert islands has proved rather serious).
>
> Japan's purchase of the materials will usually be by f.o.b. contract for which it will pay inconveniently generously from the viewpoint of other raw material importers like Britain. Japan will not try sufficiently to screw down producer prices, but the computers of Japanese importers and shippers will control the rate of shipments, the rate of shipping arrivals, the levels of onshore inventories—and thus have considerable influence over any prices which the Japanese think are improper. This could give them considerable political, as well as overwhelming commercial, weight in these areas, including the most important one.[47]

The control of logistics rather than that of resource production itself serves to palliate economic nationalism in the resource-producing country, simultaneously enables Japan indirectly to exercise controls over the supply of resources, and reduces the risk, as well as the potential cost, of nationalization, because Japan's capital is not tied up, and the vessels easily can be withdrawn. The facilities and mode of transportation that are uniquely custom-made to fit the specific technical requirements of Japan's logistics alone will give Japan a monopsony position, hindering the entry of other resource-importing nations. An intensive use of modern technology on logistics also enables Japan to compensate for increases in f.o.b. resource prices. A substantial reduction in transportation costs is crucial for Japan not only to acquire resources at a lower cost but also to diversify the supply sources by bringing into an economically attractive range those suppliers who are too distant to be competitive in supplying Japan. Kiyoshi Kojima points out:

> If an index of 100 is used to indicate freight costs for iron-ore between Australia and Japan using a small vessel (60,000 DW type), it costs 185 from Australia to Europe or 188 from Australia to the U.S.A. The cost is reduced to 81 between Australia and Japan by the use of specialized bigger vessels (160,000 DW type).
>
> By comparison, the ocean transport distance of Brazilian iron-ore to Japan is the longest, and it was thought earlier that this ore would never prove to be competitive. But with the development of so-called triangle transport (that is, oil is first transported from the Persian Gulf to Europe, then the carrier sails in ballast to Brazil in order to load iron-ore destined for Japan), freight costs are lowered significantly thereby enhancing the competitiveness of the Brazilian ore.[48]

The control of logistics is no doubt made easier by the existence of the *keiretsu* groups—and in particular, their respective trading companies—which can organize a vertically as well as horizontally integrated system of business operations. In Kozo Yamamura's words: "Even if trading companies themselves do not provide the transportation, they can coordinate shipping times and locations to reduce the cost per unit of goods transported. Transportation costs are also reduced because of facilities and arrangements made at ports of origin and destination. Such facilities and arrangements can be characterized as having a large fixed cost and small marginal costs."[49] The economical spread of such "a large fixed cost" among many companies is made possible primarily within the industrial group each trading company represents but if necessary among the groups as well. Large overseas development projects are increasingly carried out as inter-*keiretsu* ventures.

Conclusions

This chapter examined how Japan's ethnocentric policy to industrialize, despite her exiguous resource endowments, has trapped her ever more inextricably into depending upon overseas resources (and equally important, into a nearly irreversible process of destroying the natural environment of her limited territory). Japan's very effort to strengthen herself industrially has increased her vulnerability to outside forces, a vulnerability long latent under the fortuitous circumstances of most of the period after World War II, but suddenly revealed by recent adverse developments in the world market of resource supplies. Because Japan's vulnerability remained hidden for so long, it was all the more serious when finally it was exposed, leaving the nation pitifully helpless, as evidenced by the Arab oil embargo.

Japan now is struggling to restore a modicum of self-sufficiency in energy and food and is attempting to restructure her industry so that it will become less resource-dependent. At the same time, she is pushing ahead with a D & I strategy overseas to secure stable supplies of vital industrial resources—with an ever-growing propensity to curry favor with the resource-rich developing countries by making attractive concessions and offering technological and economic assistance. Indeed, it is ironical that Japan's industrial ethnocentrism has forced her to accept more and more "polycentric" or local-interest-oriented approaches in her overseas extractive investments.

Yet Japan is shrewdly taking advantage of the exposure of her vulnerability and appears to be finding a new and effective way to secure resource supplies through the application of systems-focused strategies to her D & I investments and, through the increased control of logistics, to regulate indirectly the vital flow of resources from the supply sources to the home market. Japan is strengthening her economic ties with resource-rich advanced countries by way of technological cooperation (that is, Joint R & D for sources of energy) and with resource-rich developing countries through stepped-up development assistance programs.

Chapter 6

Conflict with Local Interests: Economic, Sociocultural, and Political Factors

JAPANESE firms rushed to set up large numbers of plants overseas, they did so rapidly, and particularly toward the end of the 1960s and in the early 1970s, this development tended to create friction with local interests. Hostility was openly expressed in Thailand and Indonesia by violent anti-Japanese demonstrations during Prime Minister Kakuei Tanaka's disastrous "goodwill" trips to five Southeast Asian countries in January 1974. The problem was aggravated by the initial inexperience of the Japanese in overseas ventures and their somewhat callow disregard of local attitudes as well as by the unfamiliarity of local people with Japanese ways of conducting business. But there are many more important and fundamental reasons for local ill will toward Japanese business. This chapter examines both the "purely" economic and the sociocultural and political sources of that friction.

Economic Sources of Friction

Regional and Industrial Concentration

Japanese industry has advanced upon Japan's neighbors en masse. By the end of March 1975, nearly 70 percent of Japanese manufacturing ventures were concentrated in Asia (approximately 40 percent of the value of Japanese manufacturing investment). Compared with other regions, Asia hosts a relatively large number of small-scale ventures.

Moreover, these Asian ventures are intensively concentrated

in five economies: Hong Kong, South Korea, Taiwan, Thailand, and Indonesia; these alone account for as much as 73 percent of Japan's overseas ventures in Asia and nearly 30 percent of her global total. Because of their significant size, Japanese investments now take a 7 to 10 percent share of fixed capital formation in these Asian countries.[1] Elsewhere in the world, Brazil is another popular host country; more than half of Japan's investments in Latin America are located there.

Although Japan's global investments are only about one-eighth of those of the United States, Japan is now the foremost investor in Thailand, South Korea, Taiwan, and Indonesia, and has already attained or is about to attain the second position in other developing countries such as the Philippines, Malaysia, and Brazil. In these countries, Japanese ventures are centered in light manufacturing industries, notably textiles and electric appliances. This pattern is again more distinctive in Asia than anywhere else with more than one-half of Japan's investments in these industries located there. In fact, Japanese interest now dominates these industrial sectors in the developing host countries where labor-intensive manufacturing industries are being developed mostly with the help of outside capital and technology.

It is also worth remembering that Japan's ascent to the position of major investor in the developing countries has taken place only recently and in a short span of time. It is then easy to understand how great the impact of so massive and rapid an incursion of Japanese industry must have been, both socially and economically, on the host countries. Because criticism of Japanese firms and their business practices overseas grew as their numbers swelled, a new nonprofit organization, Japan Overseas Enterprises Associations (JOEA), was formed in Tokyo in 1974. It is designed "to serve as a coordinator, an adviser, a mediator, a consultant, and a trouble shooter for Japanese corporations expanding their operations abroad, especially in developing countries."[2] The organization selected seven countries—South Korea, the Philippines, Singapore, Thailand, Malaysia, Indonesia, and Brazil—as the host countries where utmost caution should be exercised by Japanese firms to prevent friction with local interests.

Strong Trade Orientation

Japan's overseas manufacturing investments have been made in many instances because her exports were threatened by the tariffs and quotas set up by foreign countries: they were designed to circumvent trade barriers and to preserve export markets. This type of investment is known as "tariff factories." At present, for example, many Japanese manufacturers are motivated to set up shop in Australia, which has lately imposed severe restrictions on manufactured imports from Japan. Indeed, this defensive motivation was most predominant in the early stages of Japan's multinationalism prior to the mid-1960s, as shown in chapter 3 in the analysis of the postwar development of Japan's overseas production.

The motive of circumventing trade restrictions is perhaps the most familiar one: many U.S. firms invested in the European Economic Community (EEC) for this reason. But Japan's tariff factories in developing countries had one unique feature: tariffs themselves were often raised by the local governments at the urging of *investing* Japanese companies. In some instances, a given investment was implemented only on the condition that competing imports would be curbed or completely prohibited once the local venture started production. The intention was clear; the investing firm wanted to be treated as if it were an "infant industry." In fact, such a demand for protection was not rare during the period when the developing countries vied with each other in attracting direct foreign investment, and may still be made in those much less developed countries that are barely industrialized but are eager to attract foreign capital and technology for their economic development. The Japanese practice is noted in a criticism expressed by a scholar in Singapore:

The view is often encountered that, in the past, Japanese foreign investment policy has really been "very selfish" in the sense that it has been unconcerned with economic benefits to host countries. Investing only in countries where they could obtain protection, the Japanese have sought primarily to capture host markets. . . .

[T]he usual Japanese insistence on tariff protection has in effect meant guaranteed profits on the consumer items produced. In certain instances—when, for example, the prolonged use of tariffs has led to the shoring up of inefficient units and stagnant industries—the economic result for host countries has been negative. Critics of the Japanese practice allege that the quest for protection characterizes the Japanese *modus operandi* in such countries as Indonesia, Malaysia, Singapore, Taiwan, and Thailand.[3]

Because Japanese manufacturing ventures have lately become increasingly export-oriented and because the import-substitution phase of economic development in many Asian countries is now largely over, the Japanese practice of insisting on protection is no longer so prevalent. Nevertheless, an interview with an executive of a leading Japanese textile manufacturer confirmed that the firm and its competitors frequently had engaged in such a practice in the past. This sort of arrangement undoubtedly enabled some ventures to enjoy "guaranteed profits," and it may partially explain the relatively high profitability of Japanese ventures in developing countries. However, the profitability of these ventures, although high, might not be so exorbitant; an excessively high rate of return, if it existed, would have been eliminated, in part by the entry of other firms, especially their compatriots and competitors, and in part by host country taxes on excessive profits. In addition, there was a good economic reason for the demands of Japanese firms for tariff protection. For local production in developing countries often meant a substantial increase in production costs due to scaled-down operations, because the local markets were necessarily small and lacked opportunities for scale economies. In many cases Japanese manufacturers could have continued to supply the local markets with exports more cheaply and more profitably than local production could. Therefore, in order to make their locally produced goods salable, they found it necessary to ask for tariff protection against imports; otherwise their local production would have been ruined by competition from their own exports and those of their competitors shipped from Japan. The smaller the domestic market of a developing host country, the less efficient the operation of a new venture and hence the greater the demand for protection. The result was usually a formidably high tariff rate to "protect" Japanese interests and resultant high prices for the local consumers.

Another source of strain, perhaps more important, soon developed in the process of import substitution. The local production of goods hitherto imported from Japan is undertaken supposedly to reduce the need for imports and thereby to economize on the use of meager foreign reserves of the host countries. But it does not necessarily accomplish this end; it may, in fact, aggravate the host countries' balance of payments. For Japanese tariff factories usually take the form of knock-down or assembly operations and support the export of plant equipment, parts, and components from Japan. As a result, this type of overseas venture does not necessarily reduce the value of Japan's exports as it starts to put out end-products in much larger numbers than its previously imported counterparts. In fact, the export value of capital goods and semi-finished products often comes to exceed the previous value of the end-product exports, which now are restricted by trade controls. A study made by the MITI on this export-creating effect of Japan's overseas manufacturing investment estimates that in 1973 the value of investment-induced exports was as much as $3,090 million, whereas the value of exports replaced by overseas production was $1,650 million.[4] In other words, overseas production is, so far, definitely a positive factor in Japan's balance of payments, as it encourages, on the whole, about $2 worth of new exports for every $1 worth of exports replaced. This necessarily means that host countries' balance-of-trade positions have deteriorated as they have become more dependent on Japan for the imports of capital goods and intermediate products.

In addition, they have discovered that their new dependence on supplies of industrial inputs from Japan is placing them in a more perilous position than was their previous dependence on the imports of finished products. For the imports of finished products may be suspended temporarily without any adverse direct effect on domestic production, or the imports may even be secured from countries other than Japan. But the imports of semi-finished industrial materials that the newly established "domestic" factories need for their operation cannot be cut back so easily or purchased elsewhere. In other words, the import substitution directed at finished products has created a new and more "locked-in" import dependency. On the theoretical level, this reduced elasticity of the host country's over-all import demand for Japanese goods provides Japanese industry with an opportunity to exercise greater monopolistic power than before. If, for example, there is no possibility of purchasing parts and components from any suppliers except the Japanese source, elasticity is zero, and the Japanese producer can administer the prices for input materials—a familar cause of tension associated with the so-called transfer pricing. (This problem of import dependency seems more prevalent and serious in Latin American countries that emphasize import-substitution policies, attracting foreign manufacturing ventures, particularly in R & D-based, modern industries with high product differentiation.)

One incidence of the increased vulnerability discussed above is illustrated by the following episode: "Hong Kong depends on Japan for 70 percent of its total plastic imports. Its imports from Japan have decreased due to a series of industrial explosion accidents which occurred in petroleum plants in Japan in

1973. This has compelled quite a few companies to suspend their production operations."[5] When, in the wake of the Arab oil crisis, serious supply shortages of petroleum-based secondary materials occurred throughout 1974, the dangers inherent in the newly evolved pattern of dependency on the Japanese economy were driven home to Asian economies. To ameliorate the situation for Asian industries (and for their own overseas ventures), should such supply shortages recur, the Japanese are now investing in overseas production of intermediate raw materials in those Asian countries where raw materials can be processed. The recent move of Japan's textile industry to produce polyester filaments in Indonesia exemplifies this trend.

In addition to the newly emerging pattern of import dependence described above, there is a more basic disequilibrium in the over-all trade relationship between Japan and her Asian neighbors. Japan exports high-value-added manufactures which have high income elasticities, and imports only raw materials or low-value-added manufactures, which have relatively low income elasticities. Despite recent increases in the price of primary goods, which brought about comfortable trade surpluses for natural-resource-exporting countries such as Indonesia, Malaysia, and the Philippines, these countries are unhappy about the asymmetrical trade pattern, which some critics describe as "a new form of colonialism." In fact, the present trade surpluses may even be giving resource-exporting countries a false sense of security, because their exports to Japan are concentrated in one or two primary commodities such as timber, oil, iron ore, copper ore, and bauxite.

For another group of Asian countries exemplified by South Korea and Taiwan, which have huge trade deficits with Japan, the situation is even worse. Because these countries are poor in natural resources, they cannot bargain as strongly as the other group. The only way for them to escape from huge trade deficits with Japan is to diversify trade and investment partners, as in the case of Singapore. Yet the fledgling manufacturing industries in these countries are so locked into import dependence on industrial materials from Japan that they cannot easily extricate themselves.

The increased economic subordination of other Asian countries to Japan was brought about because Japan, having a huge trade surplus, did not attempt to correct the trade imbalance by increasing her imports from the deficit countries or decreasing her exports; rather she plugged the gap with more capital investment (that is, to counterbalance a surplus on her trade account with a deficit on her capital account). The result was domination by Japanese interests in exactly those countries that had a trade deficit with Japan. Thus Japan's trade domination was reinforced by her investment domination in such countries as South Korea, Thailand, and Taiwan.

The problem of Asian countries' heavy trade dependence on Japan is perceptively observed by Donald C. Hellmann:

> The size and distribution of economic intercourse with East Asia also leave Japan wide room for policy maneuver. No single country takes much more than 3 per cent of the total of Japanese trade. Conversely, however, Japan in no case takes much less than 25 per cent of bilateral trade and is involved in more than 30 per cent with virtually all major non-Communist nations in the region. A decision by Tokyo regarding trade can have a profound impact on any of these countries without seriously hurting the Japanese economy, but no nation in the region has the capacity to bring truly significant pressure on Japan. The great inequality involved in the bilateral relationships and the asymmetry of the trade and investment flow make it inappropriate to describe the regional web in terms of interdependence.[6]

As it would be expressed in the economic theory of exchange, Japan's Asian partners have found themselves placed in a position very close to "perfectly competitive traders" in commercial exchange with Japan (that is, one country's action cannot affect Japan's trade significantly), while Japan has succeeded in consolidating her position as a "monopolistic trader" (that is, Japan's action can affect each of the other Asian countries seriously). In addition, Japan's trade position is now further strengthened by her overseas investments in Asian countries, which are now dependent on Japan for intermediate industrial materials.

Labor Resource Utilization

Because of an increasing shortage of factory workers at home, Japanese firms have been attracted to neighboring Asian countries where the supply of labor is abundant. This type of labor-resource-seeking venture serves to raise Japanese firms' marginal efficiency of capital, which has tended to decline recently due to rising wages (and often, sheer unavailability of workers for some categories of work). Those Japanese firms most adversely affected by the tightening labor market are, for the most part, small- and medium-sized enterprises. Their operations normally can be transplanted to low-labor-cost countries with a relatively small cost of "scaling-down" diseconomies, because they are less capital-intensive and relatively more efficient at operating on a small scale. In addition, some large Japanese enterprises are transferring the labor-intensive subsegments of their corporate production (for example, assembly production of semi-conductors) to labor-abundant countries.

The use of workers who are willing to toil at very low real wages, other things being equal, naturally leaves a large "rent" to entrepreneurs. In many cases, wages in Asian countries are kept low purposely by their governments to encourage the inflow of foreign capital and technology and to promote the export of labor-intensive products. Some developing countries, such as Taiwan and Singapore, go so far as to prohibit strikes. Labor unionism is practically nonexistent in these countries and in others where the masses are unemployed. Furthermore, Japanese ventures operating in such an environment rely on the lowest wage group of workers in the local labor market, because their operations are technologically unsophisticated. For example, it is said that in South Korea "Japan-related operations pay the lowest wages of all foreign-capital enterprises."[7]

The Japanese themselves are fully aware of the low wages paid by their enterprises overseas and are somewhat apologetic about them. Kazuji Nagasu observes:

> The dual structure of wages in Japanese industry—the great disparity between organized workers in large industries and workers in medium and small industries—is gradually being modified as high economic growth and the labor shortage take effect at home. At the same time, I think our old wage system is being exported overseas with Japanese business. The pattern of miserable wages for low-skilled, unorganized labor has been reproduced on a larger scale in Southeast Asia. Japanese corporations have moved into Thailand, Indonesia and South Korea in search of cheap labor; wages are a fraction of those paid in Japan. Those countries claim that Japan is using low wage scales to reap enormous profits, and I see no way to defend our position.[8]

Thus the dual structure of wages that has existed within the Japanese economy and that has permitted trade competitiveness in labor-intensive goods is now being shifted across borders, although still retained by Japanese industry.

On a theoretical level, the existence of unorganized labor is supposed to lead to the phenomenon that economists call "monopsonistic exploitation." In the absence of collective bargaining by trade unions the entrepreneurs, in order to maximize profits, can equate the marginal revenue product of labor to the marginal expense of labor instead of to its supply curve.[9] Yet this theoretical consideration is perhaps irrelevant for the labor-resource-utilizing ventures, because the supply curve of local labor, instead of being an upward-sloping curve, which gives rise to a difference between the marginal expense of labor and its supply curve, is quite possibly nearly horizontal at a very low (subsistence) wage rate because of the existence of surplus labor in developing countries. Hence, the problem of labor exploitation, if it exists, is not marginal, as envisaged in the theory of monopsonistic exploitation (a phenomenon that occurs in the absence of organized labor) but is rather more fundamental—the absolutely low level of wages which leaves, after the payment of a total wage bill, an abnormally large residual income (or rent) for the complementary factors, such as capital and technology, owned by foreign entrepreneurs.

Paul Streeten has aptly described the utilization of local labor by foreign enterprises:

> It is foreign, not domestic, capital, know-how, enterprise, management and marketing that are highly mobile internationally, and that are combined with the plentiful, but internationally immobile, domestic, semi-skilled labour. One set of factors (enterprise, management, knowledge and capital) are in relatively *inelastic* supply *in total*, but easily moved around the world and therefore in *highly elastic* supply *to any particular country*. The other factor, labour, is in *highly elastic* supply domestically but *immobile* across the frontiers.
>
> Specialization between countries follows not different commodity groups but different factors of production; the poor countries specializing in low-skilled labour, leaving the rewards of enterprise, capital, management and know-how to the foreign owners of these scarce, but internationally mobile, factors. The situation is equivalent to one in which plentiful unskilled or semi-skilled labour itself, rather than the product of labour, is exported. For the surplus of the product of labour over the wage, resulting from the co-operation of other factors in less elastic supply, accrues to foreigners.[10]

There is another important angle in the use of low-cost labor by Japanese enterprises. In the static theory of factor movement, the wage rate in a relatively labor-abundant country is supposed to rise with an inflow of capital, whereas that in a labor-scarce country to decline with an outflow of capital. In the final equilibrium, the two countries' wages are to be equalized. Capital, a relatively abundant factor in the labor-scarce country, will enjoy a rent from the use of abundant labor overseas. Or the same result, as Streeten observes, can be obtained if labor, instead of capital, moves from the labor-abundant country to the labor-scarce country. In order for wages to be equalized, however, it must be assumed, among other things, that the same line of labor-intensive industrial activities exists in both countries. But, contrary to these assumptions used in the standard theory of factor movement, the capital outflow from Japan is designed to transform Japan's own industrial structure both by transferring low-technology, labor-intensive industries to low-wage countries and by advancing further into high-technology, capital-intensive industries at home (that is, by the purposeful creation of a dual structure across her national borders). Wages in the host country normally tend to rise as labor-intensive productive activities are transplanted, but wages in Japan will rise even more, because operations requiring low skills are increasingly being replaced with the higher-value-added operations at home. Thus, a vertical international division of labor at different technological levels is fostered by Japan's overseas investment; the Japanese are specializing in higher-yielding industrial operations while the nationals of the host countries are concentrating on relatively low-yielding activities. (It is no wonder, then, that Japan's labor unions are not particularly opposed to Japanese overseas investments in labor-intensive industries.)[11]

Furthermore, there is no real possibility of labor movement to Japan from other Asian countries; the symmetrical relationship between capital and labor transfers envisioned in the theory of factor movement does not hold. Although one may speculate upon various schemes of economic integration similar to that of the EEC as possible forms of economic cooperation in Asia, Japan benefits from the nonexistence of such an arrangement. For if Japan belonged to a common market like the EEC, for example, with South Korea, Taiwan, and Hong Kong, there would be an inflow of low-cost labor from these neighboring countries. The result would be the continued existence of low-technology, labor-intensive industries in Japan, and consequently the upgrading of Japanese industry would be retarded. In addition, such labor migration, if it occurred, would surely cause social tensions, with problems similar to or perhaps even more aggravated than those experienced in West Germany, France, and the Netherlands with the influx of low-skilled workers from outside the EEC.

Thus, Japan's overseas investments in labor-intensive industries requiring low-skilled workers serve as a vital mechanism to houseclean and upgrade her industrial structure and to create in the process new opportunities both for capital to enjoy a monopoly rent from her overseas investments and for labor to attain higher skills. Labor-abundant developing countries are thus effectively used by Japan through her labor-resource-oriented investments, as a rung on the industrial ladder up which she may climb toward a more sophisticated, higher-technology economy as profits from overseas ventures are plowed back for this national objective. This theory is expressed most straightforwardly by a former MITI official:

> While certain segments of the industrial structure are being encouraged, there must be modification of those industries where productivity is low, where technology is stagnant and where there is reliance on simplistic intensified use of labor. . . . The solution of this problem is to be found according to economic logic, in progressively giving away industries to other countries, much as a big brother gives his out-grown clothes to his younger brother. In this way, a country's own industries become more sophisticated.[12]

One may argue that although the developing countries are subordinated as junior economic partners in this relationship, this is not necessarily deleterious to their interest, because the industries that can utilize their abundant factor of production, labor, are developed with the assistance of Japanese capital and technology. "[C]omparative profitabilities in trade-oriented foreign direct investment conform to the direction of potential comparative costs and, therefore, complement each other. In other words, foreign direct investment going from a comparatively disadvantageous industry in the investing country (which is a potentially comparatively advantageous industry in the host country) will harmoniously promote an upgrading of industrial structure on both sides and thus accelerate trade between the two countries."[13]

Japan has recently moved to eliminate barriers to the importation of labor-intensive manufactures from the developing countries in order to promote the more "harmonious" trade relationship envisaged above. Japan's adoption of the GSP for developing countries' exports is a first step in this direction, although it still leaves much to be desired. With further liberalization of import restrictions in Japan, a mutually complementary relationship could develop in the future. Nevertheless, a more fundamental issue about the vertical international division of labor of this sort stays unresolved. For the developing countries are not likely to remain forever satisfied with their specialization in less sophisticated, low-technology industries, which are controlled by foreign interests with an unfavorable distribution of income on their side. A serious source of tension always resides in this type of economic relationship.

Sociocultural and Political Sources of Friction

The Tradition of Insularity

The Japanese have a strong tradition of idiosyncratic national characteristics, because their culture has been formed within the confines of a geographically small island nation over many centuries. For approximately 200 years, from the mid-seventeenth century to the mid-nineteenth century, Japan intentionally secluded herself from the influence of the West. The opening of Japan's full-scale contact with the West in the late nineteenth century had considerable effect on Japanese society, especially in legal and institutional arrangements, but the unique modes of Japanese thought and behavior inherited from the feudalistic past have stayed largely intact.

Japan's trade, her major transboundary linkage with the rest of the world, has not brought with it many significant interactions with other countries on the sociocultural level, despite its phenomenal expansion after World War II. Trade relationships are essentially "impersonal," devoid of direct sociocultural interaction between the countries concerned; only inanimate objects, commodities, move between the countries. In contrast, the direct foreign investment now emerging as another major international linkage is an economic activity involving close human contacts and common work experience and therefore an interplay of sociocultural factors on the personal level.[14] Because Japan's manufacturing investment is concentrated in labor-intensive industries, opportunities for close human interactions and the chances for human conflict are considerable—probably much greater than those of Western counterparts, which tend to be centered mainly in large-scale, capital-intensive industries.

Largely as a result of Japan's insular tradition, the Japanese are poor social mixers in the international community (that is, in the outside world), and feel uncomfortable with foreigners and, for that matter, in any alien environment. Chie Nakane explains:

> The Japanese are often thought by foreigners to be very reserved. A more accurate description would be that Japanese on the whole are *not sociable*. This is partly because once outside their immediate orbit, they are at a loss for appropriate forms of expression. They have not developed techniques for dealing with persons "outside," because their lives are so tightly concentrated into their "own" groups. Within these groups, the Japanese could not be described as reserved. In virtue of the sense of unity fostered by the activities and emotions of the

group, each member is shaped to more or less the same mould, and forced to undergo the kneading effects of group interaction whether he likes it or not. The individual Japanese has little opportunity to learn sociability. Whatever security he feels is derived from aligning and matching himself with group purpose and plan; his circle is all he knows, and there is little real functional value in mere socializing.[15]

This observation applies to the general behavioral pattern of the Japanese in their relationships with each other at home. It is easy, therefore, to understand their extreme "shyness" with foreigners. Not only is theirs a group-oriented way of life, but from early childhood they have little opportunity at home to socialize with foreigners. They are taught at school about foreign countries, their different cultures, and languages—but always as something completely outside their own "system." Thus the average Japanese are gauche in their social interactions with foreigners and appear taciturn to outsiders.

Their taciturnity is further aggravated by their poor linguistic capability. Mizuo Kuroda, director-general of the Bureau of Public Information and Cultural Affairs, Japan's Ministry of Foreign Affairs, admits this weakness:

We have to increase our diplomatic and other efforts in proportion to the increase in our economic presence. Economic cooperation, technical assistance, cultural exchange, etc., should be more extensively promoted.

However, the insularity of the Japanese people is a heavy handicap in such efforts of ours. The number of Japanese capable of engaging in activities in the field of international exchange is lamentably limited. . . .

The heaviest handicap for Japanese working overseas lies, in most cases, in the language barrier. The Japanese weakness in speaking foreign languages is now legendary. It may derive from our national character—we are introverts and shy. . . .[16]

Thus their communication problem is no doubt a decisive factor in their tendency to remain isolated from the local population.

The Japanese stationed overseas have acquired a reputation for sticking together in groups, particularly in their activities outside their work. Professor Nakane also explains their clustering propensity as a way of defending themselves from a culture shock they experience overseas, a shock exacerbated by such an insulated home environment: "One should imagine how strong the culture shock is for a man who has come out of his homeland for the first time in his life. Not only the scenery changes, but also the entire rhythm of life, including the reactions of people. This culture shock makes him stick to his own way, which is the only way he can pull himself out of a state of disorganization. Thus, a Japanese will become more Japanese, thereby divorcing himself from the reality before him."[17]

Chie Nakane advances a typology concerning the reaction behavior of Japanese experiencing culture shock overseas, and observes that a majority of Japanese typically react by retreating into their own system (that is, by forming an exclusive enclave in the foreign community), but that there are also some significant number of Japanese who "escape" into the local community:

> One of the distinguishable characteristics of [the] Japanese . . . is the strong attachment to Japanese culture, as indicated by the fact that their companions are always found among the local Japanese where they are stationed. Further analysis of such a Japanese behavior pattern reveals that it is not because of mere "Japaneseness," it is more correct to say that it is the habit of strong one-way affiliation. As a matter of fact, in Southeast Asia there are many cases where an individual Japanese has become one of [the] locals divorced from his own people. There are some Japanese who have remained in the country after having married local women and establishing businesses in the local community. These Japanese usually sever their relationships with their own people: In a sociological sense they become non-Japanese. They think that these Japanese have become fishes of another pond. In this sense, the degree of localization

of a Japanese is extremely high, which is quite different from the case of Chinese or Indian people who wherever they may go, and no matter how long they may stay, maintain strong networks with their own people.

In comparison with these people, the nature of the sociological relationship for Japanese is quite different. The function and strength of Japanese personal ties depends to a great extent on the situation in which individuals are placed. The maintenance of a close relationship requires tangible and constant dealings. Therefore, a set of persons who meet frequently develops a group feeling and takes on a kind of exclusive character. One's affiliation to a group naturally becomes singular.

This is why it is not easy for a Japanese man who is overseas to have equally close relations with members of the local Japanese community and also the local people who belong to entirely different groups. It can be only done by those who are quite sophisticated and outward looking and who at the same time have already acquired the firm confidence of their Japanese colleagues. Otherwise, one is too busy cultivating friendship with members of his own community to establish a closer relation with locals who are outside the group. If a man who looks for [a] closer relation with locals is not [a] fully accepted member of [the] Japanese community, he goes to the locals and the relationship with his own people tends to become weaker—such men normally try to keep themselves outside of the local Japanese community.

Indeed, for a Japanese, it requires special talent and techniques to cross freely the boundary between the local Japanese community and others. . . .[18]

This observation is limited to Japanese in Asian countries. The Japanese stationed in advanced Western countries, particularly in the United States, seem not so polarized in their behavioral pattern, however. There are many who can "freely cross the boundary." In the developing countries the Japanese normally "protect" themselves from a lower local standard of living by forming an enclave, and those who have become "locals" may be looked down upon by their compatriots. Thus, the local community is a "less preferred" entity, and not much effort is made by the Japanese to acclimate themselves. By contrast, the local community in an advanced Western country is a "more preferred" entity socially, culturally, and economically, and the Japanese are eager to adopt the local way of living. Enclaves in the advanced countries, if they exist, serve to avoid the sheer inconvenience of communicating in the local language or to alleviate the deep-seated inferiority complex held by the majority of the prewar generation of the Japanese toward Westerners. The propensity of the Japanese to be assimilated into the local community is thus much higher when they are in the advanced countries than in the developing countries. Particularly in the United States, the prevalence of egalitarian social values (emanating from the existence of heterogeneous ethnic and racial groups, the predominance of the middle-income class, widespread education, and a high standard of living) facilitate socializing between the Japanese and the local people, as well as between the incoming Japanese and the "localized" Japanese.

As Japanese overseas ventures become more polycentric in ownership and management, Japanese stationed overseas can no longer remain ethnocentric in their personal behavior. The tendency of the Japanese toward isolation so far observed abroad is due in no small part to a lack of the polycentric orientation of their overseas business itself. With the waning of ethnocentric philosophy in Japanese overseas business and with a gradual replacement of the prewar generation of Japanese businessmen by the young, more internationally educated generation, the behavior of Japanese businessmen will probably "improve." After all, it is important to realize that the postwar generation now is more than half the Japanese population. The youngsters are, it is said, quickly losing "the notorious shyness of their forebears" and can "effortlessly ease themselves into the international society—a feat almost unthinkable for older generation Japanese."[19]

Overemployment of Japanese Nationals

Japanese factories overseas are often criticized for the excessive use of Japanese nationals dispatched from the home offices. Although criticism is at times exaggerated, there is a strong tendency on the part of Japanese parent companies to staff foreign operations with employees sent from Japan. Since such a practice means fewer opportunities for employment and job training for the local community, local resentment is natural. Reportedly, the MITI, keenly aware of the problem of overstaffing factories with Japanese nationals, included in its set of guidelines governing the conduct of Japan's overseas ventures a rule that at least thirty local people should be hired for each Japanese brought from home.[20]

Local criticism made Japanese firms aware of this problem, and they now consciously reduce the number of Japanese nationals assigned to their overseas posts. But overemployment of Japanese was probably very common in the early days of Japan's multinationalism. During the 1950s and 1960s an overseas assignment was considered a reward or a privilege by company employees; such an assignment was in many cases made on the basis of seniority. This "elite" image of overseas assignment has rather eroded in recent years, however, because of an increase in the number of such opportunities available and because overseas pleasure travel is now within the reach of the average Japanese.

But foreign assignments are still eagerly sought by newly recruited, young employees who are either single or who, if married, have no school-age children. These people are willing to go to practically any foreign country, because overseas posts normally mean both higher financial rewards and more varied cultural and social amenities than can be enjoyed in overcrowded Japan. There is also the lure of adventure in overseas assignment. It is said that Japanese youth crave "variety, more visible rewards, challenge, and even adventure in their work," and that "overwhelming majorities of high school and college graduates desire to work overseas at some time or other."[21] Indeed, it is the general trading companies, airlines, travel agents, and other overseas-venture-active companies that attract a large number of job applicants from school graduates each year.

Naturally, advanced Western countries are more popular as places of assignment than developing countries, because it is the former that offer such cultural opportunities as visits to museums, operas, symphonies, and other recreational facilities, many of which are, in fact, dreams of most Japanese. On the other hand, however, assignments in developing countries often offer a comfortable life—usually with a couple of domestic servants, a luxury the Japanese cannot afford at home.

Japan's high cost of living is another factor that makes foreign assignments attractive. Tokyo is probably the world's most expensive city. Costs of housing and meat in particular are prohibitively high. It is no wonder that Western corporations operating in Japan usually keep the number of personnel sent from home to a minimum and employ as many locals as possible. Even with extra compensation for services overseas, the managers of Western corporations—and their families in particular —are generally unhappy about staying in Tokyo.

The Japanese who can escape sardine-packed commuter trains, cramped company houses, and congested industrial cities are blessed in comparison with their Western counterparts as well as with their compatriots who must stay at home. It should, moreover, be noted that in 1973, the fiftieth anniversary of the worst earthquake in Japanese history, pessimism suddenly surged, because a major earthquake is believed to occur about every 50 years—an apocalyptic feeling that the end of Japan might be at hand. A science fiction tale, *Japan Sinks*, a best seller later made into a film, no doubt fueled such a fear to a considerable extent, but it is not an unreasonable one; in present overcrowded conditions, a couple of million Japanese might fall victim to a major quake. Although the Arab oil crisis and the subsequent economic recession diverted the attention of the public, there still persists a deep-seated frustration because there is no way to prevent the recurrence of a major earthquake. With this frustration is commingled a sense of helplessness in the face of overcrowded conditions and a deteriorating natural environment. There are, indeed, many Japanese who would be happy to migrate overseas if appropriate opportunities were granted. Thus, while Western multinational corporations may be finding their personnel less than eager to be stationed in Tokyo, there is, by and large, no such pressure on Japanese corporations operating abroad.

In addition to the attractiveness of overseas living, Japan's unique managerial practice of lifetime employment and promotion based on seniority may also contribute to the tendency to overemploy Japanese nationals in her overseas ventures. For new overseas managerial and supervisory posts could be used to solve problems of internal overcrowding in many Japanese corporations. In this connection it is interesting to note what a Japanese business journal points out as one of the major reasons why it thinks "much greater investment overseas and greater utilization of industrial sites abroad . . . must be pursued":

> Basically, a population of 110 million is simply too large for the Japanese Archipelago. It can be said that the present living standard is the best that can be expected if this number is to be supported on these islands alone. If an improvement in the standard of living is desired, we must be prepared for a number of side effects, such as further deterioration of our environment and greater critcisms from abroad. From this standpoint, the Japanese personnel that would be needed [overseas] . . . and the resultant emigration would be developments that would be greatly welcome by these overcrowded islands.[22]

The above argument does not present a strong case. Overseas assignments are minuscule relative to either Japan's total labor force or her population; the number of Japanese nationals currently employed by their overseas ventures is possibly no more than 40,000.[23] Nevertheless, it does reflect the attitude of the Japanese toward overseas working opportunities created by their direct foreign investments.

The geographical distribution of Japan's overseas ventures, numbers of Japanese stationed abroad, and numbers of local people employed by these ventures are compared in figure 6.1. As of 1971, although only 22.4 percent of Japan's overseas ventures were located in North America (Canada and the United States), this region accounted for as much as 45.3 percent of the total number of Japanese personnel stationed abroad but for only 16.9 percent of the total number of local people employed by Japanese ventures. In contrast, Asian countries, in which 39.3 percent of Japan's overseas investments were located, absorbed 26.2 percent of the Japanese stationed overseas and had the largest share of the total local labor force working for Japanese ventures, 63.5 percent. These patterns indicate that Japanese operations in North America are relatively more intensive in the use of personnel dispatched from Japan, while those in Asia are relatively more intensive in the use of local labor. This is exactly in line with the fact that Japanese ventures in Asia are mainly designed to use low-cost labor, while those in North America are mostly commercial- and service-oriented industries. But a greater Japanese presence in North America and other Western countries than in economically backward developing countries is also attributable to better living conditions and less open antagonism against the Japanese in the former, as mentioned above. According to a more recent survey made by the MITI in 1975, the average number of Japanese nationals stationed per venture is highest in North America, 19.9; in Europe 8.6; in Oceania 4.7; in the Middle East 3.9; in Africa 2.8; in Latin America 1.9; and in Asia 1.2.[24]

Thus there is a tendency to dispatch Japanese personnel abroad, but the problem of overemployment of Japanese nationals has often been exaggerated through misunderstanding. When a Japanese plant is set up for the first time in a particular

Figure 6.1

Geographical Distributions of Japan's Overseas Ventures,
Japanese Personnel Stationed Abroad, and Local Personnel
in Japanese Ventures, 1971

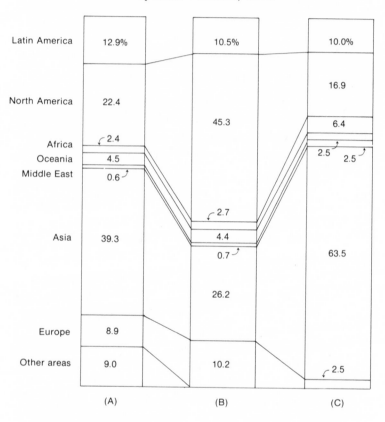

(A) Japanese overseas ventures, based on number of ventures as of the end of 1971.
(B) Japanese businessmen stationed overseas. (The share of other areas is excluded.) (Assignment longer than one year.)
(C) Local personnel in Japan's overseas ventures. (The share of other areas is excluded.)

Source: Compiled from data in MITI, *Nihon Kigyo no Kokusaiteki
Tenkai* [International spread of Japanese enterprises], p. 92 and appendix
p. 7 as presented in Ozawa, "Sociocultural Problems," p. 9.

foreign community, natives are both curious and ignorant. For example, as *The Wall Street Journal* reported, American NTN Bearing, a subsidiary of Tokyo Bearing, had been considered a "mystery plant" in the Chicago community until it held an open house to dispel rumors of various sorts; for example, it was said that "the Japanese firm was flying whole planeloads of workers to Chicago from Japan to work at rock-bottom wages" and that "when their 90 day visas expired they would be shipped home, only to be replaced by a fresh crew of workers from Japan."[25] This sort of episode illustrates that the old image of Japanese workers is still prevalent in the West and, perhaps more important, that Japan's overseas ventures lack experience in public relations.

Another important source of misunderstanding is the hiring practice that prefers persons of Japanese descent, a practice that inevitably suggests that the ventures are overstaffed with Japanese nationals. The main reason for this practice is that the employment of local Japanese descendants helps establish better communications both inside and outside the firm, because most Japanese are, as discussed above, not fluent in local languages. The reverse is also often true; local people who speak Japanese (one of the most difficult languages to master) may be rare, except in some Asian countries such as Taiwan or South Korea.

Also, some Japanese overseas ventures require the use of Japanese nationals or persons of Japanese descent. Overseas investments in the service sectors (hotels and recreational facilities) are in many cases aimed at catering to Japanese tourists and businessmen. A prime example is Japanese investment in Hawaii. "While Japanese-Americans make up 27 percent of the total population of Hawaii, they comprise 70 percent of all the employees of Japanese firms. Together with the 17.8 percent of Japanese nationals employed by these firms, a total of 88 percent of all employees are of Japanese extraction. The number of Japanese nationals per firm averages out to 4.8 persons. In many cases the owner of the firm and one or two close associates make up the entire Japanese staff of a firm. It is also remarkable to note that the highest number of Japanese nationals employed by any firm is sixteen. Hence the charge sometimes heard that local workers are being replaced by Japanese nationals seems to be without foundation."[26] It should be noted here that Japanese ventures in Hawaii are mostly small-scale operations concentrated in the tourist industry. The number of Japanese nationals stationed elsewhere in the United States is much higher, particularly in commerce-related activities (trading companies). Moreover, the presence of a large number of Japanese tourists and transient businessmen attracted by their own ventures further intensifies the impression that the Japanese are overstaffing in Hawaii and elsewhere.

Political Factors

Because Japanese direct foreign investments are concentrated in developing countries, they are affected by the precarious political situations existing there. In these countries income distributions are invariably skewed, with a wide gap between the ruling elites and the masses, the local governments in power representing the interest of the former but scarcely the latter. Democracy or any system of political representation is still in a rudimentary stage of development, and the governing authorities are largely isolated from the people—not infrequently kept in power by the exercise of authoritarian rules such as martial law, as has been seen in Thailand, Indonesia, South Korea, and the Philippines.

Thus political instability is a common feature of developing countries. In fact, some argue that industrialization, especially in its early stages, disturbs the system of traditional values and mores, aggravates the problems of urbanization with a conversion of rural "disguised" unemployment into "open" unemployment in the cities,[27] and leads to a state of sociopsychological derangement and ennui—a cause of political dissatisfaction and instability.[28] Hence, the more rapid the pace of industrialization, the greater the possibility of political unrest.

It is against this political backdrop that Japan's overseas ventures operate. Precisely because multinational corporations reputedly serve as an engine of industrialization, they are inevitably held responsible for the social and economic malaise associated with economic development. Besides, a view commonly prevails that the benefits of economic development fostered by multinationals are not equitably distributed among different social groups. Robert W. Cox contends: "The pattern of growth promoted by private foreign investment has accentuated the discrepancy between geographical poles of growth and the hinterland—between the São Paulos and the Nordestes—and has exacerbated inequalities in the distribution of incomes between social groups within countries, in large part because of the very limited employment-creating effect of this kind of growth."[29]

To the extent that Japanese ventures in developing countries —other than those in the extractive industries—are intended to use low-cost labor, they do contribute to the creation of employment. Yet they are frequently looked upon as "exploiters" whose exploitation is sanctioned by the totalitarian host government; this view is held both by social critics deeply concerned about widening income inequality and by social groups who are not allowed to partake of the immediate fruits of development. "Regimes which rely substantially upon MNCs to produce growth have consciously sacrificed the 'less fit,' among whom the social marginals loom larger and larger. This is politically possible only if the less fit remain unable to protest effectively, and if such protest as they do make can be effectively repressed. Repression becomes a political condition for a pattern of growth which generates marginality. But the coercive state has its own autonomy, and the military-bureaucratic regimes born of this process acquire through it also in time the ability to extract greater concessions from the foreign investors they have admitted."[30]

Thus, by necessity, Japanese overseas ventures establish close cooperative ties with local government officials and local business interests—and this collaboration is, unfortunately, often accompanied by corruption. Indeed, it appears to be an open secret that Japanese businessmen—and for that matter American and European as well—are actively engaged in "business-by-payoff" practices. According to Gunnar Myrdal:

> Western business representatives never touch on this matter publicly, but, as the writer can testify, in private conversation they are frank to admit that it is necessary to bribe high officials and politicians in order to get a business deal through and to bribe officials both high and low in order to run their businesses without too many obstacles. They are quite explicit about their own experiences and those of other firms. These bribes, they say, constitute a not inconsiderable part of their total costs of doing business in South Asian countries. Although hardly any foreign company can make it an absolute rule to abstain from giving bribes, it is apparent that there is a vast difference in regard to the willingness to bribe, not only between companies but also between nationalities. Among the Western nations, French, American, and, especially, West German companies are usually said to have the least inhibitions about bribing their way through. Japanese firms are said to be even more willing to pay up.[31]

This type of practice by multinationals may help create a close relationship with local government officials but certainly alienates the multinationals from the general public. Bribery or not, a close collaboration between foreign business interests and the local elite itself worsens existing tensions between the elite and the masses for whom social critics often appear as spokesmen. In this connection, it is pertinent to note a statement made by an executive of a Japanese company after the anti-Japanese demonstrations during Prime Minister Tanaka's Asian tour, as quoted by Kazuji Nagasu: "The trouble was completely unexpected. As far as we could tell from our contacts with Southeast Asian businessmen, relations were quite amicable. Government officials also appreciate our presence because it helps them to develop their local automobile industries."[32] Nagasu is quite right in emphasizing the statement and pointing out that "Japanese officials maintain close contact only with officialdom in the host country. The Japanese *zaibatsu* confer only with their counterparts in other countries. Both groups meet the 'local people' only in the most formal and elegant settings. Discussions take place over tables laden with sumptuous food and the drinks flow freely. It is naturally appropriate for the side proffering the aid to be warmly welcomed and gain a sense of acceptance, but do all the people in the host country get invited to the party?"[33] In this sense, Japan's overseas ventures in developing countries remain essentially an "enclave." But this is perhaps what is generally expected of foreign investment in developing countries, and Japanese investment is not unique. "The multinational corporation . . . has different impacts upon periphery countries according to what stage of development they are in. In countries at a primary stage of modernization they are likely to take the form of enclaves with little interaction with the rest of a population but highly significant for local governments and economies. At a high stage of development, on the contrary, they are likely to be intermeshed throughout the entire social and political network prevailing in a country and to have indirect impacts for which they take few responsibilities."[34]

There is another angle of Japanese multinationals' collaboration with the local elites that leads to heightened social tension and resentment in many Asian countries (that is, their economic involvement with overseas Chinese businessmen). Japanese companies, when they first moved into other Asian markets, found it necessary to cultivate cordial relationships with overseas Chinese interests, which controlled local distribution and finance. It was a rational choice for many Japanese manufacturers to choose as their partners in their new local ventures those Chinese merchants who used to be their import agents.

In general, the Japanese found much closer cultural and motivational affinities in the Chinese than in the local people. However, there is a deep-seated resentment against the economic dominance of overseas Chinese in such Asian countries as Indonesia, Malaysia, and Thailand. The Japanese, by joining economic forces with this particular local interest, unwittingly have made themselves targets of local resentment. For overseas Chinese are in many instances not even officially regarded as truly "local" partners, as is the case with Malaysia. Note the incidence of anti-Japanese demonstrations in Indonesia in which Chinese-owned stores of Japanese car dealerships were destroyed. Raul S. Manglapus observes:

> The Japanese embassy in Jakarta has confirmed that more than 70 percent of Japanese investors in Indonesia have taken on ethnic Chinese as their joint-venture partners. This is particularly interesting in a country where thousands of Chinese were killed in the bloodbath of 1965 and where attempts at assimilation (including forced adoption of Indonesian names) have not been a spectacular success. The changing of names, in fact, appears to have camouflaged the continued Chinese control of the economy. . . .
>
> Soedjatmoko, the distinguished Indonesian intellectual and consultant to the Indonesian Planning Board (BAPENAS), warns of the "hidden political cost" for the future in the Japanese rush, "due to lack of time," to nonindigenous or Chinese partners in order to make quick profits. He suggests that a Japanese shift to long-term lending and long-range profit-taking might encourage the Japanese investors to take on less-prepared and lesser-financed indigenous partners and head off what appears to be an eventual political explosion.[35]

Conclusions

Drawing mainly upon Asian experiences, this chapter has analyzed some of the significant sources of friction between investing Japanese firms and the local interests of the host countries.

Most of these sources are inherent in the new international economic relationships that Japan has woven through the peculiar patterns of her direct foreign investment, such as the regional and industrial concentration of Japanese overseas ventures, their support of trade in favor of Japan, and a vertical international division of labor in which developing countries are subordinated technologically.

This situation is further aggravated by the unique behavioral patterns of Japanese business organizations and of the Japanese themselves. More important, however, the politico-economic structure of developing countries is such that Japanese investors of necessity collaborate with the local elites, the privileged whose interests are protected in many instances by autocratic regimes.

In response to waves of anti-Japanese demonstrations and rising complaints about the "ugly Japanese," Japanese government and industry have introduced behavioral standards or codes to prevent undesirable activities. Yet the behavioral problem is, after all, only contributory, not the basic source of tension. More fundamental reasons for friction are the newly emerging patterns of economic relationship created by Japan's direct foreign investment and the perilous politico-economic environment of developing countries, both largely the outcome of the very process of the transitional stages of economic development. Until the developing countries attain both a high standard of living with a more equitable distribution of income and a system of democratic political representation, these basic sources of tension will not be eliminated.

Chapter 7

General Assessment

Momentum and Accommodation

A number of Japanese institutions have ventured to predict the size of Japan's future overseas investments. For example, in March 1972 the Japan Economic Research Center forecast that by 1980 the outstanding balance of Japan's overseas investments would have increased tenfold from its 1967 level of $2.7 billion to $27.3 billion, a level surpassed only by the United States and West Germany, and that about one-half of the total (50.8 percent) would be in ventures designed to serve the supply of natural resources (mainly, mining), about one-fourth (26.2 percent) in manufacturing designed to use low-cost labor and to capture local markets, and the rest (23.0 percent) in service-related ventures (banking, insurance, commerce, and leisure industries).[1] Then, in July 1974, the center offered a revised forecast. Assuming Japan's economic growth rate to be 5 percent, Japan's overseas investments would grow at 24 percent per annum and by 1980 reach a total of $38.5 billion. If the growth rate were 9 percent, overseas investments would be $46.0 billion by 1980.[2]

Another prediction made in April 1974 by the Mitsui Bank, a leading private bank, was more optimistic.[3] It suggested that the outstanding value of Japan's overseas investments would reach $48.7 billion in 1980, about fourteen times the 1970 level of $3.6 billion. According to the bank's prediction, 40.0 percent would be in resource-oriented ventures, 37.0 percent in manufacturing, and 22.0 percent in service sectors. It also foresaw a further shift in the distribution of investments by region: the share of developing countries would rise from 49.1 percent in 1970 to 55.0 percent in 1980, while that of industrialized countries would fall. Interestingly enough, it also predicted that by 1980 the Communist countries would attract approximately $1.5 billion worth of Japan's direct investments, accounting for 3 percent of the total.

These projections were followed in 1974 by a study made by the Industrial Structure Council, an advisory organ of the MITI. It predicted that by 1985 the outstanding total would amount to $93.5 billion.[4]

The sharply increasing trend suggested by these forecasts reflects a rising awareness by both government and industry of the national need to transfer and to expand productive activities abroad and a conviction that such a scheme of global production for Japan will be accommodated in the rest of the world without serious strain. Government and industry are aware that the domestic factors that generate "push effects" on Japan's overseas investments—rising wages and the resulting loss of competitiveness in the labor-intensive segment of manufacturing activities, a growing shortage of industrial sites for pollution-prone industries, continued dependency on open-market transactions to secure vital industrial resources and the resulting need for the D & I version of investment—have intensified. Moreover, government and industry anticipate a further strengthening of "pull effects" on Japan's productive activities abroad, particularly from the developing countries. One such prospect exists in Southeast Asian countries, where ever-growing labor populations are expected to impel their governments to seek an increased inflow of Japanese capital and technology in order to create employment opportunities.[5] Similarly, Latin American countries, hitherto dominated by U.S. investments, are increasingly turning to Japan for alternative economic assistance, as is best exemplified by Brazil. Countries in the Middle East are likewise strengthening their economic ties with the Japanese economy in connection with their efforts to industrialize. Africa is still virgin territory—its rich natural endowment and vast potential market await development. There will also be more commercial ties with the Communist countries, which, despite their ideological conflict with the capitalistic mode of industrialization, are pragmatically inclined to acquire advanced technologies, capital for large-scale projects, and export markets.[6]

Paradoxically, a recent shift of bargaining power away from the multinational corporation toward the host countries, particularly those with resource-rich endowments, is in many ways a favorable turn of events for Japanese industry, which has just begun to participate in the worldwide game of multinationalism. Until quite recently, the world's key resources were largely controlled by a handful of powerful Western interests, so that Japan was able to obtain only the spillover of resource supplies generated by those Western interests. Fortunately the supplies were both abundant and secure, and Japan actually benefited as a buyer without direct involvement in resource exploration. But increasing demand for industrial resources, coupled with the new political power gained by capitalizing on power struggles between the Western and the Socialist bloc, have helped the resource-rich developing countries to begin to effectively control access to their national resources. That access is now open equally to Japan and to Western interests. International bidding is becoming a standard procedure.

In addition, the developing countries now increasingly restrict the entry of foreign capital in key extractive industries and other strategically important sectors—mostly with the establishment of state enterprises that either preclude foreign participation or demand a majority share in ownership and management. Here Japanese multinationals on the whole are more accommodating; they are more inclined to work out compromises with the demands of the host countries than are their U.S. counterparts. It is well known that, while U.S. multinationals may insist on complete or majority ownership, Japanese firms are more often than not quite willing to accept minority ownership. Richard J. Barnet and Ronald E. Müller, for example, observe:

> The new flexibility that permits poor countries to demand competitive bidding is a consequence of the sharpening economic competition among the rich countries, which more and more have similar resource needs. Until the late 1950's or early 1960's (depending upon the region), U.S.-based global companies dominated foreign investment almost everywhere. But between 1965 and 1971 the growth rate of German and Japanese foreign investment was approximately triple the U.S. rate. In many cases the Japanese have been able to offer better terms than the Americans. (The Minister of Fuels of a Latin American country told us that Japanese, German, and East European companies were bidding for mineral concessions which fifteen years ago would have gone as a matter of course to a U.S. corporation. The Japanese, he explained, offered much the best terms.) Indeed, it frequently happens that the Japanese, who are significantly increasing their investment in Brazil among other places in Latin America, are able to outbid the Americans.[7]

According to a survey made by the MITI in 1975, minority ownership (less than 50 percent equity ownership) accounts for 43.9 percent of 3,214 Japanese overseas ventures surveyed, while wholly-owned operations (more than 95 percent equity ownership) account for 39.3 percent.[8] Minority ownership is as high as 59.7 percent in Asia and reaches 72.9 percent in the Middle East and Africa. In contrast, the minority ownership of U.S.-based multinationals is on the average as small as 8.3 percent.[9]

The Japanese firms have a high propensity to "cooperate" because the social and the private benefits of overseas investment are immeasurably high for the Japanese economy—in most cases the former are clearly higher than the latter. The outward expansion of Japanese enterprises results from their struggle to escape from the Ricardo-Hicksian trap of industrialism, a phenomenon that does not exist in the United States. The majority of Japanese manufacturers investing overseas are "immature" in size and technological sophistication by Western standards. Trading companies are exceptions, but by themselves they are incapable of becoming multinational investors; they are organizers, requiring as their joint-venture partners manufacturers or resource-processors. On the other hand, U.S. multinationals, most of which are R & D-based manufacturers, are moving outward by themselves more or less as an organic growth of individual business organizations, displaying the oligopolistic, discrete behavior of the Galbraithian technostructure. Overseas production is, then, a postponable luxury for most U.S. manufacturers, as pointed out by Richard E. Caves: "[B]ecause information costs associated with undertaking a foreign investment are both heavy and relatively fixed, small but rising firms that might someday find direct investment profitable may rationally postpone it until their penetration of the home market is more advanced."[10]

For Japan, in contrast, overseas production has suddenly emerged as a national requirement encompassing practically the entire spectrum of her industries and enterprises, small and large alike. The segments of industrial activities that are no longer suitable, environmentally or otherwise, for the Japanese economy need to be transplanted abroad, and overseas resources now must be developed more directly to insure supplies. Whether or not the individual firms affected have gained an advantage because of size and developed an internal structure mature enough for overseas production is almost immaterial and they are all compelled to expand abroad—hence the extension of organizational assistance by trading companies to Japanese manufacturers, particularly small ones; the unique formation of mutually supportive group investments (within, as well as between, industrial groups) as a way of compensating for small size; and the provision of government loans, subsidies, and other incentives to promote direct foreign investment. The underdeveloped state of the Galbraithian technostructure, then, in most Japanese firms is compensated for by the unique formation of Japan's *macro-technostructure*.

Furthermore, overseas investment is now viewed as an essential device by which to upgrade Japanese industry and to make Japan's foreign economic aid more "effective." The Japanese government's integration of overseas investment in both its over-all economic growth strategy and its foreign economic policy sharply contrasts with the rather vacillating attitude of the U.S. government toward its own multinationals. The U.S. government "has not even made up its mind whether to recognize the existence of the MNE [multinational enterprise] in foreign economic policies, much less whether it is good or how it should be treated."[11] Ironically, the nature and size of the U.S. economy —the existence of diversified interests among vigorously competing economic units which is the mainspring of oligopolistic U.S. multinationalism—seems in part responsible for the lack of solid and unified government support, for it is difficult for the government to come up with a policy impartial to competing interests.[12] To be sure, before World War II, American corporations played an important role as agents of the political domination of the United States over Latin America; and in the postwar years (particularly in the 1950s and the early 1960s), the U.S. political hegemony of the free world was, in turn, the "necessary" if not a "sufficient" condition for U.S. corporations to dominate the world market as multinationals. "The Multinational corporation has prospered because it has been dependent on the power of, and consistent with the political interests of the United States."[13] But against the backdrop of a steady decline of U.S. power, U.S. multinationals with their expanding overseas operations inevitably began to act outside the sphere of influence of their home country and often against their national interests; as a result, the United States is politically ambivalent about its multinationals. By comparison, the growth of overseas investment by Japanese corporations has just begun to be promoted by the government, essentially to meet Japan's national interests.

The Japanese economy is engaged in a desperate search for a stable supply of overseas resources, having been trapped in an abnormal pattern of heavy resource consumption. In order to make her overseas extractive ventures as palatable to the host country as possible, Japan is offering these ventures more and more in the form of what may be called "a development assistance package." It includes the downstream processing stages of the extractive industries, complete with the development of infrastructure (power, transport, and communications), if required, and a variety of related manufacturing ventures. In particular, processing activities are likely to be transferred from Japan at a much faster pace than from any other industrialized countries—partly because of Japan's environmental constraints and, perhaps more importantly, because in the past she has "tended to purchase raw materials at a lower stage of processing than other developed countries."[14] Because Japan is the major buyer of unprocessed resources in several countries, this monopsonistic position also facilitates her overseas investment in processing activities by assuring a minimum scale of operation.

The development assistance package has begun to emerge as a major formula in Japan's bilateral economic assistance program, as demonstrated in such countries as Indonesia and Brazil, and it is definitely in the interest of the Japanese economy to continue to move in this direction. "Because of its unusually strong foreign exchange position and investment capability, Japan in the 1970s is in a better position than any other power to take the lead in more ambitious development programs if it can make the decision to do so and design a program that expands its welcome rather than increases suspicions or hostility toward it."[15]

Indeed, a peculiar match of economic interest between Japan and the Third World is in the making with respect to the transfer of resource-processing activities, the establishment of labor-intensive industries, the transfer of "intermediate" technologies (which are more suitable to the local conditions than those used in capital-intensive manufacturing), and the relatively strong export orientation of Japan's overseas ventures.

In this regard Japan's multinationalism is definitely taking a a unique evolutionary path. The ultimate modal form of multi-nationalism—if it is allowed to take its own course unhampered by the parochial interventions of nation-states—is said to be "geocentric," the final stage being one in which "the international corporation has no country to which it owes more loyalty than any other, nor any country where it feels completely at home,"[16] and in which the operations of the corporation are internationally integrated (the corporation acquires and organizes into production various factor inputs from and at different places in the world and markets products worldwide under the least-cost and the maximum-profit principle).

This situation is no doubt the best for multinationals and for pure economic efficiency, but the realization of such a world is increasingly impeded by economic nationalism in the host countries, particularly those developing ones which now prefer to see—and often demand—a more nationally integrated operation of the multinational corporation. There are good economic reasons behind this attitude; the developing host countries desire to increase value-added operations by internalizing industrial linkages that can be captured through a vertical and horizontal integration of industry at home. Put more simply, the operations of a truly geocentric multinational firm are incompatible with the interests of the developing countries. After all, nationally integrated operation is the only effective way to avoid the economic costs of so-called transfer pricing by multinationals.

Because truly geocentric multinationalism is unattainable because of the strong desire of the developing host countries to pursue a more locally integrated, self-contained form of industrialization, the host country orientation increasingly exhibited by Japanese industry is probably a "second-best" solution. This orientation is practically a prerequisite for resource-development investment, because the supply of natural resources is far more country-specific than are other factors of production such as labor and industrial sites. Besides, it is in natural resource development that the marketplace is most politicized, and political considerations often override economic calculation. Hence, by necessity, Japan's overseas extractive ventures will be custom-tailored to the specific needs of the host countries, and will be more and more vertically integrated locally. But this trend is also advantageous for Japanese industry. For group investment offers them a way of becoming more effective in establishing locally integrated operations because the majority of Japanese firms seeking overseas production are not large enough to set up internationally integrated operations. In short, a host-country-oriented bilateral multinationalism—in contrast to a globally oriented geocentric multinationalism—will be a predominant operational mode of Japanese enterprises in the resource-abundant countries.

Concurrent with this growing bilateralism of economic ties with the resource-rich regions, a vertical international division of labor will continue to be pursued by Japanese industry with the resource-poor but labor-abundant developing regions. The production of products that are less capital-intensive, less so- phisticated, and less value-added will continue to be phased out of Japan's industrial structure and transplanted to low labor- cost countries—mostly to Asian countries as in the past, but increasingly to Latin American countries and possibly to some African countries in the future. These investments in labor-in- tensive manufacturing, for the most part, will take the form of joint ventures with local interests—partly to save capital and partly to reduce friction with local interests. Many of these manufacturing ventures either will be export-oriented at the be- ginning or will become so oriented eventually. It is through this development that advanced Western economies, the United States in particular, are most likely to be confronted with the problem of import invasion in their declining labor-intensive industrial sectors. Interestingly enough, therefore, Japan's overseas production will more directly threaten the interest of U.S. labor unions than will the overseas production of U.S. multinationals, who are often blamed for the problem of manufactured imports. U.S. overseas investment has a relatively small impact on domestic employment. Raymond Vernon explains:

> With the activities of United States-based multinational enterprises strongly concentrated in industries where oligopoly prevails, one implication begins to be evident. The products that have been prominent as "problems" in the exports of developing countries to the United States are a quite different group from those in which multinational enterprises tend to concentrate. The goods that are the focus of complaints by labour and business in the United States generally come from industries that are well dispersed in structure, not industries that are highly concentrated. For the most part the goods involved in such complaints are highly standardized products, sold in international markets by many different sources according to standard specifications. . . . Textiles are the case *par excellence.* . . .[17]

From the viewpoint of labor unions and import-injured industries in the United States (even though they may not be aware of this), Japan's multinationals are actively engaged in the manufacturing of the "problem" products. In this respect, U.S. multinationals may be scapegoats for the activities of their Japanese brethren.

In contrast, Japan already has opened up her domestic market to the "problem" imports to a much greater extent than any of the other industrialized countries. "By 1973, according to the United Nations Conference on Trade and Development Secretariat in Geneva, developing countries were supplying more than 25% of Japan's total imports of manufactured products. This was much higher than the 17.5% share of U.S. manufactured imports held by developing countries and the 3.2% in the European Free Trade Association countries. Of total imports of manufactured products from developing countries by 21 industrial countries, Japan accounted for more than 14%."[18]

Although this development has not been without problems at home, Japan is inclined to capitalize on its positive impact: sharply increased import competition from the developing countries—both at home and in the third-country markets— spurs Japanese industry to raise its technological level and take up more sophisticated lines of production. An upgrading structural transformation is being forced upon Japanese industry. In this respect the Japanese economy is perhaps structurally flexible; in Europe the migration of low-skilled workers tends to perpetuate the existence of low-technology industries, and in the United States strong labor unions likewise hinder the relocation of low-technology industries overseas. No other industrial country, at the moment, is so bent on transforming her industrial structure as is Japan. In addition to transplanting overseas the labor-intensive, low-value-added end of her dual industrial structure, Japan is fostering the growth of high-technology industries such as computers.

As Japan's industrial technology advances pari passu with her industrial transformation toward more knowledge-based sectors, Japan's manufacturing investments in advanced Western countries will be further encouraged. Equipped with technological advantages, Japanese firms will then be able to manufacture more competitively in the highly developed oligopolistic markets of the United States and Europe. Because these Japanese ventures are allowed to penetrate the advanced countries' markets without as much restriction as they are confronted with in the developing countries, the Japanese are likely to set up wholly- or majority-owned ventures and to exhibit ethnocentric characteristics in contrast to the relatively strong polycentric orientation of Japanese investments in the developing countries.

Beneficiary of the Era of Multinationalism

As this book has emphasized throughout, overseas investments are a national desideratum for Japan, a policy officially encouraged and wholeheartedly supported by the Japanese public—including the labor unions. Consequently, various government measures designed to defray the private cost and to realize the social benefits of overseas production are socially justified. In fact, among the industrialized countries Japan is benefiting perhaps the most in this age of multinationalism. Japan has traditionally striven to better her economic lot by supplementing her meager endowments of natural resources with international trade. She has made the best use of trade opportunities. Now multinationalism offers a superior alternative for Japan to escape from the domestic confines of limited economic resources. For she can now utilize overseas resources more effectively than was allowed through the sole medium of international trade because overseas production makes it possible to acquire both *importable* and *unimportable* foreign resources, and it is the latter kind of resources (industrial land and labor) whose shortages at home have emerged as constraints on Japan's economic growth.

As a matter of fact, the exiguity of natural resources at home is about to serve again as a positive factor; it imposes no restraint on Japan in directly seeking the best supplies of economic resources through overseas investment. The position of the multinational firm is superior to the national one, as stressed by Raymond Vernon: "The national enterprises will acquire human resources and capital at their own national prices; the multinational enterprise at the best prices available to it anywhere. The national enterprises will import goods and services

at world market prices; the multinational enterprises at the
marginal cost to the system."[19]

Japan benefited immensely as an importer of resources in the
open market throughout the postwar period, because resources
were then in abundant and relatively stable supply overseas and
their "world market prices" were favorably low—lower than
in some industrialized countries whose industry had to use their
own domestic resources purchased above the world-market
price. Now that resource supplies increasingly are controlled by
the exporting countries, the situation has changed drastically; it
is no longer either economical or safe for Japan to secure resources in the open market. She must seek as much control as
possible of hitherto untapped stocks of resources in addition to
securing the conventional flows of developed resources. Fortunately, there are still plenty of resources left in the world. The
developing countries in particular are eager to seek economic
and technical assistance for the development of their resources,
and Japan is more than willing to collaborate with the Third
World.

Thus Japan is endeavoring to transform herself from her
early postwar position of a price taker (or a perfectly competitive buyer) in "open" world resource markets into that of a
monopsonistic buyer in "closed" resource markets so that she
can acquire vital resource supplies "at the marginal cost to
the system" (that is, retaining to herself decisions over output,
if not decisions over prices). Japan is adroitly capitalizing on
the present global trend of this particular form of economic integration in the factor market, a trend called multinationalism.

Appendix

Data on Japan's
Direct Foreign Investment

THE statistics on Japan's direct foreign investment used by the
MITI are based on those applications for overseas ventures approved by the Japanese government (the Ministry of Finance)
and not on investments actually carried out. Consequently, they
do not reflect actual capital outflows from Japan, reinvestment
of profits by the existing overseas ventures, or capital raised locally in overseas markets. Koichi Hamada explains: "Statistics
on the flow of Japanese investment abroad can be obtained from
two sources. One source is the Ministry of Finance which gives
the authorisation to projects proposed under the Foreign Exchange and Foreign Trade Control Law (1940). The number
of projects approved and the scale of projects are reported. The
other source is Balance of Payments Statistics compiled by the
Bank of Japan. As can be imagined, the first figure is usually
larger than the second, indicating that there exists a substantial
lag in the actual transfer of funds behind authorisation."[1]

Indeed, there is a considerable lag; for instance, from 1951
to 1965, the ratio of the actual outflow to the approved amount
was 44.4 percent; from 1965 to 1970 38.5 percent; and from
1971 to 1972 34.9 percent.[2] Thus there seems to be a decline
in the ratio of the actual outflow to the approved amount in
recent years. This may be due in part to an increase in the average size of Japan's overseas investment. For, in general, the
larger the size of investment, the longer the preparatory work
involved before a project is actually implemented. Japan is now
increasingly engaged in large-scale resource-development ven-

tures which require a relatively long period of preparatory activities. A recent prolonged recession also caused the cancellations and postponement of many investment projects.

Yet the actual amount of Japan's overseas investment may not be so far off from the amount approved by the Japanese government when the capital raised overseas and the reinvestment of profits are taken into consideration. Yoshihiro Tsurumi states: "Upon the basis of my own fieldwork in and outside Japan, I estimate that the actual level of assets controlled by Japanese investments is generally at least twice the level of direct investments authorized by the Bank of Japan."[3] (However, he does not explain the basis of his estimates.) No doubt, the amount of capital raised or plowed back outside Japan will increase in the future. For the time being, however, the amount of direct foreign investment approved by the Japanese government serves as a good proxy for the actual amount invested, because the amount of capital raised and reinvested overseas seems, so far, roughly to match the amount of delayed or cancelled capital outflows from Japan.

Table A.1   Japan's Direct Foreign Investment by
Financial Category at the End of Fiscal 1974
(in millions of U.S. dollars)

Financial category	Cumulative value approved	%
Securities investment	7,011	55.4
Direct overseas loan	4,642	36.6
Acquisition of real estate and direct overseas investment	608	4.8
Establishment of branch offices	404	3.2
Total	12,665	100.0

Source: MITI, Wagakuni Kigyo, 1975, p. 232.

Table A.2 Labor Force by Age Group in Japan

Age group	1955 (X1,000)	%	1960 (X1,000)	%	1965 (X1,000)	%	1970 (X1,000)	%
15-19	5,230	12.4	4,530	9.9	4,050	8.4	2,950	5.7
20-29			11,870	26.2	13,180	27.4	14,600	28.2
	20,210	47.8						
30-39			10,620	23.4	11,860	24.6	12,400	23.9
40-64	14,740	34.8	16,020	35.3	16,800	34.9	19,450	37.6
65 and over	2,120	5.1	2,320	5.1	2,290	4.6	2,300	4.4
Total	42,300	100.0	45,360	100.0	48,180	100.0	51,700	100.0

Source: Economic Planning Agency, *Economic Survey of Japan (1970-1971)*, p. 104.

Table A.3 High School Graduates Entering the Labor
Force in Japan, 1960-1969

Year	Junior High School A (X1,000)	B	C %	Senior High School A (X1,000)	B	C %
1960	1,770	683	38.6	934	573	61.3
1965	2,360	625	26.5	1,160	700	60.3
1966	2,134	523	24.5	1,557	903	57.9
1967	1,947	446	22.9	1,603	941	58.7
1968	1,847	386	20.9	1,601	941	58.9
1969	1,737	324	18.7	1,497	883	58.9

Source: Economic Planning Agency, *Keizai Yoran*, 1971, p. 253.
Note: A = Number of school graduates
 B = Number of school graduates entering employment
 C = B/A

Table A.4 Proportion of Young Compared to Total Population
in Selected Asian Countries

Country	Year of census	(A) Total population	(B) 19 years old and under	B/A %
1. Burma	1954	2,677,719	1,301,787	48.6
2. Cambodia	1962	5,728,771	3,043,535	53.1
3. China (Taiwan)	1968	13,473,471	7,298,638	54.2
4. Hong Kong	1969	3,990,400	1,950,200	48.9
5. India	1970	550,376,000	284,038,000	51.6
6. Indonesia	1965	97,634,000	50,350,000	51.6
7. Japan	1969	102,648,000	34,309,000	33.4
8. South Korea	1970	31,793,000	16,199,800	50.9
9. West Malaysia	1968	9,030,236	4,925,779	54.6
10. Pakistan	1961	90,282,674	47,617,446	52.7
11. Philippines	1968	35,883,000	20,609,000	57.4
12. Singapore	1970	2,074,507	1,051,273	50.6
13. Thailand	1960	26,257,916	13,818,635	52.6

Source: U.N., *Demographic Yearbook*, 1970, pp. 538-546.

Table A.5 Key Ratios of Japan's Direct Foreign Investment (DFI) Compared to Those of Other Major Countries

	Year	Accumulated value of direct foreign investment (in millions of U.S. dollars)	Share of DFI in DAC countries %	Ratio of DFI to GNP %	Ratio of DFI to export %	Per capita DFI (in dollars)
Japan	1967	1,458	1.4	1.2	14.0	15
	1974	12,663	5.6	2.8	22.8	115
United States	1967	59,486	57.1	7.4	191.7	299
	1974	118,613	52.5	8.5	120.4	560
West Germany	1967	3,015	2.9	2.4	13.9	50
	1974	15,258	6.7	4.0	17.1	246
United Kingdom	1967	17,521	16.8	15.8	121.1	319
	1974	32,633	14.4	17.1	84.5	582

Sources: Selected from MITI, *Tsusho Hakusho*, 1976, pp. 294-295. MITI data are from the Export-Import Bank of Japan; U.N., *Multinational Corporation in World Development*; Dresdner Bank, *Merkbatter fur den Aussenhandel*; U.S. Department of Commerce, *Survey of Current Business*, and IMF, *Balance of Payments Yearbook* and *International Financial Statistics*.

Notes

Preface

1. Some Japanese are upset by this characterization of their economy and become quite defensive about the symbiotic relationship between their government and industry. They do not need to be. After all, the United States has been described similarly by Cohen and Mintz in *America, Inc.* Indeed, there is no such a thing as a "free market" in this ever-inter-dependent world economy in which economic issues have become top-priority items in the execution of foreign policy by any industrial country.

2. Among the most recent publications are Yoshino, *Japan's Multinational Enterprises* and Tsurumi, *The Japanese Are Coming.* They are both written from the viewpoint of business administration; they focus largely on the managerial aspects of Japan's overseas ventures.

Chapter 1

1. Ministery of International Trade and Industry (MITI). *Tsusho Hakusho,* 1976, pp. 294-295. It should be noted that Canada's relatively high rate of growth in direct foreign investment also reflects the overseas (third-country) investment activities of American subsidiaries in Canada.

2. In comparison, the United States has a long history of overseas manufacturing operations, as may be expected from its dominant role as the home country for a majority of multinationals in the world. James W. Vaupel and Joan P. Curhan point out that 187 U.S. companies currently in operation had already as many as 116 manufacturing subsidiaries overseas back in 1913; the number rose to 715 in 1939, 988 in 1950 and 3,646 in 1967. The overseas expansion of U.S. firms thus has been rather long and gradual in development, though it has gained momentum in recent years. Vaupel and Curhan, *Making of Multinational Enterprise,* quoted in Vernon, *Sovereignty,* p. 61.

3. Three related concepts, ethnocentrism, polycentrism, and geocentrism, were introduced into the analysis of multinationalism by Perlmutter, "Tortuous Evolution of the Multinational Corporation," pp. 9-18.

4. Kogiku, "Japan's 'Doubling National Income Plan,' " p. 538.

5. Ibid., p. 541.

6. Patrick and Rosovsky, "Japan's Economic Performance," in Patrick and Rosovsky, eds., *Asia's New Giant,* pp. 45-46.

7. Trezise and Suzuki, "Politics, Government, and Economic Growth in Japan," p. 794.

8. Economic Planning Agency, *Economic Survey of Japan—1970-1971*, p. 72.

9. It should be stressed here that the senile sector contracted only in relative but not in absolute terms throughout the 1950s and the 1960s, although many industries in this sector are now contracting absolutely. "It must be kept in mind that these changes in the relative importance of industries occurred within the context of overall rapid growth. Even industries in relative decline grew absolutely, in fact rapidly in comparison with other industrial nations." Patrick and Rosovsky, "Japan's Economic Performance," in Patrick and Rosovsky, eds., *Asia's New Giant*, pp. 20-21.

10. Small and Medium Enterprise Agency, *Chusho Kigyo Hakusho*, 1976, pp. 2, 3, 8.

11. Trezise and Suzuki, "Politics, Government, and Economic Growth in Japan," p. 772.

12. Ibid., p. 776.

13. Heller, "Factor Endowment Change," p. 283.

14. Patrick and Rosovsky, "Japan's Economic Performance," in Patrick and Rosovsky, eds., *Asia's New Giant*, p. 17.

15. In addition to a noticeable jump in the value of overseas investment approved from $275 million in fiscal 1967 to $557 million in fiscal 1968, Japan has become a net capital-exporting country ever since 1968 in terms of her balance sheet of foreign assets and liabilities. This phenomenon is pointed out by Kitamura, "What Posture Should Japan Take in Its Overseas Expansion?" p. 49. Thus, the year 1968 clearly marked a watershed in Japan's overseas investment.

16. These implicit requirements are cited in Frank and Hirono, eds., *How the United States and Japan See Each Other's Economy*, p. 59.

17. For an excellent discussion of the nature of Japan's industrial reorientation policy, see Kojima, *Japan and a New World Economic Order*, pp. 120-147.

18. For an analysis of Japan's postwar experience in assimilating foreign technologies and developing trade competitiveness, see Ozawa, *Japan's Technological Challenge*.

19. The high ratio for Europe exists not because Europe is a more important export market for Japan than the United States but because other categories of investment in Europe are much smaller than in the United States.

20. The ratio has recently declined because of increased shares for manufacturing and services. But at the end of 1972, for example, the ratio of extractive investments was as high as 36.8 percent for Japan, compared to 35.7 percent for the United States, 7.2 percent for Britain, and 5.3 percent for West Germany. MITI, *Wagakuni Kigyo*, 1974, p. 84.

21. Vernon, *Sovereignty*, pp. 7, 11.

22. Horst, "Firm and Industry Determinants," p. 261.

23. Helleiner, "Transnational Enterprises," p. 110.

24. Vernon, *Sovereignty*, p. 12.

25. There are only a few exceptions: "It is usually said to be unique to Japan, but there are three exceptions. There are two trading companies in West Africa—United Africa Company and the Swiss Trading Corporation—and *Societé Général* in Belgium. All of them are much smaller in capital and volume of trade and very much simpler in the range of activities. These three trading companies, along with the Japanese trading companies, arose in the second half of the nineteenth century, though it is difficult to say which was the first, especially as they developed gradually" (Bieda, *Structure and Operation of the Japanese Economy*, pp. 202-203).

26. Young, "Internationalization of the Japanese General Trading Companies," p. 78.

27. "General Traders in Japan," p. 26.

28. Toyo Keizai, *Kaigai Shinshutsu*, p. 2.

29. For a concise discussion of the historical development of trading companies, see Yamamura, "General Trading Companies in Japan," pp. 161-210.

30. A study made in 1971 by the Export-Import Bank of Japan reported that compatriot Japanese competition accounted for as much as 40 percent of local competition in Asian countries (see *Wagakuni Kaigai Toshi*, 1971, p. 29).

31. MITI, *Keizai Kyoryoku*, 1973, as summarized in "Japan's Economic Cooperation," p. 17.

32. Mikesell, *Economics of Foreign Aid*, p. 194. The strong ethnocentric nature of Japan's economic aid is stressed by Hasegawa, *Japanese Foreign Aid*.

33. Economic Planning Agency, *Economic Survey of Japan—1970-1971*, pp. 116-117.

34. "Japan's Economic Cooperation," p. 17.

35. Ibid., p. 19.

36. MITI, *Tsusho Hakusho*, 1976, p. 268.

37. The Japanese name of this organization is *Kaigai Boeki Kaihatsu Kyokai*.

38. These organizations are called, in Japanese, *Chusho Kigyo Kinyu Koko, Kokumin Kinyu Koko*, and *Shoko Kumiai Chuo Kinko*, respectively.

39. MITI, *Wagakuni Kigyo*, 1976, p. 25. The survey is based on the replies of 1,361 firms whose total accumulated value of securities investment corresponded to 78.4 percent of the total value of securities investments made by Japanese firms as of March 31, 1975.

40. Heller and Heller, *Japanese Investments*, p. 51.

41. A MITI survey reported in *Asahi Shimbun*, April 1, 1976, p. 9.

42. This practice led to a swift decline in production costs with the familiar phenomenon of an "experience curve" effect, and the firms were able to operate at a relatively small profit margin with lower prices. These advantages are discussed in Shimizu, "Financing Foreign Operations," in Ballon and Lee, eds., *Foreign Investment*, pp. 211-225. Admittedly, this practice is highly risky. Once a recession strikes and sales fall, companies are then left with a heavy debt burden and may go bankrupt. The 1974-1978 recession amply revealed this vulnerability.

Chapter 2

1. Dunning, "Determinants," pp. 289-336; Hufbauer, "Multinational Corporation," in Kenen, ed., *International Trade*, pp. 253-319; Parry, "International Firm," pp. 1201-1221; United Nations, *Multinational Corporations; Impact of Multinational Corporations*; and *Summary of Hearings*.

2. Dunning, for example, states: "The second line of research which needs pursuing is a more systematic analysis of the distinctiveness of (multinational enterprises [MEs]) and alternative forms of market penetration, by country and industry. . . . Why is the broad industrial pattern of the Japanese MEs different from that of their U.S. and European counterparts?" "Determinants," p. 329. Vernon also observes: "there are stages in the process of developing new theory when it pays to emphasize the inductive rather than the deductive phase of the cerebrating process. Though a considerable amount of observation has been done concerning the factors affecting the decisions of the U.S. firms as they establish themselves overseas, much less has been done regarding the behavior of European and Japanese firms" (see "Program of Research," in Bergsten, ed., *Future of International Economic Order*, p. 97).

3. Hymer, *International Operations*; Kindleberger, *American Business Abroad*; and Caves, "International Corporations," pp. 1-27. The references cited here are certainly not meant to be exhaustive; there are many other works bearing on this particular theory.

4. Cooper, *Economics*, p. 88.

5. Baranson, "Technology Transfer," p. 437.

6. Kindleberger, *American Business Abroad*, pp. 13-14.

7. Vernon, "Future of Multinational Enterprise," in Kindleberger, ed., *International Corporation*, p. 383.

8. Galbraith, *Economics*.

9. This neoclassical economic characteristic is noted by McNulty in connection with his analysis of the evolution of the concept of competition: "Economic Theory," pp. 639-656.

10. Galbraith, *Economics*, p. 167.

11. Ibid., pp. 169-170.

12. Organization for Economic Cooperation and Development (OECD), *Gaps*, p. 198.

13. For this view, see Vernon, "International Investment," pp. 190-207; and *Sovereignty*.

14. Vernon, *Manager*, p. 208.

15. Perhaps an exception is the home video tape recorders (VTRs) recently commercialized by Japanese firms ahead of their foreign competitors. There are two variants of home VTR technology; the Betamax technology developed by Sony and licensed to Sanyo and Toshiba, and the Video Home System (VHS) commercialized by the Matsushita group (Victor, Matsushita Electric, Sharp, and Hitachi). Leading U.S. companies quickly concluded business tie-ups with the two Japanese groups to market home VTRs; Zenith with Sony and RCA with Matsushita.

16. Magee, "Multinational Corporations," pp. 301-302.

17. This "factor proportions account" of trade was originated by Heckscher and expanded by Ohlin, *Interregional and International Trade*.

18. Rybczynski, "Factor Endowment," pp. 336-341.

19. Mundell, "International Trade," pp. 321-335.

20. The theorem states: "The maintenance of the same rates of substitution in production after the quantity of one factor has increased must lead to an absolute expansion in production of the commodity using relatively much of that factor, and to an absolute curtailment of production of the commodity using relatively little of the same factor." Rybczynski, "Factor Endowment," p. 338.

21. See Flatters, "Commodity Price Equalization," pp. 473-476; Krauss, "Commodity Trade," pp. 797-801; Ozawa, "Commodity Trade," p. 668; Krauss, "Commodity Trade: Reply," pp. 669-670.

22. Schmitz and Helmberger, "Factor Mobility," pp. 791-797.

23. Kojima, "Macroeconomic Approach," pp. 1-20.

24. Kojima, "International Trade," pp. 1-12.

25. Ibid., pp. 4-6. Kojima presents his complements model as more "distinctly" complementary than the one shown by Purvis, "Technology," pp. 991-999.

26. Johnson, "Survey of Issues," in Drysdale, ed., *Direct Foreign Investment*, p. 2, as quoted by Kojima, "International Trade," p. 6.

27. Kojima, "International Trade," pp. 6-7.

28. Ibid., p. 7.

29. Ozawa, *Transfer of Technology*, referred to by Kojima, "International Trade," p. 7. An extensive quotation appears in Kojima, "Transfer of Technology," and in Kojima, *Kaigai Chokusetsu Toshi*, pp. 146-153.

30. Roemer, in *U.S.-Japanese Competition*, carries out an excellent statistical study of Japan's international competitiveness (manifest in manufacturing exports and overseas investment) as compared to the

United States, the United Kingdom, and West Germany. His analysis is based on a four-stage hypothesis, which he modestly describes as "too simplistic to provide a theory of direct investment," but "intended only to provide a framework for purposes of discussing international economic competition." He explains his stage hypothesis as follows: "A developed capitalist country which becomes involved in significant international competition is seen as passing through four stages. These four stages are demarcated by various turning points in its world shares of trade and investment in manufactures. In the first stage, the country's share in world exports of manufactures starts to rise. In the second stage, the rise in its trade share slows (or its trade share becomes stable), and its share in world direct foreign investment in manufactures starts to rise. In the third stage, its trade share in manufactures starts to fall, but its investment share continues to rise. In the fourth stage, its trade share continues to fall and its share in manufacturing foreign investment starts to fall also" (p. 131).

One basic weakness of the stage hypothesis (and for that matter, any stage theory stretching over a long span of time) is the underlying assumption that a latecomer is viewed as (or "programmed" into) going through the same stages as his predecessors. But particularly when it comes to the recent experiences of overseas investment, the world (a set of international parameters, both political and economic to which the predecessor-investor once reacted) has drastically changed; the follower-investor is now confronted with an entirely new set of global parameters that calls for different adaptive behavior and strategies—hence different implications for competitive relationship among the nations. Furthermore, Japan's opting for overseas production is being influenced more strongly by quite different domestic macroeconomic circumstances.

31. Kojima, "International Trade," p. 8.

32. Caves, "International Corporations."

33. Ibid., p. 1.

34. The "bandwagon" effect is treated as an oligopolistic reaction in Knickerbocker, *Oligopolistic Reaction.*

35. The difference between their industrial policies is emphasized in Abegglen and Rapp, "Competitive Impact of Japanese Growth," in Cohen, ed., *Pacific Partnership*, p. 21.

36. Hicks, "Mainspring," pp. 336-348; and "Future of Industrialism," pp. 218-229. A theoretical examination of the impulse concept is also presented in Hicks, *Capital and Time*, chapter 10.

37. Hicks, "Future of Industrialism," pp. 128-219.

38. For an excellent analysis of the *keiretsu* group, see Bieda, *Structure and Operation*, pp. 208-221.

39. A detailed analysis of the staggered entry of industrial groups into the petro-chemical industry (a case involving low-density, high-pressure

process polyethylene) is presented by Peck with Tamura, "Technology," in Patrick and Rosovsky, eds., *Asia's New Giant*, pp. 553-558.

40. Ohkawa and Rosovsky, *Japanese Economic Growth*.

41. This decline in NNW is referred to in Bennett and Levine, "Industrialization and Social Deprivation," in Patrick, ed., *Japanese Industrialization*, p. 447.

42. Johnson, "Economic Benefits," in Hahlo, Smith, and Wright, eds., *Nationalism and Multinational Enterprise*, pp. 165-166. For a similar view, see also Kindleberger, *American Business Abroad*, p. 35.

43. Hymer, "Multinational Corporation," in Bhagwati, ed., *Economics*, pp. 113-140.

44. Leibenstein, "Allocative Efficiency," pp. 392-415.

45. Ibid., p. 404.

46. In addition to the immigrant-psychology effect, the Japanese manufacturers who have set up shop in the United States seem to be unexpectedly finding that they also possess another source of X-efficiency in the form of their paternalistic managerial system based on bottom-up decision-making process, a system that seems conducive to raising labor productivity in their U.S. shops. This phenomenon was recently described:

"On the assembly line of a U.S. company in Atlanta, Georgia, 35 American women put together transistor panels in a prescribed set of steps. In Tokyo, at another plant of this company, 25 Japanese assemblers use the same technology and the same procedure to manufacture the same part. The only real difference between the two lines is their productivity; the Japanese workers turn out 15% more panels than do their American counterparts 7,000 miles away.

"In Sony Corporation's plant at San Diego, California, some 200 Americans make 17- and 19-inch television sets on an assembly line that is identical with Sony's typical assembly line in Japan; the American workers produce as much for Sony in San Diego as the Japanese assemblers do for Sony in Tokyo.

"What is more, our interviews with 20 other Japanese companies operating in the United States suggest that, in many instances, they are outperforming American companies in the same industries" (Johnson and Ouchi, "Made in America," p. 61).

The X-efficiency that Japanese firms reportedly enjoy is an advantage they stumbled on only after they started to manufacture in the United States (in fact, they had probably had not been aware of it until the Johnson-Ouchi study was made and its findings publicized). Such efficiency is still an isolated incident, occurring only on a limited scale in Japanese manufacturing activities in the United States. There is no guarantee that Japanese-style paternalistic management would work on an extended basis in the United States or in any other alien environment. It should be noted that such an advantage is neither firm-specific nor in-dustry-specific, but culture-specific. Further, its appearance in the United States may even be a cross-cultural phenomenon, because it is possible that only Americans particularly attracted to such paternalistic manage-ment earnestly sought employment, and that the Japanese company con-sciously recruited only individuals psychologically attuned to its pater-nalistic philosophy.

47. When the Shiseido cosmetics firm advanced into New York and Paris in the mid-1960s, its move was reportedly intended to improve the image of its products at home lest it lose out to foreign competitors such as Max Factor, Revlon, and Avon, which were expected to sell directly in the Japanese cosmetic market. Japan was then about to liberalize re-strictions on imports and inward foreign capital investment. Takashi-maya, one of Japan's leading department stores, also opened a New York branch store on Fifth Avenue, which was very small and quite unprof-itable, but allowed its main store in Tokyo to advertise as the sole Japa-nese department store with a branch store on Fifth Avenue in New York City.

Honda Motor's recent decision to set up an assembly plant (initially motorcycles but eventually passenger cars) in the United States ahead of Toyota and Nissan is no doubt partly motivated not only by a desire to enter the U.S. market directly but also by one to boost its market share in the Japanese market dominated by the other two competitors. Although Honda is the world's largest motorcycle producer, it began to produce passenger cars as recently as 1967. Whether Honda can firmly establish itself as another auto maker at home crucially rests on its suc-cess in overseas markets, particularly the U.S. market.

Chapter 3

1. Japan ranked only after the United States and the United Kingdom in terms of total capital invested in Asia. By the end of 1972, Japan had invested $1,390 million (the value of investments approved by the gov-ernment), while the United States by then had invested $3,402 million and the United Kingdom $2,420 million. MITI, *Tsusho Hakusho*, 1974, p. 418.

2. A concise examination of Japan's economic cooperation policies is presented in Caldwell, "Evolution of Japanese Economic Cooperation," in Malmgren, ed., *Pacific Basin Development*, pp. 23-60.

3. Naya and Schatz, "Trade, Investment, and Aid," in Malmgren, ibid., p. 75.

4. See Table A.1.

5. See Table A.2.

6. "As a result, wages of employees in their 50s in major corporations decreased markedly in relation to those of younger employees. In 1955,

these older workers earned three times as much as did workers aged 20-24, but in 1970, slightly over two times as much" (Economic Planning Agency, *Economic Survey of Japan—1970-1971*, pp. 103-106).

7. These various measures are described in Hsing, *Taiwan*, pp. 189-222.

8. Sekai Shuho, *Nihon Kigyo*, p. 39.

9. For example, Matsushita Electric (Taiwan), which was initially a small venture aimed at the local market, has grown to be one of the largest manufacturers in Taiwan with increasing export sales, so much so that it received a medal from the Board of Foreign Trade of the Republic of China in 1970 for its achievement in export promotion.

10. The economic logic of export processing zones is discussed in Wall, "Export Processing Zones," pp. 478-489.

11. Japan Chamber of Commerce, "Taiwan no Rodo Jijo to Kogyo-yochi no Genjo," p. 2.

12. Japan Chamber of Commerce, "Taiwan ni okeru Nikkei Kigyo," p. 2.

13. Computed from data in Industrial Development and Investment Center, *Overseas Investment*.

14. Cole and Lyman, *Korean Development*, p. 99. This book provides an excellent analysis of South Korea's political and economic relations with Japan after World War II.

15. Awanohara, "Sweet and Sour Affair," p. 54.

16. For a detailed description of South Korea's official measures to promote foreign capital inflow, see Yang, "Foreign Investment," in Drysdale, ed., *Direct Foreign Investment*, pp. 242-257.

17. "Japanese Enclave Taking Shape at Korea's MAFEZ," *Business Asia*, May 7, 1971, pp. 150-151.

18. Singapore began to transform its entrepôt economy into an industrial one by establishing the Economic Development Board in 1961. Once designated by the board as a "pioneer" industry contributing to Singapore's industrialization and export, any manufacturing operation, whether foreign-owned or locally-owned, would be given preferential tax treatments, including tax exemption on corporate income, tax reduction on export profits, and tax credit for interest paid on foreign loans and for royalties and technical assistance fees. The Employment Act and the Industrial Relations Acts of 1968 were legislated for the purpose of improving the labor climate for industry by prohibiting strikes. Singapore's industrialization effort also included the opening of an industrial park in Jurong. For a description of Singapore's investment incentive programs, see, for example, Agnelli, "Singapore," pp. 27-32.

The Jurong Industrial Park in Singapore did not, however, immediately attract Japanese enterprises on a similar scale to KEPZ and MAFEZ. Singapore is geographically much farther away from Japan than Taiwan and South Korea are. A greater distance means, in addition to a rise in transport costs, an equally greater sociocultural distance, which imposed a psychological barrier for many Japanese businessmen who had only lately begun to gain experience in producing overseas.

19. Hong Kong, a British protectorate, is Singapore's twin city in many respects—from geographical characteristics to cultural heritage. With an influx of refugees and returning residents from Communist revolution-torn China, notably from such Chinese commercial centers as Kwangtung and Shanghai, Hong Kong's population swelled by about one million between 1945 and 1956. But those immigrants provided Hong Kong with industrial capital, technology, and entrepreneurial skills as well as an abundant supply of low-cost labor, all of which combined to contribute to Hong Kong's industrialization. Industrial development was further fostered by its traditional laissez faire economic system: low taxation on business profits, weak trade unions, and the lack of legislation protecting workers (for example, no minimum wage law and no restrictions on working hours). Hong Kong quickly transformed itself from a trading entrepôt city into an industrial one. A short, but excellent examination of Hong Kong's postwar history is presented in Rabushka, *Changing Face of Hong Kong*.

20. Shimabukuro, "Economy of Singapore," p. 20.

21. "They did not appear to be much affected by the provision of the Pioneer Ordinance. . . . The anticipated formation of the Federation of Malaysia during 1962-63, on the other hand, was a very important motivating factor, not only in bringing manufacturers to Singapore but also in increasing the size of plant and equipment investment" (Ryokichi Hirono, "Japanese Investment," in Hughes and Seng, eds., *Foreign Investment*, pp. 93-94).

22. Some ventures, such as oil refining (a joint venture of Maruzen Oil and Toyo Menka) and the manufacture of diesel engines (a joint venture of Yammar Diesel, Nichimen, and Mitsui), were forced to close down.

23. Notable examples are textile ventures such as Malaysian Textile Industry (a subsidiary of Teijin) and Singapore Textile Towels (a joint venture of Mitsubishi, a group of Japanese textile firms and local interest), which were set up to export their products, mostly to advanced countries.

Some successful and relatively large-scale investments were also made. The prime examples are Jurong Shipyard, and Jurong Shipbuilding, both established by Ishikawajima-Harima Heavy Industries in joint ventures with the Singapore government; Bridgestone Malaysia (a tire manufacturing venture of Bridgestone); Singapore Cement (a joint venture of Onoda Cement and Mitsui); Pan Malaysia Paint (a 40 percent joint venture of Nippon Paint); and printing and book-binding ventures set up by leading Japanese printing companies (Dai Nippon and Toppan). On the whole, however, "[c]ompared to recent entrants like General Electric,

Rollei, and Philips, most of [Japanese investments] are small or medium-sized" (Ong, "Japanese Investment in Singapore," in Ballon and Lee, eds., *Foreign Investment*, p. 306).

24. For the investments by the U.S. electronics industry in Singapore and other Asian countries, see Chang, *Transfer of Technology*.

25. Japan External Trade Organization (JETRO), *Kaigai Shijo Hakusho*, 1972, p. 63.

26. Shimabukuro, "Economy of Singapore," p. 20. He also points out that although Western petroleum companies used Singapore as a supply depot for explorations and drilling projects, Japanese companies preferred to work directly from Japan.

27. U.S. Tariff Commission, *Economic Factors*, p. A-90, quoted by Chang, *Transfer of Technology*, p. 27.

28. Tilton, *International Diffusion of Technology*, pp. 139-140.

29. Unpublished data compiled by MITI.

30. Rabushka, *Changing Face of Hong Kong*, pp. 13-14.

31. Silcock, "Outline of Economic Development 1945-65," in Silcock, ed., *Thailand*, p. 13.

32. These measures included the establishment of the Board of Investment in 1959 and the legislation of the Promotion of Industrial Investment Act in 1960. Ibid., p. 230.

33. The profitability of these Japanese manufacturing ventures was on the whole high partly because of rather excessive promotional benefits accorded by the Board of Investment of Thailand (such as increased tariffs or even the outright prohibition of imports to protect the "infant" ventures and numerous tax concessions). "While tax incentives such as the five-year tax holiday are provided by many other Asian countries also, the concessions for protection of industries are more liberal in Thailand than those in most other countries of the region. These protectionist measures have encouraged monopoly and restrictive practices and seem to be one reason why the ratio of value-added to fixed assets has been very high in spite of the very obvious inefficiencies in the industrial sector" (Marzouk, *Economic Development*, p. 234).

According to a survey made by the Bank of Japan, as many as 70 percent of Japanese investments in Thailand succeeded in showing profits within 3 years and paying dividends within 5 years. JETRO, *Kaigai Shijo Hakusho*, 1972, p. 100.

34. "Japan, which is the leading foreign investor in Thailand, attracts special attention. The presence of Japanese in Thailand is conspicuous not only in industry but in export-import, in wholesale trade, and in banking and services as well" (Viravan, "Foreign Investment," in Drysdale, *Direct Foreign Investment*, pp. 233-234).

35. For an analysis of changing climate for multinational corporations in Thailand, see Chaimungkalanont, "Role of Multinational Corporations," pp. 297-336.

36. *Nihon Keizai Shimbun*, October 27, 1971, p. 4.

37. *Mainichi Shimbun*, October 2, 1971, p. 9.

38. *Japan Economic Journal*, September 15, 1971, p. 15.

39. Computed from data given in MITI, *Wagakuni Kigyo*, 1974, p. 80.

40. Awanohara, "A Sweet and Sour Affair," p. 54.

41. Wall, "Export Processing Zones," p. 485. The political relations between Japan and South Korea were frequently strained by a series of incidents such as the "Dae-Jung Kim kidnapping incident" of August 1973, the arrest of two Japanese youths by the Korean authorities in spring 1974, and the attempted assassination of President Park by a Korean resident in Japan in August 1974. Despite these thorny diplomatic issues, however, their relationship was brought back to "normalcy" through pragmatic compromises made by both countries—mainly because South Korea needed more economic aid from Japan and because Japan recognized that South Korea was vitally important to her peace and security. See Kim, "Japanese-South Korean Relations," pp. 981-995.

42. It should be noted, however, that so far as the value of projects approved by the Filipino government from 1968 to 1975 is concerned, Japanese investment ranks second to that of the United States. JETRO, *Kaigai Shijo Hakusho*, 1976, p. 101.

43. Ibid., 1975, p. 114.

44. MITI, *Keizai Kyoryoku*, 1975, p. 393. The original data are from the Bank of Japan. The figures cited are not on an approval basis but on an actual investment basis.

45. Ibid., p. 393.

46. "Multinationalization of Japanese Firms (2)," pp. 35-36.

47. But the latter two countries' outright grants were much higher than those of Japan. MITI, *Keizai Kyoryoku*, 1975, p. 395. More recently (in November 1976), Japan extended to Indonesia a loan equivalent to $136.7 million for the latter's economic development projects. The loan is reportedly repayable in thirty years with a ten-year grace period and carries an annual interest rate of 3 percent. "Japan Signs Accord for Loan to Indonesia," *Wall Street Journal*, November 22, 1976, p. 25.

48. A similar pattern is exhibited in Malaysia: In 1974 Japan gave Malaysia economic aid, inclusive of long-term official loans, worth $36 million, in contrast to $7.4 million by Britain, $4 million each by Australia and the United States, and $3.8 million by West Germany. MITI, *Keizai Kyoryoku*, 1975, p. 375.

49. The discussion on the Asahan project presented here is partly based on "Asahan Aluminum Project," pp. 15-17 and Stockwin, "Asahan," pp. 42-43.

50. Japan has not set up any significant "show-case" venture in the resource-rich Malaysia equivalent to the Asahan project. In terms of the

Japanese government's participation, a steelmaking venture, Malayawata, deserves to be mentioned. It is a successful joint venture of the Malaysian government (51 percent ownership) and a group of Japanese firms (a 49 percent ownership shared by Nippon Steel, Nittetsu Kosan, Mitsui, and Mitsubishi). The venture, which started its operation in 1965, is a small but integrated steel mill. Its unique feature is that it uses charcoal derived from discarded rubber trees, instead of coke, in iron smelting operations—a feature cited by the World Bank as a model for its unique technological adaptation to local environment. Initially, the venture's operation was unprofitable, due mainly to weak demand conditions and competition from cheaply imported steel products. But it turned profitable in early 1969 "partly because of better world prices, and mainly because of the Malaysian Government's decision to levy import duty" on competing imports. See "Multinationalization of Japanese Firms (2)," p. 23. Herein lies a clear advantage of the tie-up with the local government, and this advantage is consciously exploited elsewhere by Japanese industry in its joint ventures with the host government.

51. Stockwin, "Asahan," p. 43.

52. The five groups are (1) Sumitomo Chemical and Sumitomo Shoji; (2) Nippon Light Metal, C. Itoh, Nissho-Iwai, and Nichimen; (3) Showa Denko and Marubeni; (4) Mitsubishi Chemical and Mitsubishi Corporation; and (5) the Mitsui Group.

53. A $800 million petro-chemical complex on a small island off Singapore takes the form of an equal partnership between the Singapore government and a group of Japanese firms led by Sumitomo Chemical and backed up by the Japanese government. The core plant will use locally refined oil mainly to produce 300,000 tons of ethylene annually. The Japanese side will reportedly be represented by an investment company made up of twenty-three Japanese firms, and the OECF is to supply 30 percent of the initial capital of 180 million yen.

54. MITI, *Keizai Kyoryoku*, 1972, pp. 109-113 and *Sankei Shimbun*, March 26, 1972, p. 4.

55. Japan Tariff Association, *Tokkei Kanzei*; MITI, *Hattentojokoku*, 1971; and MITI, *Tsuho Hakusho*, 1972, pp. 303-305.

56. *Nishizawa, Tokkei Kanzei no Zenbo*, pp. 128-129.

57. *Nihon Keizai Shimbun*, November 8, 1971, p. 2.

58. *Nihon Keizai Shimbun*, October 17, 1971, p. 4.

59. MITI, *Keizai Kyoryoku*, 1972, p. 111.

60. MITI, *Tsusho Hakusho*, 1974, p. 269.

61. *Japan Economic Journal*, January 28, 1975, p. 20.

62. At the end of March 1973, Japan's direct foreign investment in textiles totaled $690 million in value and 434 in number of ventures, out of which the Asian region accounted for $460 million and 314 ventures, *Japan Economic Journal*, February 4, 1975, p. 20, and Industrial Bank of Japan, "Textile Industry in Japan," pp. 19-36.

63. This particular security issue is emphasized, for example, in Sigur, "Japan's Broadening International Role," pp. 17-30.

Chapter 4

1. This comparison is based on capital outflows from Japan and does not take into consideration locally borrowed money. Because the United States is an important financial center of the world to which Japanese industry often turns for capital, the percentages cited here may be somewhat distorted. Nevertheless, the over-all differences noted between the United States and Canada are still valid.

2. The competitive relationship between U.S. mass-merchandisers and Japan's trading companies (as well as Japan's newly emerged merchandisers) in their overseas procurement activities is stressed in Yoshino, "Multinational Spread of Japanese Manufacturing Investment," pp. 357-381.

3. An interesting study made by MITI reveals the importance of technology as a decisive factor in Japanese manufacturing ventures in the United States. The study considered, on a hypothetical basis, how well Japanese manufacturers would have fared in production costs compared to their U.S. counterparts if they had invested and manufactured in the United States. It was assumed that the Japanese would have used the same technology they used at home but paid the prevailing U.S. wages in accordance with the U.S. pattern of labor share in the total product, and that the Japanese would have been subject to their own domestic value-added ratio. For the manufacturing sector as a whole, the "cost relative" of the investing Japanese firms in 1963 was estimated to be almost four times as high as that of U.S. manufacturers. But it improved to about three times as high in 1968, and narrowed further to less than twice as high in 1973. MITI, *Tsusho Hakusho*, 1972, pp. 346-347, and 1974, p. 428.

If the trend continues, it probably would be shown that within the next few years Japanese manufacturers could produce goods in the United States almost as efficiently as their U.S. counterparts. (The same MITI study estimated that in 1970 Japanese manufacturers had already become more efficient than Italian, British, or Danish manufacturers.) However, the MITI study, using the average level of Japanese productivity for the manufacturing sector as a whole, necessarily neglects diverse individual cases. Some Japanese firms already possess some technical skills equivalent or even superior to those of U.S. firms in certain manufacturing operations.

4. The innovation-conducive environment of the U.S. market and the resource- and market-orientation of Japanese ventures in the United States discussed in this section were previously explored in Ozawa, *Japan's Technological Challenge*, pp. 92-99.

5. JETRO, *Kaigaishijo Hakusho*, 1974, p. 54.

6. Anderson, "Angling for Capital," p. 1.

7. "Japanese Firms (2)," pp. 14-15.

8. Ibid., pp. 10-12, and "Japanese Firms (1)," pp. 6-9.

9. JETRO, *Kaigaishijo Hakusho*, 1975, p. 41.

10. JETRO, *Kaigaishijo Hakusho*, 1974, p. 54.

11. *Brazilian Bulletin*, December 1975, p. 2.

12. U.S. Department of Commerce, *Foreign Economic Trends*, p. 12.

13. An excellent analysis of the incentives given by Brazil to foreign investors is found in Gordon and Grommers, *United States Manufacturing Investment*.

14. A detailed analysis of Japanese immigrants is made in Smith, *Brazilian Society*, pp. 153-179: The first group consisted of 781 persons (158 families). Brazil turned to Japan for the supply of farm workers, since it had difficulty recruiting them from its traditional supplier, Italy, due to the prohibition imposed by the latter's government. From 1908 to 1923, a total of 32,266 Japanese immigrants arrived in Brazil—only 2.5 percent of all immigrants. As a result of the Japanese government's encouragement of emigration in the early 1930s, the Japanese became the predominant group of immigrants. Immediately after World War II only a handful migrated to Brazil. It was only after 1952 that the immigration of the Japanese again became substantial, numbering 4,912 in 1956.

15. *Business Week*, September 14, 1968, p. 172. Mitsui's investment was made in 1967. It is a wholly-owned company of Mitsui and called Fertilizante Mitsui Industria e Comercio. It started with an initial capital of $1,250,000.

16. Roper, *Investment in Latin America*, p. 10.

17. Ishikawajima-Harima's overseas investments in Brazil and elsewhere are described in "Multinationalization (3)," pp. 15-18.

18. The details of the USIMINAS project are given in "Multinationalization (2)," pp. 22-23.

19. The unwillingness of American chemical firms to yield in ownership was pointed out by Professor Peter Evans of Brown University in a seminar presented at M.I.T. on November 7, 1975.

20. *Japan Economic Journal*, September 21, 1976, p. 2.

21. For the examples cited here and other Japanese ventures, see the recent issues of Economic Intelligence Unit (E.I.U.), *Quarterly Economic Review on Brazil*.

22. Metz, "Brazil's Vale," p. 1.

23. JETRO, *Kaigaishijo Hakusho*, 1975, p. 186.

24. *Japan Economic Journal*, November 20, 1973, p. 1.

25. *Japan Economic Journal*, November 27, 1973, p. 2.

26. The current functions and duties of the JPDC are described in Jukagaku, *Nihon no Kaigaishigen Kaihatsu*, pp. 54-57. See also Johnson, *Japan's Public Policy Companies*, pp. 123-125.

27. *Japan Economic Journal*, February 12, 1974, p. 2.

28. *Time*, February 11, 1974, p. 28.

29. This fact is clearly illustrated by the following episode: "On a hot day in July, 1973, a Japan Air Lines jumbo jet lifted off from Amsterdam's Schiphol Airport and was very soon hijacked by a band of Palestinian guerrillas. Changing its course to the southeast it put down at Dubai in the United Arab Emirates. In Dubai, at the time, there was only one resident Japanese. He was not a diplomat, nor an accredited correspondent of any newspaper—he was a representative of Japan's leading trading organization, the Mitsubishi Corporation. Eventually, the jumbo jet left Dubai and, landing at Benghazi in Libya, the passengers were freed and the plane was blown up. Not surprisingly, there were two representatives of the Marubeni Corporation in Benghazi and they, together with the five members of that company's Tripoli office and representatives there of Mitsui & Co. and of Sumitomo Shoji Kaisha were very active in caring for the passengers of the plane and in conveying messages to Tokyo" (Takeda, "Japanese Trading Companies," p. 407).

30. *Japan Economic Journal*, February 12, 1974, p. 12.

31. *Japan Economic Journal*, April 23, 1974, p. 1.

32. *Wall Street Journal*, June 14, 1974, p. 6.

33. *Asahi Shimbun*, April 6, 1976, p. 9.

34. Franko, "Multinational Enterprises," pp. 313-314.

35. *Business International*, May 3, 1974, p. 142.

36. Hymans, "Japan and Sheikhs," p. 38.

37. *Japan Economic Journal*, September 14, 1976, p. 1.

38. MITI, *Tsusho Hakusho*, 1976, pp. 296-297.

39. JETRO, *Kaigaishijo Hakusho*, 1975, p. 139.

40. The present behavior of Japanese industry in Europe fits the pattern envisaged in the second stage of international competition, one of the four stages discussed in Roemer, *U.S.-Japanese Competition*.

41. Gregory, "Invasion of Europe," p. 80.

42. JETRO, *Kaigaishijo Hakusho*, 1975, pp. 140, 147.

43. Gregory, "Japan's New Multinationalism," pp. 122-129.

44. JETRO, *Kaigaishijo Hakusho*, 1975, p. 128.

45. A detailed article-by-article analysis of the treaty is given in Millar, "Japan and Australia," pp. 28-42.

46. JETRO, *Kaigaishijo Hakusho*, 1975, pp. 205-206.

Chapter 5

1. Resource Study Committee, *Kokusaika Jidai*, p. 2.

2. MITI, *Tsusho Hakusho*, 1971, p. 338.

3. *Japan Times*, January 3, 1975, p. 2.

4. MITI, *Tsusho Hakusho*, 1977, Tokyo, 1977, p. 360.

5. Economic Planning Agency, *Keizai Hakusho*, 1974, p. 114.

6. FAO (United Nations Food and Agricultural Organization), *Yearbook of Fishing Statistics*, 1972, as quoted in *Japan Times*, June 5, 1974, p. 9.

7. Economic Planning Agency, *Keizai Hakusho*, 1974, p. 114.

8. "Fisheries Industry," p. 16.

9. Economic Planning Agency, *Keizai Hakusho*, 1974, p. 112.

10. MITI, *Tsusho Hakusho*, 1974, p. 87.

11. MITI, *Tsusho Hakusho*, 1973, p. 229.

12. Ibid., p. 230.

13. Whitlam, "Japan and Australia," p. 2.

14. Reported by UPI in *Japan Times*, May 21, 1973, p. 11.

15. Kojima, "Japan's Resource Security," mimeo, p. 13.

16. Head, "Canada's Pacific Perspective," p. 18.

17. Bieda, "Future Australia-Japan Trade Relations," p. 157.

18. *Japan Economic Journal*, December 21, 1976, p. 6.

19. *Japan Times*, April 24, 1974, p. 1.

20. *Wall Street Journal*, April 24, 1974, p. 12.

21. Dirks, "Japan Ups Investment Overseas," p. 11.

22. Meadows et al., *Limits to Growth*.

23. "Whaling in Japan," p. 24.

24. *Japan Times*, December 15, 1974, p. 10.

25. *Japan Economic Journal*, December 17, 1974, p. 1.

26. MITI, *Tsusho Sangyo Gyosei Shihan Seiki no Ayumi* [A Quarter Century of Trade and Industrial Administration], pp. 302-305, referred to in Johnson, *Japan's Public Policy Companies*, p. 122.

27. Bieda, *Structure and Operation of Japanese Economy*, p. 45.

28. Johnson presents a concise description of the postwar government policy for the coal industry in *Japan's Public Policy Companies*, pp. 127-131.

29. The original plan made public in 1973 aimed at building a 60 million-kilowatt capacity.

30. *Japan Times*, January 10, 1975, p. 2.

31. According to a study made in 1976 by the MITI with the use of a twenty-three-sector input-output table for the Japanese economy, there was some "significant" sign of a decline in the demand for natural resources because of a change in industrial structure in 1974. The study attributed 73.6 percent of that year's decline (2.2 percent) in the over-all demand for resources to a recession-caused decrease in the aggregate demand, 19.4 percent to a resource-saving shift in industrial structure, and 7.0 percent to the residual factors. Reported in *Asahi Shimbun*, June 5, 1976, p. 9.

32. MITI, *Tsusho Hakusho*, 1971, p. 343.

33. *Japan Economic Journal*, January 21, 1975, p. 6.

34. "Food Policy Complexities Mount," p. 10.

35. Economic Planning Agency, *Keizai Hakusho*, 1974, p. 118.

36. *Japan Times*, February 5, 1975, p. 12.

37. *Japan Economic Journal*, October 22, 1974, p. 5.

38. For an excellent survey of Japan's agricultural ventures overseas, see Dirks, "Japan Ups Investment Overseas."

39. "Food Policy Complexities Mount," p. 9.

40. Dirks, "Japan Ups Investment Overseas," p. 8.

41. The OFCF was established for the purpose of promoting the extension of technical and economic cooperation to developing countries. By the end of 1976 it had granted more than thirty loans worth nearly $9 billion to Japanese fishery firms for their overseas ventures in developing countries such as Mexico, Guinea, the Solomon Islands, Yemen, Senegal, and Indonesia. The funds used by the OFCF are directly provided by the Japanese government in the form of subsidies. Then the OFCF allocates loans directly to Japanese firms which in turn extend loans to or make investments in local ventures—the multiple-layer credit system discussed in chapter 1. See "Major Protein Source," p. 12.

42. MITI, *Wagakuni Kigyo*, 1974, p. 78.

43. "Fisheries Industry," p. 16.

44. Kawasaki Steel's $230-million sintering plant, currently under construction, in the Philippines is "essentially part of the company's number 6 blast furnace complex at Chiba, with which it is supposed to dovetail." And Kobe Steel's plant in Qatar will produce the billets which will be shipped to Japan for further processing. "Business Brief," p. 80.

45. Goodman, "Social Organization of Decision Making," in Apter and Goodman, eds., *Multinational Corporation*, pp. 64-65.

46. Yoshino aptly calls the *keiretsu* "a system-based oligopoly" in "Multinational Spread of Japanese Manufacturing Investment," p. 363.

47. Macrae, "Pacific Century, 1975-2075?" p. 30.

48. Kojima, "Japan's Resource Security," mimeo, pp. 8-9. For citing the Brazilian ore as an example, he makes reference to Hama, "Japan's Iron-steel Industry and Australian Iron Ore," in Kojima, ed., *Australia, Japan*, pp. 84-86.

49. Yamamura, "General Trading Companies in Japan," in Patrick, ed., *Japanese Industrialization*, p. 162.

Chapter 6

1. MITI, *Tsusho Hakusho*, 1975, p. 430.

2. Reported in *Japan Times*, July 19, 1974, p. 9.

3. Ong, "Japanese Investment," in Ballon and Lee, eds., *Foreign Investment*, p. 314.

4. MITI, *Tsusho Hakusho*, 1975, p. 434.

5. "Japan's Trade," p. 14.

6. Hellmann, *Japan and East Asia*, p. 100.

7. "Japan-ROK Economic Relations under Fire," p. 17.

8. Nagasu, "Super-Illusions," p. 156.

9. For a standard textbook treatment of this economic analysis, see, for example, Ferguson and Gould, *Microeconomic Theory*, pp. 416-449.

10. Streeten, "Policies towards Multinationals," p. 394.

11. This is in marked contrast to the generally unfavorable impact of U.S. overseas investment on its employment, as observed by Robert Gilpin:

"The effect of foreign investment is to decrease the capital stock with which Americans work; this decreases the productivity of American labor and real wages below what they would have been if the foreign investment had not taken place. By one estimate, the annual rate reduction in labor's income is around $6 billion. This is obviously a rough estimate but it serves to indicate that the export of capital benefits the owners of capital and management more than labor as a whole" (U.S. Senate, Committee on Labor and Public Welfare, "The Multinational Corporation and the National Interest," Washington, D.C.: Government Printing Office, 1973, p. 18, quoted in Barnet and Müller, *Global Reach*, p. 298). Gilpin's analysis is clearly within the "static" theory of factor movement. The adverse effect of U.S. overseas investment continues so long as an appropriate structural adjustment of the U.S. economy is not emphasized.

12. Quoted in Rapp, "Japan's Industrial Policy," in Frank, ed., *Japanese Economy*, p. 55.

13. Kojima, "Macroeconomic Approach," p. 1.

14. The various forms of transboundary linkages of the multinational corporation in contrast to those of trade, including the human-relations linkage stressed here, are discussed in detail in Kolde, *Multinational Company*, pp. 12-33.

15. Nakane, *Japanese Society*, pp. 130-131.

16. Kuroda, "Some Basic Elements," p. 389.

17. Nakane, "Social Background," p. 120.

18. Ibid., p. 124.

19. *Japan Economic Journal*, April 13, 1976, p. 20.

20. Ibid., March 13, 1973, p. 2.

21. Passin, "Changing Values," p. 832.

22. "Changing Industrial Structure," pp. 43-44.

23. Estimated from a sample figure given in MITI, *Wagakuni Kigyo*, 1975, p. 205. It is, however, predicted by the Industrial Structure Council of MITI that the number will reach approximately 90,000 by 1985.

24. Ibid., p. 91.

25. *Wall Street Journal*, October 11, 1972, p. 12.

26. Heller and Heller, *Japanese Investment*, pp. 102-103.

27. Lewis, *Development Planning*, pp. 76-78.

28. For this view of the political consequences of industrialization,

see, for example, Huntington, *Political Order*; Weiner and Hoselitz, "Economic Development," pp. 172-184; and Ake, "Modernization," pp. 576-591.

29. Cox, "Labor," p. 350.

30. Ibid., pp. 350-351.

31. Myrdal, *Asian Drama*, Vol. II, pp. 946-947.

32. Nagasu, "Super-Illusions," p. 150.

33. Ibid., p. 151.

34. Apter, "Charters, Cartels, and Multinationals," in Apter and Goodman, eds., *Multinational Corporation*, p. 19. He refers to Johnson, "Ideology," in Johnson, ed., *Economic Nationalism*, pp. 124-141.

35. Manglapus, *Japan in Southeast Asia*, pp. 64, 66.

Chapter 7

1. Japan Economic Research Center, *Japan's Economy in 1980*, pp. 10-11.

2. Quoted in Kobayashi, "Japanese Approach to 'Multinationalism,' " pp. 177-178.

3. Mitsui Bank, "Takokuseki Kigyo to Ginko," pp. 20-24.

4. Quoted in *Shukan Toyo Keizai* (weekly), September 28, 1974, p. 72.

5. In this connection, Drucker's observation is pertinent: "In the next ten years are the years in which the developing countries will both most need the multinationals and have the greatest opportunity of benefiting from them. For these will be the years when the developing countries will have to find jobs and incomes for the largest number of new entrants into the labor force in their history while, at the same time, the developed countries will experience a sharp contraction of the number of new entrants into their labor force—a contraction that is already quite far advanced in Japan and in parts of Western Europe and will reach the United States by the late 1970s. And the jobs that the developing countries will need so desperately for the next ten years will to a very large extent require the presence of the multinationals—their investment, their technology, their managerial competence, and above all their marketing and export capabilities" ("Multinationals," p. 134).

6. All in all, Japanese industry still can expand its overseas productive activities when the present level of such activities is measured against its GNP, per capita income, and exports. In 1974, for example, the ratio of overseas investment to GNP was only about 3 percent for Japan, compared to 17 percent for Britain, 8.5 percent for the United States, and 4 percent for West Germany. For other comparisons, see table A.5.

7. Barnet and Müller, *Global Reach*, pp. 202-203.

8. Computed from the results of a MITI questionnaire survey, which had a response rate of 50.2 percent but which covered 78.4 percent of

the total value of overseas equity investment made by Japanese firms as of March 31, 1975. MITI, *Wagakuni Kigyo*, 1976, pp. 157-160.

9. Computed from the 1967 data based on 187 U.S.-controlled multinational enterprises as shown by Vaupel and Curhan, *Making of Multinational Enterprises*, quoted in Vernon, *Sovereignty*, p. 141.

10. Caves, "Industrial Organization," in Dunning, ed., *Economic Analysis*, p. 130.

11. Behrman, "Multinational Enterprise," in Sethi and Holton, eds., *Management*, p. 21.

12. Vernon states: "Small countries, as a rule, can be counted on to support the one or two multinational giants that may be based in their economies; in any international dispute in which governmental support might matter, the Netherlands can almost surely be counted on to rally to the support of Philips Electric, or Switzerland to the support of Ciba. When the National Iranian Oil Company becomes a multinational enterprise, as is not unlikely over the next decade or so, it will almost certainly be able to count on the unequivocal support of Iran.

"From the viewpoint of an American firm, however, U.S. government support is somewhat more problematic, and that problematic quality is not unrelated to the size of the American economy. At the very least, the U.S. government has to consider the interests of other U.S.-based firms. This may sometimes argue for supporting the interests of some imperiled enterprise all the harder, in a special application of the domino theory; but it may also argue for turning a deaf ear and a blind eye to the plight of any single company. If International Petroleum wants the U.S. government's help in dealing with the Peruvian government, as it sure did in the 1960s, America has to weigh the risk of a backlash against other U.S. interests in Peru. If General Motors wants American help to break into the Spanish markets, as it was trying to do in the spring of 1974, the United States has to weigh that plea against the opposition of Ford and Chrysler. Beyond that, there are bilateral questions of military relations, regional questions of inter-American relations, multilateral questions of U.N. relations, and so on, to be taken into account, questions which may be of less complexity in the eyes of a smaller country. Indeed, there may even be times when, in the interest of high politics, the U.S. government may have to take some initiative that places in peril all multinational enterprises based in the United States" ("Multinational Enterprises," in Apter and Goodman, eds., *Multinational Corporation*, pp. 56-57).

13. Gilpin, *U.S. Power*, p. 41.

14. Krause and Sekiguchi, "Japan and World Economy," in Patrick and Rosovsky, eds., *Asia's New Giant*, p. 388.

15. Langdon, *Japan's Foreign Policy*, p. 195.

16. Kindleberger, *American Business Abroad*, p. 182.

17. Vernon, *Operations*, p. 3.
18. Gregory, "Opening a Door," pp. 92-93.
19. Vernon, "Location," in Dunning, *Economic Analysis*, p. 111.

Appendix

1. Hamada, "Japanese Investment Abroad," in Drysdale, ed., *Direct Foreign Investment*, p. 174.
2. Mitsui Bank, *Chosa Geppo*, no. 469 (1974), p. 121.
3. Tsurumi, "Multinational Spread," in Apter and Goodman, eds., *Multinational Corporation*, pp. 121-122.

Bibliography

Books and Monographs

Barnet, Richard J. and Müller, Ronald E. *Global Reach: The Power of the Multinational Corporation.* New York: Simon and Schuster, 1974.

Bieda, Ken. *The Structure and Operation of the Japanese Economy.* New York: Wiley, 1970.

Chang, Yu Sang. *The Transfer of Technology: Economics of Offshore Assembly, The Case of Semiconductor Industry.* New York: United Nations Institute for Training and Research, 1971.

Cohen, Jerry S. and Mintz, Morton. *America, Inc.: Who Owns and Operates the United States.* New York: Dial, 1971.

Cole, David C. and Lyman, Princeton N. *Korean Development.* Cambridge, Mass.: Harvard, 1971.

Cooper, Richard N. *The Economics of Interdependence.* New York: Council on Foreign Relations, 1968.

Ferguson, Charles E. and Gould, John P. *Microeconomic Theory.* Homewood, Ill.: Irwin, 1975.

Frank, Isaiah and Hirono, Ryokichi. *How the United States and Japan See Each Other's Economy.* New York: Committee for Economic Development, 1974.

Galbraith, John K. *Economics and the Public Purposes.* Boston: Houghton Mifflin, 1973.

Gilpin, Robert. *U.S. Power and the Multinational Corporation.* New York: Basic Books, 1975.

Gordon, Lincoln and Grommers, Engelbert L. *United States Manufacturing Investment in Brazil, 1946-1960.* Boston: Harvard Business School, 1962.

Hasegawa, Sukehiro. *Japanese Foreign Aid: Policy and Practice.* New York: Praeger, 1975.

Heller, H. Robert and Heller, Emily E. *Japanese Investments in the United States: with a Case Study of the Hawaiian Experience.* New York: Praeger, 1974.

Hellmann, Donald C. *Japan and East Asia.* New York: Praeger, 1972.

Hicks, John R. *Capital and Time: A Neo-Austrian Theory*. Oxford: Clarendon, 1973.

Hsing, Mo-Huan. *Taiwan: Industrialization and Trade Policies*. London: Oxford, 1971.

Huntington, Samuel P. *Political Order in Changing Societies*. New Haven, Conn.: Yale, 1968.

Hymer, Stephen H. *The International Operations of National Firms*. Cambridge, Mass.: M.I.T., 1976.

Japan Economic Research Center. *Japan's Economy in 1980 in the Global Context*. Tokyo: Japan Economic Research Center, 1972.

Johnson, Chalmers. *Japan's Public Policy Companies*. Washington, D.C.: American Enterprise Institute, 1978.

Jukagaku Kogyo Tsushinsha. *Nihon no Kaigaishigen Kaihatsu* [Japan's Overseas Resource Development]. Tokyo: Jukagaku Kogyo Tsushinsha, 1976.

Kindleberger, Charles P. *American Business Abroad: Six Lectures on Direct Investment*. New Haven, Conn.: Yale, 1969.

Knickerbocker, Frederick T. *Oligopolistic Reaction and Multinational Enterprise*. Boston: Harvard Business School, 1973.

Kojima, Kiyoshi. *Japan and a New World Economic Order*. Tokyo: Tuttle, 1977.

————. *Kaigai Chokusetsu Toshi Ron* [Theory of Foreign Direct Investment]. Tokyo: Diamond, 1977.

Kolde, Endel J. *The Multinational Company: Behavioral and Managerial Analyses*. Lexington, Mass.: Heath, 1974.

Komatsu, Sakyo. *Nippon Chimbotsu*. Tokyo, 1973. English translation by Michael Gallagher, *Japan Sinks*. New York: Harper & Row, 1976.

Langdon, Frank C. *Japan's Foreign Policy*. Vancouver: University of British Columbia Press, 1973.

Lewis, W. Arthur. *Development Planning*. New York: Harper & Row, 1966.

Manglapus, Paul S. *Japan in Southeast Asia: Collision Course*. New York: Carnegie Endowment for International Peace, 1976.

Marzouk, Girgis A. *Economic Development and Policies: Case Study of Thailand*. Rotterdam: Rotterdam University Press, 1972.

Meadows, Donella H., *et al. The Limits to Growth: A Report for the Club of Rome's Project on the Predicament of Mankind*. New York: University Books, 1972.

Mikesell, Raymond F. *The Economics of Foreign Aid.* Chicago: Aldine, 1968.

Myrdal, Gunnar. *Asian Drama: An Inquiry into the Poverty of Nations.* New York: Random House, 1969.

Nakane, Chie. *Japanese Society.* Berkeley: University of California Press, 1970.

Nishizawa, Kimiyoshi. *Tokkei Kanzei no Zenbo* [The Full Outline of Preferential Tariffs]. Tokyo: Nippon Kanzei Kyokai, 1971.

Ohkawa, Kazushi and Rosovsky, Henry. *Japanese Economic Growth: Trend Acceleration in the Twentieth Century.* Palo Alto: Stanford, 1973.

Ohlin, Bertil. *Interregional and International Trade.* Cambridge, Mass.: Harvard, 1933.

Ozawa, Terutomo. *Japan's Technological Challenge to the West, 1950-1974: Motivation and Accomplishment.* Cambridge, Mass.: M.I.T., 1974.

———. *Labor-Resource-Oriented Migration of Japanese Industries to Taiwan, South Korea and Singapore.* Economic Staff Working Paper No. 134. Washington, D.C.: International Bank for Reconstruction and Development, 1972.

———. *Transfer of Technology from Japan to Developing Countries.* New York: United Nations Institute for Training and Research, 1971.

Rabushka, Alvin. *The Changing Face of Hong Kong: New Departures in Public Policy.* Washington, D.C.: American Enterprise Institute, 1973.

Roemer, John E. *U.S.-Japanese Competition in International Markets: A Study of the Trade-Investment Cycle in Modern Capitalism.* Berkeley: University of California, Institute of International Studies, 1975.

Roper, Penelope. *Investment in Latin America.* London: Economist Intelligence Unit, 1970.

Sekai, Shuho. *Nihon Kigyo no Kaigai Shinshutsu—Asia* [Overseas Expansion of Japanese Enterprises—Asia]. Tokyo: Sekai Shuho, 1969.

Smith, T. Lynn. *Brazilian Society.* Albuquerque: University of New Mexico Press, 1974.

Tilton, John E. *International Diffusion of Technology: The Case of Semiconductors.* Washington, D.C.: Brookings, 1971.

Toyo Keizai. *Kaigai Shinshutsu Kigyo Soran* [Japanese Multinationals—Facts and Figures]. Tokyo: Toyo Keizai Shinposha, 1976.

266 Bibliography

Tsurumi, Yoshihiro. *The Japanese Are Coming: A Multinational Interaction of Firms and Politics.* Cambridge: Ballinger, 1976.

Vaupel, James W. and Curhan, Joan P. *The Making of Multinational Enterprise.* Boston: Harvard Business School, 1969.

Vernon, Raymond. *Manager in the International Economy.* Englewood Cliffs, N.J.: Prentice-Hall, 1972.

————. *The Operations of Multinational United States Enterprises in Developing Countries.* Geneva: United Nations Conference on Trade and Development, 1972.

————. *Sovereignty at Bay: The Multinational Spread of U.S. Enterprises.* New York: Basic Books, 1971.

Yoshino, Michael Y. *Japan's Multinational Enterprises.* Cambridge, Mass.: Harvard, 1976.

Contributions to Symposia or Volumes of Conference Papers

Abegglen, James C. and Rapp, William V. "The Competitive Impact of Japanese Growth." In Jerome B. Cohen, ed., *Pacific Partnership: United States-Japan Trade.* Lexington, Mass.: Heath, 1972.

Apter, David E. "Charters, Cartels, and Multinationals—Some Colonial and Imperial Questions." In David E. Apter and Louis Wolf Goodman, eds., *The Multinational Corporation and Social Change.* New York: Praeger, 1976.

Behrman, Jack N. "The Multinational Enterprise in 1976 and After." In S. Prakash Sethi and Richard H. Holton, eds., *Management of the Multinationals: Policies, Operations, and Research.* New York: Free Press, 1974.

Bennett, John W. and Levine, Solomon B. "Industrialization and Social Deprivation: Welfare, Environment, and the Post-Industrial Society in Japan." In Hugh Patrick, ed., *Japanese Industrialization and Its Social Consequences.* Berkeley: University of California Press, 1976.

Caldwell, Alexander J. "The Evolution of Japanese Economic Cooperation, 1950-1970." In Harald B. Malmgren, ed., *Pacific Basin Development.* Lexington, Mass.: Heath, 1972.

Caves, Richard E. "Industrial Organization." In John H. Dunning, ed., *Economic Analysis and the Multinational Enterprise.* London: Allen, 1974.

Goodman, Wolf Louis. "The Social Organization of Decision Making in the Multinational Corporation." In David E. Apter and

Louis Wolf Goodman, eds., *The Multinational Corporation and Social Change*. New York: Praeger, 1976.

Hama, Yoichiro. "Japan's Iron-steel Industry and Australian Iron Ore." In Kiyoshi Kojima, ed., *Australia, Japan, and the Resource Goods Trade*. Tokyo: Japan Economic Research Center, 1974.

Hamada, Koichi. "Japanese Investment Abroad." In Peter Drysdale, ed., *Direct Foreign Investment in Asia and the Pacific*. Toronto: University of Toronto Press, 1972.

Hirono, Ryokichi. "Japanese Investment." In Helen Hughes and You-Poh Seng, eds., *Foreign Investment and Industrialization in Singapore*. Madison: University of Wisconsin Press, 1969.

Hufbauer, G. C. "The Multinational Corporation and Direct Investment." In Peter B. Kenen, ed., *International Trade and Finance: Frontiers for Research*. Cambridge: Cambridge University Press, 1975.

Hymer, Stephen. "The Multinational Corporation and the Law of Uneven Development." In Jagdish Bhagwati, ed., *Economics and World Order from the 1970s to the 1990s*. New York: Collier-Macmillan, 1972.

Johnson, Harry G. "Economic Benefits of the Multinational Enterprises." In H. R. Hahlo, J. Graham Smith, and Richard W. Wright, eds., *Nationalism and the Multinational Enterprise: Legal, Economic and Managerial Aspects*. Dobbs Ferry, N.Y.: Oceana, 1973.

————. "The Ideology of Economic Policy in the New States." In Harry G. Johnson, ed., *Economic Nationalism in Old and New States*. London: G. Allen, 1968.

————. "Survey of Issues." In Peter Drysdale, ed., *Direct Foreign Investment in Asia and the Pacific*. Toronto: University of Toronto Press, 1972.

Krause, Lawrence B. and Sekiguchi, Sueo. "Japan and the World Economy." In Hugh Patrick and Henry Rosovsky, eds., *Asia's New Giant: How the Japanese Economy Works*. Washington, D.C.: Brookings, 1976.

Naya, Seiji and Schatz, Richard. "Trade, Investment, and Aid: The Role of the U.S. and Japan in Asian Economic Development." In Harald B. Malmgren, ed., *Pacific Basin Development*. Lexington, Mass.: Heath, 1972.

Ong, Hui Chong. "Japanese Investment in Singapore." In Robert J. Ballon and Eugene H. Lee, eds., *Foreign Investment and Japan*. Tokyo: Kodansha, 1973.

Patrick, Hugh and Rosovsky, Henry. "Japan's Economic Performance: An Overview." In Hugh Patrick and Henry Rosovsky, eds., *Asia's New Giant: How the Japanese Economy Works.* Washington, D.C.: Brookings, 1976.

Peck, Merton J. with the collaboration of Shuji Tamura. "Technology." In Hugh Patrick and Henry Rosovsky, eds., *Asia's New Giant: How the Japanese Economy Works.* Washington, D.C.: Brookings, 1976.

Rapp, William V. "Japan's Industrial Policy." In Isaiah Frank, ed., *The Japanese Economy in International Perspective.* Baltimore: Johns Hopkins, 1975.

Shimizu, Norihiko. "Financing Foreign Operations." In Robert J. Ballon and Eugene H. Lee, eds., *Foreign Investment and Japan.* Tokyo: Sophia University, 1972.

Silcock, T. H. "Outline of Economic Development 1945-64." In T. H. Silcock, ed., *Thailand—Social and Economic Studies in Development.* Durham, N.C.: Duke, 1967.

Tsurumi, Yoshihiro. "The Multinational Spread of Japanese Firms and Asian Neighbor's Reactions." In David E. Apter and Louis Wolf Goodman, eds., *The Multinational Corporation and Social Change.* New York: Praeger, 1976.

Vernon, Raymond. "A Program of Research on Foreign Direct Investment." In C. Fred Bergsten, ed., *The Future of the International Economic Order: An Agenda for Research.* Lexington, Mass.: Heath, 1973.

―――. "Future of the Multinational Enterprise." In Charles P. Kindleberger, ed., *The International Corporation: A Symposium.* Cambridge, Mass.: M.I.T., 1970.

―――. "The Location of Economic Activity." In John H. Dunning, ed., *Economic Analysis and Multinational Enterprise.* London: G. Allen, 1974.

―――. "Multinational Enterprises in Developing Countries: Issues in Dependency and Interdependence." In David E. Apter and Louis Wolf Goodman, eds., *The Multinational Corporation and Social Change.* New York: Praeger, 1976.

Yamamura, Kozo. "General Trading Companies in Japan: Their Origins and Growth." In Hugh Patrick, ed., *Japanese Industrialization and Its Social Consequences.* Berkeley: University of California Press, 1976.

Yong, Yoonsae. "Foreign Investment in Developing Countries: Korea." In Peter Drysdale, ed., *Direct Foreign Investment in*

Asia and the Pacific. Toronto: University of Toronto Press, 1972.

Journal Articles

Agnelli, Bernard F. "Singapore: Boom Town." *Columbia Journal of World Business* 6 (1971): 27-32.

Ake, Claude. "Modernization and Political Instability: A Theoretical Exploration." *World Politics* 26 (1974): 576-591.

Anderson, Harry B. "Angling for Capital: States Redouble Effort to Lure New Industry and Provide More Jobs." *Wall Street Journal*, July 11, 1975, p. 1.

Awanohara, Susumu. "A Sweet and Sour Affair." *Far Eastern Economic Review* 89 (1975): 52-56.

Baranson, Jack. "Technology Transfer through the International Firm." *American Economic Review* 60 (1970): 435-440.

Bieda, K. "Future Australia-Japan Trade Relations." *Australian Journal of Agricultural Economics* 14 (1970): 150-169.

"Business Brief: Raw Materials for Japan." *The (London) Economist*, Nov. 8, 1975, pp. 80-81.

Caves, Richard E. "International Corporations: The Industrial Economics of Foreign Investment." *Economica* 38 (1971): 1-27.

Chaimungkalanout, Suchint. "The Role of Multinational Corporations in Thailand." *Journal of International Law and Economics* 10 (1975): 297-336.

"Changing Industrial Structure." *Business Japan* 20 (1975): 43-44.

Cox, Robert W. "Labor and the Multinationals." *Foreign Affairs* 54 (1976): 344-365.

Dirks, Harlan J. "Japan Ups Investment Overseas to Diversify Food Sources." *Foreign Agriculture* 12 (1974): 7-11.

Drucker, Peter F. "Multinationals and Developing Countries: Myths and Realities." *Foreign Affairs* 53 (1974): 121-134.

Dunning, John H. "The Determinants of International Production." *Oxford Economic Papers* 25 (1973): 289-336.

Export-Import Bank of Japan. "Wagakuni Kaigai Toshi no Genjo" [Present Conditions of Our Country's Overseas Investment]. *Yugin Joho* [Export-Import Bank Bulletin] 11 (1971): 1-31.

"Fisheries Industry." *Oriental Economist* 42 (1974): 15-17.

Flatters, Frank. "Commodity Price Equalization: A Note on Factor Mobility and Trade." *American Economic Review* 62 (1972): 473-476.

"Food Policy Complexities Mount." *Oriental Economist* 42 (1974): 6-12.

"Foreign Trade: Preferential Tariffs Inaugurated." *Oriental Economist* 39 (1971): 36-37.

Franko, Lawrence G. "Multinational Enterprises in the Middle East." *Journal of World Trade Law* 10 (1976): 307-333.

"General Traders in Japan." *Oriental Economist* 42 (1974): 24-40.

Gregory, Gene. "Invasion of Europe Not as Great as Expected." *Business Japan* 20 (1975): 80-84.

———. "Japan's New Multinationalism: The Canon Giessen Experience." *Columbia Journal of World Business* 11 (1976): 122-129.

———. "Opening a Door to the Third World." *Far Eastern Economic Review* 91 (1976): 92-94.

Head, Ivan L. "Canada's Pacific Perspective." *Pacific Community* 6 (1974): 16-30.

Helleiner, G. K. "Transnational Enterprises and the New Political Economy of U.S. Trade Policy." *Oxford Economic Papers* 29 (1977): 102-116.

Heller, Peter S. "Factor Endowment Change and Comparative Advantage: The Case of Japan, 1956-1969." *Review of Economics and Statistics* 63 (1976): 283-292.

Hicks, John R. "The Future of Industrialism." *International Affairs* 50 (1974): 218-229.

———. "The Mainspring of Economic Growth." *Swedish Journal of Economics* 75 (1973): 336-348.

Horst, Thomas. "Firm and Industry Determinants of the Decision to Invest Abroad: An Empirical Study." *Review of Economics and Statistics* 54 (1972): 258-266.

Hymans, Henri. "Japan and the Sheikhs: A Romance Cools." *Far Eastern Economic Review* 89 (1975): 38-39.

Industrial Bank of Japan. "Textile Industry in Japan and Southeast Asia." *Japanese Finance and Industry*, No. 28 (1975): 19-36.

"Japan Buys a Stake in Burgeoning Brazil." *Business Week*, Sept. 14, 1968, pp. 168-172.

Japan Chamber of Commerce. "Taiwan ni okeru Nikkei Kigyo no Genjo to Mondaiten ni tsuite" [On the Present Conditions and Problems of Japanese Enterprises in Taiwan]. *Kaigai Kigyo to Gijutsu*, No. 2 (1970), pp. 1-15.

———. "Taiwan no Rodo Jijo to Kogyoyochi no Genjo" [Present

Conditions of Labor and Industrial Land in Taiwan]. *Kaigai Kigyo to Gijutsu*, No. 4 (1969), pp. 1-25.

"Japan-ROK Economic Relations under Fire." *Oriental Economist* 41 (1973): 14-20.

"Japanese Enclave Taking Shape at Korea's MAFEZ." *Business Asia*. May 7, 1971, pp. 150-151.

"Japanese Firms Going for Production in U.S.—(1)." *Oriental Economist* 45 (1977): 6-9.

"Japanese Firms Going for Production in U.S.—(2)." *Oriental Economist* 45 (1977): 14-15.

"Japan's Economic Cooperation: Its Present State and Problems." *Oriental Economist* 43 (1975): 17-21.

"Japan's Trade with S. E. Asia." *Oriental Economist* 42 (1974): 12-20.

Johnson, Richard T. and Ouchi, William G. "Made in America (under Japanese Management)." *Harvard Business Review* 52 (1974): 61-69.

Kim, Hong N. "Japanese-South Korean Relations in the Post-Vietnam Era." *Asian Survey* 16 (1976): 981-995.

Kitamura, Hiroshi. "What Posture Should Japan Take in Its Overseas Expansion." *Japan Economic Studies* 1 (1973): 39-55.

Kobayashi, Noritake. "The Japanese Approach to 'Multinationalism.'" *Journal of World Trade Law* 10 (1976): 177-184.

Kogiku, K. C. "Japan's 'Doubling National Income Plan' 1961-1970 and the 1976 Plan." *Weltwirtschaftliches Archiv* [Review of World Economics] 113 (1977): 511-553.

Kojima, Kiyoshi. "A Macroeconomic Approach to Foreign Direct Investment." *Hitotsubashi Journal of Economics* 14 (1973): 1-20.

———. "International Trade and Foreign Investment: Substitutes or Complements." *Hitotsubashi Journal of Economics* 16 (1975): 1-12.

———. "Transfer of Technology to Developing Countries—Japanese Type versus American Type." *Hitotsubashi Journal of Economics* 17 (1977): 1-14.

Krauss, Melvyn B. "Commodity Trade and Factor Mobility." *American Economic Review* 64 (1974): 797-801.

———. "Commodity Trade and Factor Mobility: Reply." *American Economic Review* 66 (1976): 669-670.

Kuroda, Mizuo. "Some Basic Elements of Japan's Foreign Policy." *Pacific Community* 5 (1974): 380-391.

Leibenstein, Harvey. "Allocative Efficiency V. 'X-Efficiency.'" *American Economic Review* 56 (1966): 392-415.

Macrae, Norman. "Pacific Century, 1975-2075?" *The Economist*, Jan. 4, 1975, pp. 15-35.

Magee, Stephen P. "Multinational Corporations, the Industry Technology Cycle and Development." *Journal of World Trade Law* 11 (1977): 297-321.

"Major Protein Source for Japanese Threatened." *Oriental Economist* 45 (1977): 10-13.

McDonald, Hamish. "Indonesia: Asahan Bolsters a Hard Year." *Far Eastern Economic Review* 92 (1976): 70.

McNulty, Paul J. "Economic Theory and the Meaning of Competition." *Quarterly Journal of Economics* 82 (1968): 639-656.

Metz, Tim. "Brazil's Vale Set to Supply Iron, Pulp for Japanese." *Wall Street Journal*, Sept. 24, 1976, p. 1.

Millar, T. B. "Japan and Australia: Partners in the Pacific." *Pacific Community* 8 (1976): 28-42.

Mitsui Bank. "Takokuseki Kigyo to Ginko" [Multinational Firms and Banks]. *Chosa Geppo*, No. 469 (1974), pp. 2-30.

"Multinationalization of Japanese Firms (2)—Iron and Steel, Automobiles, Textiles." *Oriental Economist* 40 (1972): 22-38.

"Multinationalization of Japanese Firms (3)—Heavy Machinery." *Oriental Economist* 41 (1973): 22-23.

Mundell, Robert A. "International Trade and Factor Mobility." *American Economic Review* 47 (1957): 321-335.

Nagasu, Kazuji. "The Super-Illusions of an Economic Superpower." *Japan Interpreter* 9 (1974): 149-164.

Nakane, Chie. "Social Background of Japanese in Southeast Asia." *Developing Economies* 10 (1972): 115-125.

Ozawa, Terutomo. "Commodity Trade and Factor Mobility: Comment." *American Economic Review* 66 (1976): 668.

———. "The Emergence of Japan's Multinationalism: Patterns and Competitiveness." *Asian Survey* 15 (1975): 1036-1053.

———. "International Investment and Industrial Structure: New Theoretical Implications from the Japanese Experience." *Oxford Economic Papers* 31 (1979): 72-92.

———. "Japan's Mideast Economic Diplomacy." *Columbia Journal of World Business* 9 (1974): 38-46.

———. "Japan's Multinational Enterprise: The Political Economy of Outward Dependency." *World Politics* 30 (1978): 517-537.

———. "Japan's Resource Dependency and Overseas Investment." *Journal of World Trade Law* 11 (1977): 52-73.

———. "Multinationalism, Japanese Style." *Columbia Journal of World Business* 7 (1972): 33-42.

———. "Peculiarities of Japan's Multinationalism: Facts and Theories." *Banca Nazionale del Lavoro Quarterly Review,* No. 115, December 1975, pp. 404-426.

———. "Sociocultural Problems of Japanese Multinationalism." *Akron Business and Economic Review* 5 (1974): 7-13.

———, Pluciennik, Moyses, and Rao, K. Nagaraja. "Japan's Direct Investment in Brazil." *Columbia Journal of World Business* 11 (1976): 107-116.

Panglaykim, J. "Setting It Up, Tokyo-style." *Far Eastern Economic Review* 86 (1974): 18-23.

Parry, Thomas G. "The International Firm and National Economic Policy: A Survey of Some Issues." *Economic Journal* 83 (1973): 1201-1221.

Passin, Herbert. "Changing Values: Work and Growth in Japan." *Asian Survey* 15 (1975): 821-850.

Perlmutter, Howard V. "The Tortuous Evolution of the Multinational Corporation." *Columbia Journal of World Business* 4 (1969): 9-24.

Purvis, Douglas D. "Technology, Trade and Factor Mobility." *Economic Journal* 82 (1972): 991-999.

Rybczynski, T. M. "Factor Endowment and Relative Commodity Prices." *Economica* 22 (1955): 336-341.

Schmitz, Andrew and Helmberger, Peter. "Factor Mobility and International Trade: The Case of Complementarity." *American Economic Review* 60 (1970): 791-797.

Shimabukuro, Yoshiaki. "The Economy of Singapore." *Oriental Economist* 39 (1971): 18-23.

Sigur, Gaston J. "Japan's Broadening International Role." *Pacific Community* 9 (1977): 17-30.

Stockwin, Harvey. "Asahan: Why Japan Said Yes." *Far Eastern Economic Review* 92 (1976): 42-43.

Streeten, Paul. "Policies toward Multinationals." *World Development* 3 (1975): 393-397.

Takeda, Jun. "Japanese Trading Companies." *Japan Quarterly* 20 (1973): 407-413.

Vernon, Raymond. "International Investment and International Trade in the Product Life Cycle." *Quarterly Journal of Economics* 80 (1966): 190-207.

Wall, David. "Export Processing Zones." *Journal of World Trade Law* 10 (1976): 478-489.

Weiner, Myron and Hoselitz, Bert F. "Economic Development and Political Stability in India." *Dissent* 8 (1961): 172-184.

"Whaling in Japan." *Oriental Economist* 42 (1974): 24-27.

Whitlam, E. G. "Japan and Australia: Pacific Partners." *Pacific Community* 6 (1974): 1-15.

Yoshino, M. Y. "The Multinational Spread of Japanese Manufacturing Investment since World War II." *Business History Review* 48 (1974): 357-381.

Young, Alexander K. "Internationalization of the Japanese General Trading Companies." *Columbia Journal of World Business* 9 (1974): 78-87.

Unpublished Paper

Kojima, Kiyoshi. "Japan's Resource Security and Foreign Investment in the Pacific." Tokyo, Hitotsubashi University, April 1977.

Public Documents

Japanese Government

Economic Planning Agency. *Economic Survey of Japan—1970-1971.* Tokyo, 1972.

————. *Keizai Hakusho* [White Paper on the Japanese Economy]. Tokyo, 1974.

Japan External Trade Organization (JETRO). *Kaigai Shijo Hakusho: Wagakuni Kaigai Toshi no Genjo* [White Paper on Overseas Market: Present State of Japan's Overseas Investment]. Tokyo, 1972, 1974, 1975, 1976.

Japan Tariff Association. *Tokkei Kanzei no Tebiki* [Manual on Preferential Tariffs]. Tokyo, 1971.

Ministry of International Trade and Industry (MITI). *Hattentojokoku ni taisuru Ippantokkei Seido ni tsuite* [On the General Preference System for Developing Countries]. Tokyo, 1971.

————. *Keizai Kyoryoku no Genjo to Mondaiten* [Present Conditions and Problems of Overseas Economic Cooperation]. Tokyo, 1972, 1973, 1975.

————. *Tsusho Hakusho* [White Paper on International Trade]. Tokyo, 1971, 1972, 1973, 1974, 1975, 1976, 1977.

————. *Wagakuni Kigyo no Kaigai Jigyo Katsudo* [Overseas Business Activities of Our National Enterprises]. Tokyo, 1974, 1975, 1976, 1977.

Resource Study Committee, Economic Council. *Kokusaika Jidai no Shigen Mondai* [Resource Problems in the Era of Internationalization]. Tokyo, 1970.

Small and Medium Enterprise Agency. *Chusho Kigyo Hakusho* [White Paper on Small and Medium Enterprises]. Tokyo, 1976.

Other Governments

Central Bank of Brazil. *Bulletin.* May 1975, June 1977.

Industrial Development and Investment Center, the Republic of China. *Overseas Investment in the Republic of China.* Taipei, 1971.

U.S. Department of Commerce. *Foreign Economic Trends and Their Implications for the United States.* Washington, D.C., 1973.

U.S. Tariff Commission. *Economic Factors Affecting the Use of Items 807.00 and 806.30 of the Tariff Schedule of the U.S.* Washington, D.C., 1970.

International Organizations

Organization for Economic Cooperation and Development (OECD). *Gaps in Technology: Analytical Report.* Paris, 1970.

United Nations. *Multinational Corporations in World Development* E. 73. II. A. 11). New York, 1973.

———. *The Impact of Multinational Corporations on Development and on International Relations,* 4 vols. (E. 74, II. A. 5, A. 6, A. 7, and A. 8). New York, 1974.

———. *Summary of the Hearings before the Group of Eminent Persons to Study the Impact of Multinational Corporations on Development and on International Relations* (E. 74. II. A. 9). New York, 1974.

Newspapers and Weeklies

Asahi Shimbun
Japan Economic Journal (International Weekly Edition of *Nihon Keizai Shimbun*)
Mainichi Shimbun
Nihon Keizai Shimbun
Nikkei Business
Sankei Shimbun
Shukan Toyo Keizai

Index

Library of Congress Cataloging in Publication Data

Ozawa, Terutomo.
Multinationalism, Japanese style.

Bibliography: p.
Includes index.
1. Corporations, Japanese.   2. Investments, Japanese.
3. Japan—Foreign economic relations.   4. Industry and state—
Japan.   I. Title.
HD2907.09   338.8′8   79-84007
ISBN 0-691-04221-7